THE COMPLETE IDIOT'S GUIDE® TO

Finance for Small Business Owners

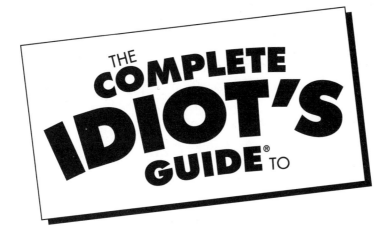

THE COMPLETE IDIOT'S GUIDE® TO

Finance for Small Business Owners

by Ken Little

ALPHA

A member of Penguin Group (USA) Inc.

ALPHA BOOKS

Published by the Penguin Group

Penguin Group (USA) Inc., 375 Hudson Street, New York, New York 10014, U.S.A.

Penguin Group (Canada), 10 Alcorn Avenue, Toronto, Ontario, Canada M4V 3B2 (a division of Pearson Penguin Canada Inc.)

Penguin Books Ltd, 80 Strand, London WC2R 0RL, England

Penguin Ireland, 25 St Stephen's Green, Dublin 2, Ireland (a division of Penguin Books Ltd)

Penguin Group (Australia), 250 Camberwell Road, Camberwell, Victoria 3124, Australia (a division of Pearson Australia Group Pty Ltd)

Penguin Books India Pvt Ltd, 11 Community Centre, Panchsheel Park, New Delhi—110 017, India

Penguin Group (NZ), cnr Airborne and Rosedale Roads, Albany, Auckland 1310, New Zealand (a division of Pearson New Zealand Ltd)

Penguin Books (South Africa) (Pty) Ltd, 24 Sturdee Avenue, Rosebank, Johannesburg 2196, South Africa

Penguin Books Ltd, Registered Offices: 80 Strand, London WC2R 0RL, England

Copyright © 2006 by Kenneth E. Little

International Standard Book Number: 1-59257-479-3
Library of Congress Catalog Card Number: 2005937200

08 07 06   8 7 6 5 4 3 2 1

Interpretation of the printing code: The rightmost number of the first series of numbers is the year of the book's printing; the rightmost number of the second series of numbers is the number of the book's printing. For example, a printing code of 06-1 shows that the first printing occurred in 2006.

Printed in the United States of America

Note: This publication contains the opinions and ideas of its author. It is intended to provide helpful and informative material on the subject matter covered. It is sold with the understanding that the author and publisher are not engaged in rendering professional services in the book. If the reader requires personal assistance or advice, a competent professional should be consulted.

The author and publisher specifically disclaim any responsibility for any liability, loss, or risk, personal or otherwise, which is incurred as a consequence, directly or indirectly, of the use and application of any of the contents of this book.

Most Alpha books are available at special quantity discounts for bulk purchases for sales promotions, premiums, fund-raising, or educational use. Special books, or book excerpts, can also be created to fit specific needs.

For details, write: Special Markets, Alpha Books, 375 Hudson Street, New York, NY 10014.

Publisher: *Marie Butler-Knight*
Editorial Director: *Mike Sanders*
Senior Managing Editor: *Jennifer Bowles*
Acquisitions Editor: *Michele Wells*
Development Editor: *Ginny Bess Munroe*
Production Editor: *Janette Lynn*
Copy Editor: *Emily M. Bell*

Cartoonist: *Shannon Wheeler*
Book Designer: *Trina Wurst*
Cover Designer: *Bill Thomas*
Indexer: *Tonya Heard*
Layout: *Brian Massey*
Proofreading: *Mary Hunt*

Contents at a Glance

Contents

14 Expanding Market Share   155

15 The Strategic Planning Budget   167

Foreword

Have you heard the story of Johnson's Neighborhood Bakery, Inc.? The store was always busy and the breads, cakes, and pastries were consistently delicious. The owner, Marc Johnson, was always on the premises and the atmosphere in the shop was friendly and accommodating. Marc, a young man, had started his business five years earlier and it quickly became a local favorite. After, what appeared to be, four successful years, Johnson moved to a larger location across the street and purchased new equipment. One year later Johnson's window displayed this sign: "Out Of Business! Thanks For Your Patronage."

What makes an apparently thriving small business suddenly close its doors? Why does a man operating an active operation from one location, fail to succeed, when he expands to a new space?

As Ken Little explains in *The Complete Idiot's Guide To Finance for Small Business Owners*, most often the reason for failure in a small business is the owner's lack of understanding of basic business financial concepts.

This book offers the owner or manager of a small business the opportunity to view the financial matters of his company through a clear and meaningful process. The author removes that "deer-in-the-headlights" look that most small business operators carry, when they are asked to discuss their company's financial statements.

The balance sheet, income statement, and statement of cash flow are described in plain *easy to grasp* language. They are shown to be useful tools in every aspect of a small business. Each is used to analyze and enhance operations, formulate budgets and raise capital, through the creation of loan packages and equity expansion presentations. Explicit examples are given, and they are explained in simple ways.

Mr. Little explains terms such as "working capital," "quick ratio," and "inventory turnover" in a manner that makes common sense and shows why knowledge of these terms is important to the success of any business. He covers marketing, advertising, strategic planning, and financing resources—all important to the success of the small business owner.

The concept of "cash is king" and the importance of cash management for small business survival are emphasized in several chapters. Ken instructs the reader that he *must* know where his cash is coming from and where it is going. This includes the forecasting of revenues and the monitoring of expenses as part of a regular routine.

Small business owners and managers will be able to glean a wealth of useful information from this book, as Ken Little has succeeded in demystifying the concepts of small business finance.

—Stephen N. Sofen

Stephen N. Sofen has been the C.F.O. of a midtown Manhattan real estate company for 23 years. He has been an accountant in both the public and private sectors, with extensive experience as a controller in the garment industry. He currently co-manages several pension and trust portfolios.

Introduction

As the owner of a small business, you carry many job titles, including the one that got you into business in the first place. Whether you own a retail store, operate a manufacturing business, or provide services of some variety, there is much more to owning a business than just doing those duties. The most important job title you have other than owner is Chief Financial Officer—and it may be the job you feel least qualified to hold.

If you look at your monthly financial statements and wonder what all the numbers mean, don't feel alone. Most small business owners have no background or education in finance and that gap is one of the leading causes of small business failure.

This book is about helping you understand your company's finances from its financial statements to its planning and budgeting process. This is a hands-on, practical guide written for people with no formal education in finance.

Your financial statements contain a gold mine of information if you know how to make the numbers work for you and that's what this book does. These numbers can help you make better decisions every day and better plans for tomorrow.

The Complete Idiot's Guide to Finance for Small Business Owners has five sections. Each section groups like subjects for easier reference.

Part 1: Numbers Are Your Friends

You're probably very good at what you do. You take pride in the products or services your company offers. Unfortunately, that's not good enough. For you and your business to survive and thrive, you need a good working knowledge of business finance—the numbers behind your business.

Not to worry. It's not as horrible as it sounds. You may never come to love the finances of your business, but after you finish this section, you'll wonder how you ever survived this long without making friends with your numbers.

Part 2: Make the Numbers Work

Your company's financial reports are just the beginning—consider them raw material. Once you have an idea of what they are all about, you can put them to work for you by applying some analysis. Don't worry, it's not that tough. This section walks you through some common financial analysis tools that will bring a deeper understanding of your business.

Here's where the real payoff comes. Using your financial statements and a few ratios, you can look at how well or poorly your company is performing in a number of key areas.

Part 3: Strategic Planning/Budgeting

Adding 5 percent to last year's budget and calling it done is not the formula for success. Strategic budgeting is part of a financial planning process that looks at the strengths, weaknesses, challenges, and opportunities facing your business and creates a financial strategy. This section looks at the budgeting process as part of the overall financial strategy.

Do you set profit goals or is profit what you hope is left over at the end of the year? What about sales goals? Many small businesses drift from one year to the next because they aren't sure where they are financially. When you understand your finances, budgeting and planning takes on a completely new meaning.

Part 4: Financing Your Business with Debt

Almost every growing business needs financing to fund new projects, new markets, acquisitions, or a variety of other needs. There are several sources to draw on for financing from short-term loans to long-term financing.

There are a number of sources for debt financing including friends and family, banks, SBA programs, and other formal lending structures. You can also use other financing techniques such as factoring and inventory financing.

Part 5: Financing Your Business with Equity

For some small businesses, there comes a time when bringing in equity partners is desirable. How you go about preparing for talks with potential investors starts with your financial statements.

While lenders and investors are concerned with many of the same financial details, there are some important differences. What is the end game? How will investors get their money and interest out of the company? This section is full of tips and guidelines for working with investors.

Document Aids

There are four types of sidebars in this book. They are little extras to point out special information or send up a red flag for a danger.

Money Talk _____

These highlight key terms in the chapter to help you translate the sometimes baffling

Notes and News

Answers and information about finance are provided here in the forms of additional sources.

CAUTION

In the Red _____

Watch out! This sidebar flags those areas where danger lurks in the form of financial traps.

Financial Aid _____

These are little known tips and hints that provide additional information to help you understand and manage your business's finances.

Acknowledgments

Thanks to Alpha Books for the opportunity to do another book in this series. As both a creator and consumer of books under *The Complete Idiot's Guide* banner, I appreciate the recognition that learning is a never-ending process.

As always, I thank my family for putting up with my mental absence while writing this book. My wife, Cyndy, in particular shouldered most of my share of the household chores during a period when she was hard pressed for time as she began serving a church as their new pastor.

Dedication

This book is dedicated to every small business owner who is still at work long after everyone else has departed for a hot meal at home. Before you sit stacks of bills, tax forms, bid requests, and last month's financial reports. You have just enough energy to tackle one stack, but not them all—which do you choose. As one of you who's "been there and done that," I urge you to pickup the financial reports and spend your remaining energy studying these gold mines of information. It won't be exciting reading, but what you learn may help you walk out the door with your employees at least a few nights each week.

Trademarks

All terms mentioned in this book that are known to be or are suspected of being trademarks or service marks have been appropriately capitalized. Alpha Books and Penguin Group (USA) Inc. cannot attest to the accuracy of this information. Use of a term in this book should not be regarded as affecting the validity of any trademark or service mark.

Part 1

Numbers Are Your Friends

You're probably very good at what you do. You take pride in the products or services your company offers. Unfortunately, that's not good enough. For you and your business to survive and thrive, you need a good working knowledge of business finance—the numbers behind your business. Not to worry. It's not as horrible as it sounds. You may never come to love the finances of your business, but after you finish this section, you'll wonder how you ever survived this long without making friends with your numbers.

Chapter 1

The Payoff

In This Chapter

- What you don't know hurts you
- If you can't measure it, you can't manage it
- Planning vs. guessing
- Information is power

What's in it for me? Your time is too valuable to not ask this question about the benefits of understanding your business's finances. So, let's get to the bottom line (that's on the income statement, by the way). Finance is the tracking and management of anything in your business that has to do with money—in other words, everything. You will never understand your business until you understand its finances. This chapter provides the motivation for mastering the math.

Ignorance Is Not Bliss

You probably didn't become a small business owner to study financial statements. You have a long "to do" list each day that seldom gets completed and spending time studying your financial statements may seem like a luxury you can't afford. This chapter makes the case that you can't afford not to take the time to study and analyze your financial statements.

Work Smart

Years ago, there were some radio ads for Dale Carnegie training courses (Carnegie was the author of the famous book, *How to Win Friends and Influence People*). The Carnegie training, still offered today, is for salespeople, managers, and others. The narrator of the ad told this story:

> A young lumberjack shows up at camp and impresses the boss by chopping down 100 trees his first week. The second week his total is an impressive 90 trees. The third week his total is 80 trees. By the fourth week, the crew boss can see the young lumberjack is on track to only chop down 60 trees, so he goes to the young man to see why he has fallen off his pace.

> The young lumberjack can't explain it. "I'm working harder each week, but felling fewer trees. The next week I work even harder and still chop down fewer trees."

> The older boss listens and asks, "Are you sharpening your axe every day?"

> "Why no," says the young man. "I don't have time to stop and do that."

This is not word for word, but the message was powerful enough to stick with me for many years. The young lumberjack was too busy to work smarter, so he worked harder and harder, but got farther behind.

> **Financial Aid** _____
>
> Budget some time each week to study your company's financial statements, even if you have to leave the premises to do it. Make that time as important as any you spend all week.

If You Don't

A great many small businesses fail not because the owner does a poor job or provides an inferior service, but because it is not run like a business. Most small business people only know one-half of what it takes to succeed. The part they are missing is how to manage and grow their business. Small business owners that succeed and thrive figure this part out or they already have this knowledge.

Unfortunately, the failure rate for small businesses is quite high. There are numerous reasons businesses fail. Here are some of the most common:

- Poor management
- Under capitalized
- Lack of cost controls
- Rapid growth

There are others such as competition, technology, and so on. However, I want to focus on these internal factors, which you have much more control over. These reasons are addressed in upcoming chapters.

Start from the Beginning

Whether you are just starting your business or have been at it for years, now is the time to start thinking differently about how you manage your business. If you are just beginning, the temptation is strong to put off anything that doesn't involve getting your business launched. It is easy to convince yourself that after your business is up and running, you'll have more time to get organized. Unfortunately, you will seldom have more time in the future and the longer you put off learning about the financial infrastructure of your business, the harder it will be to begin.

Down the Wrong Road

I know a young man who bought a landscape-related business that was doing very well; at least the young man thought so. He looked at his financial statements every month, but really focused only on the income statement to see if he was making a profit. The company was actually making a substantial profit, before taxes. However, the young man confided that he was not very happy.

He worked seven days a week during the busy planting season and six days the rest of the year. He drew a small salary from the business and had several full-time and part-time employees. The problem was he had a huge tax bill at the end of each year. The bill was so high, that he had to borrow money to pay it two years in a row.

A look at the company's organization quickly revealed a way to reduce the tax bill by 75 percent. Further examination found ways to cut costs that freed up even more cash

CAUTION

In the Red _____

You are not an expert in everything. Don't let your ego prevent you from asking for help in those areas where you don't have the experience or education, especially when it comes to taxes and legal matters.

in the business. The owner, who had a high school education, didn't believe he could understand his company's finances, so he never tried to learn. When he saw the power of what some fairly simple analysis uncovered about his business, he decided that the time investment to learn more about the management of his business was going to pay off in ways he couldn't have imagined.

The price of not knowing is very high.

Plan for Success

It is never too early to plan for success. That may seem obvious, no one starts a business to fail, however many small businesses launch with no real idea where they are going. The owner may have a notion about where he or she wants to be in terms of income, but without a map of how to get from here to there it's mostly luck if they get there.

It may seem silly to a new business owner to spend much time on financial controls when what the business desperately needs is sales, yet that's just what needs to happen. Ironically, success in the form of rapid growth, is one of the killers of small businesses. Without financial controls in place and a business owner who understands the details of the financial statements, rapid growth usually means runaway expenses. A significant cash flow can hide problems for a while, but eventually reality will strike and the owner will wake up one morning to discover he is broke and in debt up to his eyeballs.

Knowledge Is Power

You know your business. You know how to produce your products or services. That knowledge along with a desire to run your own show led you to start your own business. You are very confident about your abilities and that confidence is empowering, to use a 90s term. You can feel that same way about your company's finances, and that will be empowering as well.

Vagueness vs. Clarity

It is not uncommon to talk to small business people and find they profess to know all about their finances, yet when pushed for details are hard pressed to respond. In

h more beyond what the income statement says and
the bank account.

usiness owners are more comfortable with a fog
e afraid of what might be under the fog should it lift.

owners eagerly embrace the information if presented in
in the real world. The key is to understand how some
anage your business with greater confidence. The for-
ts don't
etation by
ou under-
don't have
see how
hese rela-
out your
day to make it

Financial Aid

Math can be intimidating to many people, but it doesn't have to be when it comes to understanding your financial statements. Once you get past the jargon, the actual math is easy.

out a strategic plan is like using a blank piece of paper
nd we might want to go there." Yet, if you walked into
lom, very few would have a real strategic plan based
ld show you.

of where you are and where you have been, it is
impossible to plot a course to where you want to be and you wouldn't know it if you
got there. The planning process, which I discuss in more detail later in this book, is
an opportunity to look at your weaknesses and make adjustments, while taking advantage of those strengths that work for your business. When you understand your
finances, there is no more guessing if this product is a "real money maker" or if that
customer is a good one.

Measure It—Manage It

There is a cliché in management circles that if you can't measure something, you
can't manage it. This may appear to take some of the "fly by the seat of your pants"
romance out of being a small business owner, but if you are interested in your

business surviving, you'll focus on understanding your business inside and out. That understanding only comes when you understand its finances and can use them to manage your business. At the core of managing your business is understanding the true costs of producing your product or service.

The Real Cost of Anything

Ask many small business people how much it costs to produce their product or service and they will rattle off parts and labor expenses, usually preceded by "about." In truth, they have no idea of the true cost of their products or services. Items they believe make money may actually lose money. Services that could be profitable with some adjustments languish, because the owner doesn't have the information needed to see the problem.

A plumber says he can install a hot water heater at a profit because he charges the homeowner the $500 retail price for the heater, but he pays $350 wholesale and charges $150 labor to install it. "That looks like a $300 profit to me," he claims. Unfortunately, he has forgotten a few items like his office expense, taxes, his truck expense, his yellow page ad, insurance, and so on. He may still make a profit if his volume is sufficient, but it is much less than $300.

Of course, you don't dump all of your expenses on one job, but you must account for and pay those expenses. What our plumber friend needed was a target for *gross margin* on each job that would allow enough to cover operating expenses and still give the company a profit. Under that scenario, maybe $300 gross margin was a fair target, but he would need to look at all of the other work he was doing to know if that were true.

Money Talk

Gross margin, also known as gross profit, is found by subtracting the direct costs of producing a product or service from the sales. The gross margin is found on the income statement.

Let's follow this example one step further. Say it took the plumber and a helper two hours to do this job. First, he has to remove the old heater, then go get the new one, and then install and test it. What if in that same two-hour period he could have done a different type of job that gave him a gross margin of $400? What if he discovered that one of his most popular jobs left him with a gross margin of only $50 for two hours of work? Which type of job should he advertise?

More important, how much do you think that plumber would give to have that information? You don't need a degree in business to see that it makes sense to put most of your efforts where they will yield the greatest results. There is nothing more frustrating than working yourself to death and not getting anywhere and not knowing why. When you know "why," it is easy to reach decisions that make sense and move your business forward.

The Real Price of Anything

Knowing your numbers is not just about identifying expenses, it is also about spotting opportunities. When you get inside your business and know it in a way that you can measure, you may find ways you can compete that were hidden before. Most of us are familiar with the "loss leader" concept—offering a product at a ridiculously low price to get customers in the door in hopes of selling them something else. Unfortunately, many small businesses offer loss leaders without even knowing it.

Aggressive pricing to land a new customer or generate traffic is a perfectly acceptable business practice if you do it as part of a focused business strategy. If you are guessing, then the results will likely be disappointing. On the other hand, when you have the numbers in front of you, you can weigh the benefits against the risks and make an informed decision. Owning a small business is risky enough without compounding the danger by guessing on important decisions like pricing.

One of the common themes you hear from small businesses is that they must charge "what the market" is charging for the same product or service. With the exception of small markets, most small business people probably don't have the means to do a comprehensive survey of the competition, so they rely on anecdotal information, which may or may not be accurate. If the competitive pricing is correct and you can't make money at that price, one of two things is happening:

- ◆ No one is making money at that price.
- ◆ Your expenses are way out of line.

In the first case, you may want to look at another product line. In the second, you can do something about it if you know what and where those expenses are. I'll talk more about pricing later in the book.

> **CAUTION**
>
> **In the Red**
>
> One of the most difficult decisions small businesses make is pricing their products or services. Small service businesses especially tend to underprice their offerings for a variety of reasons, including lack of confidence.

Hidden Assets and Liabilities

Imagine opening a shoebox in the bottom of your closet and finding it full of money! Would that be worth looking for if there was a possibility it was hiding somewhere in your house? Is there a shoebox like that in your business? I don't know, but the important question is do you know? What if I told you where to look on your financial statements to find out if you have such a shoebox?

I'm overstating things a tad here to make a point, but many small businesses do have cash tied up in their financial statements they could use to finance growth or pay off debt. However, if you don't know it's there and don't know what to do with it once you find it, that shoebox full of cash won't help you much.

There may be other assets you could put to better use if only you knew where to look and what to do with them. This is another benefit of understanding your business and its financial statements. As the owner of the business, one of your most important jobs is to see the whole picture and understand how it all fits together. If you don't know any more than your employees do, you are not managing the business.

Of course, when you start looking around your business and financial statements, you may discover that not all surprises are good ones. There may be hidden liabilities that will jump up and bite you when least expected. No one likes bad news, but it is better to identify a small problem than to be consumed by big problems.

I knew a family-owned business that, to all outward appearances, was very successful. They had several locations and close to 100 employees. It was in a highly competitive business with not great profit margins, but this company seemed to be doing just fine, until one day, the IRS showed up and shut the business down. It seems the company bookkeeper in a well-intentioned, but misguided attempt to help the company, had not been making the income tax, Social Security, and Medicare deposits for some time. The bookkeeper had been stalling the IRS for months and keeping the problem from the owner.

The owner looked at the financial statements each month, but didn't really understand anything except the income statement always showed a profit. The truth was the business was failing and the bookkeeper used the payroll tax deposits to keep the company going. That was the "profit." If the owner had known anything about the business, he would have instantly seen the problem and taken action.

Even though the bookkeeper tried to keep it from him, someone who had a basic knowledge of financial statements would have spotted the problem quickly. The price of not knowing was the owner's business. Fortunately, he was able to sell off his

equipment and other assets and pay most of
the outstanding taxes. The IRS set up a payment plan for the rest. While it's true the
bookkeeper committed the crime (even if the
intentions were not self-serving), it was still the
business owner's responsibility.

In the Red _____

Regardless of who does
your books, you are responsible
for their accuracy and for the
timely payment of taxes.

Feel the Power

Can a thorough understanding of your company's finances make it successful? Nothing
can guarantee success. However, when you are fully in control of your business, you
have the power to succeed. You can talk to bankers, investors, and suppliers with confidence because there aren't many questions they can ask that you can't answer.

Manage Your Business; Don't Let It Run Your Life

Managing a small business sometimes seems like changing a tire on a moving car.
There is never enough time to do half the things you need to do, much less those you
want to do. The truth is that many times small business owners don't effectively manage their business because they are too busy running it. The tasks of the business
become the boss.

Getting inside the heart of your business by understanding its finances and seeing the
"big picture" often reveals that many of the things you have been doing are unimpor-
tant to the success of the business. After you know what contributes to the success of
the company, you can prioritize your time and efforts to focus only on those things
that move your company forward. Later in the book, I talk about strategic planning
and getting in to the mindset of evaluating everything you do against the plan's goals.
Any activity you are doing must either move you toward your goals or be legally necessary. If it doesn't fit into one of these categories, you drop it.

This focus keeps you and your employees on task and avoids diversions that drain
time and resources from the company and you—no more chasing every potential new
product or service unless it fits your plan.

Get the Loans/Financing You Need

Securing financing for your small business can be a difficult and frustrating experience. I spend a considerable amount of time later in the book on this subject.
However, the cold reality is that financing a small business is a risky proposition.

Whether you go to a bank or pursue some other avenue, everything you do that builds confidence in your ability to manage the business will help your chances of getting the financing you need.

Lenders or investors need to know two main things before considering your application:

◆ Are you qualified to do what you say you can do?

◆ Are you capable of managing the business?

If you have no experience as a plumber, but want to open a plumbing repair business, you will raise a few eyebrows. Likewise, if you have never worked in marketing, but want to open an advertising agency, you might get some hard questions. Most people who start small businesses have some experience in the area.

The second question is usually more difficult: do you have the management skills to operate a business? If that experience is not on your resumé, then you will need to demonstrate to the potential lender some of the skills required to run a business. One of the most important skills you can show the lender is your knowledge of your company's finances. They want to know you and your company are a good investment. If you show up with some numbers scrawled on a pad of paper and no answers to simple questions, don't count on getting financial help from this lender.

Financial Aid

Lenders don't expect small business people to be financial geniuses; however they will be impressed if you can talk with confidence about your company's financial statements and any projections that are part of a loan package.

On the other hand, if you arrive with a complete financial package (if your accountant did it, that's even better) and can discuss it in detail; your chances go up dramatically. You may not get the loan, but it won't be because the lender was uncomfortable with your management skills.

Sleep Well at Night

One of the bonuses of knowing all about your company's finances is the elimination of one source of unpleasant surprises. Owning a small business is risky and anything you can do to eliminate risks will improve the odds in your favor. It is one thing for a competitor to catch you off guard or to be impacted by some other outside factor you have little or no control over. It is quite another to have your own company's finances surprise you.

Will knowing all about your company's finances guarantee you a good night's sleep? Not necessarily. The knowledge may not be pretty, but at least you'll know a problem exists and it won't be a surprise. If you know there's a problem, there's an opportunity to solve it before it becomes a disaster. If you don't know a problem exists, it may be too late to do anything by the time you discover it.

The Least You Need to Know

- What you don't know about your company's finances can hurt your business.
- Knowledge of your business and its finances gives you power and confidence.
- If you do not know all of the aspects of your business, you will have a difficult time successfully managing it.
- You should manage your business; don't let it run your life.
- If you do not have a thorough knowledge of the tax and legal aspects of your business, enlist a qualified professional to help you.

The Big Three

In This Chapter

- ◆ Reporting three ways
- ◆ Keeping things balanced
- ◆ What's coming in
- ◆ Following the cash

There are three main financial reports that will tell you almost everything you need to know about your business. You need to become good friends with them, because, in addition to helping you work smarter, these reports represent your company to the people who lend money, approve leases, or okay any other financial arrangements. This chapter provides an overview of these reports.

The Big Picture

The balance sheet, income statement, and statement of cash flows are the three most important financial reports about your business. Although they are interrelated through the way income and expenses are posted in your accounting system, each tells its own story about your business. They tell the same story to you and to anyone else looking at them.

Financial Aid _____

Some small businesses find that sharing parts of these financial reports with employees is a great way to help workers feel connected to the business.

These reports play two roles in your business: a reporting role and an operational role. The reporting role is required for a variety of business and tax reasons and must meet certain guidelines. The operational role requires more detail, but is your most important decision-making tool.

Drop Your Financial Drawers

Although you may want some privacy about your business, the reality is lenders and others who extend credit want to see the information on these reports, especially the balance sheet and income statement. In addition, even if you could manage to run a business without credit, much of the same information ends up on your personal or company's tax return, depending on how you organized the business.

Financial Aid _____

What is a "good" customer? Do you have minimum expectations in terms of profits a customer must provide? You should. For example, good customers pay on time, order consistently, and are receptive to new products or services. Think about what characteristics you want in a good customer for your business and actively seek out those types of clients.

In this reporting role, the financial statements must be current and accurate. If you use an accountant to prepare your books and statements, this shouldn't be a problem. If you do the bookkeeping yourself, take every precaution to make sure it is correct. Don't be tempted to cut corners or dress up your financial statements for lenders. Not only is it unethical, it is criminal to obtain loans or credit based on falsified financial statements. However, in most cases you don't need to get your books audited by an independent accounting firm unless your company's stock trades in a public market.

Your Best Tools

As operational tools, these reports are invaluable. They tell you where every dollar in your business is going and where it entered your company. When you can track money going through your company, you have a powerful tool for making decisions.

- Is this product/service profitable? Does it meet our minimum standards?

- Is this customer profitable? Does he or she meet our minimum standards?

- Which of these new products/services should we attempt? Why? Why not?

- What is the best use of our assets?

Your financial reports can help you make these decisions. Without information from and analysis of the significant numbers, you are guessing at any of the above decisions.

The Balance Sheet

The balance sheet is your finger on the pulse of your business. It tells you how healthy your company is, and when compared to a previous period, if its health has improved or gotten worse. You may have a strong "feeling" about the health of your business; however, the only way to know if that "feeling" is correct is by looking at the balance sheet. It will tell you precisely what's going on with the business.

Balancing Act

The balance sheet must balance. If it doesn't, something is wrong. When we look into the details of the balance sheet (that's coming up in the next chapter), you see why it's impossible for it not to balance if you do it correctly. There is a formula called the balance sheet formula that spells out how the report stays in balance:

Assets – Liabilities = *Equity*

Another way to phrase the equation is:

Assets = Liabilities + Equity

This second formula is less well-known outside financial circles and, frankly, less helpful to business people, so we'll stick with the more traditional, Assets – Liabilities = Equity. One of the main reasons for staying with this formula is that this makes sense to most business people. Assets and liabilities as reported on the balance sheet are for the most part, real tangible parts of your business.

> **Money Talk**
>
> **Equity** is the business owner's stake in the business and usually consists of what the owner originally contributed in the way of capital plus the growth of the business, less dividends paid or profits distributed to owners.

Your assets may be discounted due to depreciation and your accounts receivable may have a provision for uncollectible accounts. However, for the most part everything in your assets and liabilities columns represents real items, accounts, money, and so on.

Equity, on the other hand, constantly changes. As the assets and liabilities increase or decrease from month to month, the equity changes. Equity is your stake in the business, and depending on how healthy the company is, that stake will rise or fall. Yet, until you sell the company, it is difficult to touch your equity. Your equity is not necessarily sitting in a bank account somewhere waiting for you to cash it in.

Timing

Most companies produce a balance sheet each month and certainly at the end of the *fiscal year*. Your accountant will probably want you to have one every month. Only very small, service businesses with no debt can get by without a balance sheet for an extended period.

Money Talk

Fiscal year is the 12-month cycle of the business used for accounting purposes. It may or may not coincide with the calendar year.

Financial Aid

If your business has a seasonal nature (holiday sales, for example), that spans a traditional calendar year, you may want to consider a fiscal year that includes the whole season, such as May through April. The benefit is that you include your whole holiday season in a single fiscal year. If you used a calendar year, your holiday sales would split over two fiscal years because the old year would end Dec. 31 and the new year would begin Jan. 1.

Balance sheets give you a snapshot of your company at a particular point in time. However, it is much more meaningful if you have something to compare it to—a reference point. Many accountants and most software packages deliver a current period end to a prior period end balance sheet for comparison.

For example, you would get a year-to-date balance sheet as of June 30, 2006, compared with the year-to-date balance sheet as of June 30, 2005. Keeping the periods the same makes comparisons valid. This pattern repeats until the end of your fiscal year, when your accountant produces the final balance sheet for the year.

Of course, if you have chosen an odd fiscal year like one that ends on the last Tuesday in November, for example, year-to-year comparisons may not work out so well. Odd fiscal years can mean some years may have more than or fewer than 52 weeks, which might throw numbers off enough to be make comparisons confusing. Most companies tie their fiscal year to the calendar year (January through December), but this is not necessary and may not even be the best choice in certain circumstance. A May through April fiscal year works just fine if that fits your business cycle better.

The Income Statement

The income statement is usually the first of the three financial statements most business owners look at because it tells them if the company made money or not. You may also hear the income statement called the profit and loss statement, or P&L. This is the home of the proverbial bottom line. However, there is much more to the income statement than just the bottom line. It is a powerful tool that can help you mange one of the keys to success: containing expenses.

Same and Different

Income statements for small businesses are quite different in format and content from the income statements produced for publicly held companies. The income statements you find in annual reports contain very little detail and get to the point quickly. Their function is to report the major categories of the income statement without bogging the reader down in detail.

The small business owner, however, must have the detail, because that's where he or she will find the keys to making business decisions. The income statement lists all categories of expenses and separates those directly related to the production of the product or service from general administrative expenses. Obviously, publicly traded companies produce the same type of reports; they just are for internal use.

Regardless of the level of detail, the income statement arrives at the same bottom line: net income. Before you get to net income, you may see "income before taxes" or some other qualified income category. If you have shareholders, you can calculate the net income or *earnings* as earnings per share. This is a simple calculation. Take your earnings and divide by the number of outstanding shares to get earnings per share.

Money Talk

Earnings are the same as net income.

Timing and Format

You will want an income statement each month to track your progress. It is important to follow your profit or loss and very important to stay on top of your expenses. Except for the tiniest of businesses, this is vital information that you need each month.

Like all financial reports, the income statement works best with a point of reference. Many companies find that an income statement with multiple points of reference provides a wealth of information for management decisions. For example, your income statement might have one of these formats:

Possible Income Statement Column Headings

Month	Budget	Difference	Percent Variance
Month	Year-to-Date	Budget	Percent Variance
Month	Month Last Year	Difference	Percent Variance

It is not unusual for a small business owner to have an income statement with a combination of these formats or a different format that suits a business need. It is also possible to see an income statement in more than one form. However you make your income statement, make sure the format provides you with the information you need to make decisions.

The Statement of Cash Flows

Cash is the lifeblood of your business, or any business for that matter. Many management consultants will tell you that as a business owner, your top priority is managing cash, which can mean many different things. However, one principle is clear: you must manage your cash carefully to avoid financial disaster. Some current accounting methods make it hard to follow what is happening with your cash. The statement of cash flows is a tool that takes information from the other two financial reports (balance sheet and income statement) and creates a way for you to "follow the money."

By Another Name

The statement of cash flows is still known to some as the "sources and uses of funds" statement. Many find this more descriptive than the currently popular title. Whatever you call it, the report is still the important "third leg of the stool" of financial reports.

Because of accounting conventions, neither the balance sheet nor the income statement tells you how much cash your company has at its disposal. The statement of cash flows goes beyond what's in the bank and answers questions about the *liquidity* of your company. Do you have the cash in hand or readily available to meet your current obligations? Where does your cash come from and where does it go?

When items such as depreciation show up on the income statement as deductions (more about this in Chapter 4), it distorts the company's cash position. Depreciation is an expense, but not a cash expenditure. This means you deduct it as an expense when computing your company's net income, but no cash is involved in the transaction. The deduction lowers your net income for tax purposes. When we look at the statement of cash flows in detail in Chapter 5, you will see depreciation added back to net income, since no cash changed hands. This is one of the main functions of the statement of cash flows—reconciling accounting conventions with the "real world" management need for information.

Money Talk _____

Liquidity in this context refers to how easily your company can come up with the cash it needs to meet daily obligations.

In the Red _____

Running out of cash is one of the worst disasters a company can face. To stay in business requires drastic steps, including short-term borrowing, mortgaging or selling assets, and other solutions that may help the symptom, but do nothing for the problem.

Parts

The statement of cash flows has three major parts:

- ◆ Cash from operations
- ◆ Cash from investing
- ◆ Cash from financing

The sum of these sections is compared to the reference point or beginning balance to give you an increase or decrease in cash.

Financial Aid _____

Your business should show a steady increase in cash from operations. If it isn't, it could be a sign of serious trouble.

The most important section is cash from operations, because here is where your company is either generating cash flow or not. Investors and lenders look to this area and expect to see growth from period to period. They don't want to see a company making money off investments but continually taking in less cash through operations.

Timing

The statement of cash flows is a financial report I would recommend you look at every month. If you do your own books and use older software, it may not produce a statement of cash flows or it may not offer much in the way of flexibility. If you use an accountant, it is worth the extra money to see the report on a regular basis.

You'll want to compare the current month to a reference point or points in time to gain a perspective on what is happening in your business. Your accountant can help you decide the best reference, whether it is the previous month or previous year for your particular business. You will also want a year-end cash flow statement to accompany the other two major financial statements, the balance sheet and the income statement.

All the information for the statement of cash flows comes from the balance sheet and income statement, so those reports must be current.

Wrapping It Up

The "big three" financial reports all tell their own stories as we'll see in detail in coming chapters. However, it is when you put them together that you see the whole picture. Although it may seem like information overload, once you become more familiar with these reports, you will find they read quickly and you can spot problems and opportunities easily.

There is a world of difference in working with your own financial statements and reading words on the page of a book. Whenever possible, have your company's financial reports out as you go through these chapters. Because reporting formats vary, what is in the book may not track your reports exactly, but it will be close enough for you to follow.

The Least You Need to Know

- The balance sheet is your finger on the pulse of your business at a particular point in time.

- The income statement tells you if your company is making a profit or suffering a loss during a specific period of time.

- The statement of cash flows helps to explain the increase or decrease in cash on the balance sheet and follows the cash flows in your business.

- These three financial reports contain a wealth of information about your business you can use to make better decisions.

The Balancing Act

In This Chapter

- Checking your company's pulse
- Assessing your assets
- Listing your liabilities
- Retaining equity

You may be tempted to skip over the balance sheet when looking at your financial statements because it doesn't tell you if you're making a profit or not. That would be a mistake. The balance sheet tells you how healthy your company is and whether it can meet current and future obligations. This chapter explains the balance sheet and its various components.

A Financial Checkup

Take a set of financial reports (balance sheet, income statement, and statement of cash flows) from an ailing company to its banker and the first document he or she will probably look at is the balance sheet. That's

Without knowing the terms and information behind the numbers on a balance sheet, it is hard to make sense of the report. However, the more you learn about the balance sheet, the easier it is to see the logic of its construction.

where the banker will find most of the information needed to determine whether the company can survive or not.

The balance sheet is a financial checkup on the health of your company. It is a snapshot of a particular point in time and, when compared to a previous period, tells you if your company's health is getting better or worse. It can tell you much more if you understand the terms and categories found on the balance sheet.

The Preliminaries

Before we look at a typical small business balance sheet, it is important to get some preliminary considerations behind us. The most important of these are format and dates.

Format

There are two generally accepted formats for a balance sheet: one is the account format and the other is report format.

The account format presents the assets in the left column and the liabilities and equity in the right column. For example:

Current assets	$500	Current liabilities	$200
Long-term assets	$200	Long-term liabilities	$150
Other assets	$100	Total liabilities	$350
Total assets	$800	Shareholder's equity	$450
		Total liabilities + equity	$800

This format has the advantage of placing the numbers for assets and liabilities side by side for easier comparisons. The major drawback is that this format makes it very difficult to compare this balance sheet to another from a different period for reference.

The report format uses all the same headings and numbers, but starts with assets at the top and lists liabilities next, then shareholder equity accounts. For example:

Current assets	$500
Long-term assets	$200
Other assets	$100
Total assets	**$800**
Current liabilities	$200
Long-term liabilities	$150
Total liabilities	$350
Shareholder's equity	$450
Total liabilities + equity	**$800**

The obvious advantage of this format is that you can list numbers from other periods in adjoining columns as reference points. This allows to you see how your company is doing. Of course, this is a very simple example, but if you have to pick a format, I strongly recommend the report format because of the ease in comparing with previous periods.

Financial Aid

You study the balance sheet with two purposes in mind. The first is to look at the current period and the second is to compare it to the reference period. The ease of comparison is why I recommend the report format.

Dates

I briefly touched on the importance of dates for your fiscal year in Chapter 2, and I want to expand on that before going into the details of the balance sheet.

As I mentioned, if you are just starting your business, stick with a calendar-based fiscal year. By this, I mean a fiscal year that begins on the beginning of one month and ends 12 months later on the last day of the month. January through December is the most common fiscal year, although any 12-month cycle will work.

Some companies pick an odd ending to their fiscal year, such as the last Tuesday in November. Unless there is a compelling business reason for using such an odd date, don't do it. It will throw off any comparisons you want to make with future years

Financial Aid _____

Closing out your books for the end of your fiscal year can be simple or complex depending on the nature and size of your business. Think about those logistics when picking a yearend.

because your fiscal year may, or most likely may not, have 12 months. I am sure your accountants will agree that if you are going to choose an odd yearend fiscal year, you need a very strong business case to support this choice.

This is not to say you are stuck with the same fiscal year forever. You may find that, because of changing business circumstances, it is important to change your fiscal year. Under these conditions, it is an acceptable business practice. Your accountant can show you how to make it happen.

Breaking It Down

The balance sheet must balance. It's as simple as that. Looking at the two formats above, you can see the way it works—assets on one side (or on the top), balancing with liabilities and equity on the other (or on the bottom). To really understand the balance sheet, we need to get inside and look around. This is not an accounting book, but it relies on accounting to produce the financial reports, including the balance sheet. If you are going to use the balance sheet effectively, you need to understand the terms used in it and the reasoning behind it.

The Formula

Remember our balance sheet formula: Assets – Liabilities = Equity? If you think about it, this is a formula you are already familiar with and use on a frequent basis. If you own a house that is worth $250,000 (asset) and you have a $150,000 mortgage (liability), then your equity must be $100,000.

If Tom Cruise buys the house next door and the value of your house shoots up to $500,000, what is your equity? Answer: $500,000 – $150,000 = $350,000.

The same thing happens in your business, although it is unusual for assets to rise without some rise in liabilities. For example, you buy a building, increasing your assets, and finance part of the price, increasing your liabilities. You may also sell an asset, such as a building, which would lower your liabilities also. You can turn the balance sheet formula around to Assets = Liabilities + Equity if that helps you visualize the relationship.

What Are Assets and Liabilities?

It is easy to identify our personal assets: our house, car, furniture, stocks, bank accounts, and so on. The same is true of your business, however thanks to the accountants and the IRS, you need to be more precise in how you define assets. The same goes for liabilities. Generally, what you owe now or in the future falls into the liability category somewhere.

Let's look at the balance sheet of a typical small business so we can examine the individual parts. You'll notice that it has much more detail than the two format examples I used above. This balance sheet is in the report format, but I'll not include any reference point since we're interested in understanding the components and not the numbers.

> **CAUTION**
>
> **In the Red**
>
> Hiding assets or understating the value of an asset is not a good idea. Likewise, overstating the value of an asset for purposes of improving your balance sheet will get you in trouble.

Assets

Current Assets		
Cash	$15,000	
Marketable Securities	$10,000	
Accounts Receivable	$367,000	
Inventory	$125,000	
Prepaid Expenses	$10,500	
Total Current Assets	$527,500	
Property and Equipment		
Building	$2,021,500	
Equipment	$200,000	
Furniture and Fixtures	$5,000	
Accumulated Depreciation	($58,500)	
Total Property and Equipment	$2,168,000	
Other Assets		
Deposits	$1,000	
Total Other Deposits	$1,000	
Total Assets	$2,696,500	

continues

continued

Liabilities and Equity

Current Liabilities

Accounts Payable	$215,000
Sales Tax Collected	$10,000
Accrued Payroll Taxes	$10,000
Bank Notes	$10,000
Current Portion of Long-Term Debt	$75,000
Total Current Liabilities	$320,000

Long-Term Liabilities

Loans Payable	$2,284,000
Total Long-Term Liabilities	$2,284,000
Total Liabilities	$2,604,000

Equity

Retained Earnings	$62,500
Paid in Capital	$30,000
Total Stockholder's Equity	$92,500
Total Liabilities and Stockholder's Equity	$2,696,500

You can see from this example that the formula Assets - Liabilities = Equity is balanced and that the reversed formula Assets = Liabilities + Equity is also correct. Our goal here isn't to study the numbers, but to get an idea of the information behind the numbers. To do that, we need to break the balance sheet down into its three main parts: assets, liabilities, and equity.

Covering Your Assets

Your company's assets fall into one of three categories:

- Current assets
- Long-term assets
- Other assets

Most of the assets will fall into either the current or the long-term category. It is important to get assets in their proper pigeonhole because it will affect how certain ratios come out when we get into the analysis chapters later in the book.

Current Assets

The call on current assets is simple: anything you can convert into cash in less than 12 months should go in this category. You will be able to categorize some assets immediately (stocks, for example), while others may take some thought. Your company uses current assets to pay immediate bills and it would be in serious trouble if this category dried up.

Cash is king and queen. It is the ultimate in *liquidity*. This category includes not only what is in your bank account, but also what cash may be on premise(s). For example, retail stores need cash to transact daily business and if you have several locations, you may have a significant sum of money on site at these locations. This item on the balance sheet includes all your company's cash at all locations on the day of record for the balance sheet.

Marketable securities include stock in publicly traded companies owned by your company. Not all small businesses hold stock, but yours might. These stocks should trade on a major exchange with enough liquidity that you could sell them at a fair market price.

Money Talk

Liquidity refers to how easily you can convert an asset into cash. Common stocks are highly liquid because you can quickly sell them on the open market, while land is highly illiquid because finding a buyer could take a long time.

If you extend credit to customers, you have accounts receivable. This money is usually available, although it may take some time to collect all of it. Later in the book, I'll show you how to examine your accounts receivable for problems and opportunities.

Inventory refers to products you hold after manufacture or for later re-sell. These items are assets, however not all companies use the same method to account for them. Your accountant will help you figure out the best method for your business. This is an important decision because it may have major tax consequences for your company.

Prepaid expenses include items or services your company must pay in advance. Annual insurance premiums might fall in the category. It is considered an asset because you have already purchased the benefit. In many cases, if you canceled the benefit, you would receive some of the money back.

Property and Equipment

You can also call this category Long-Term or Fixed Assets. Assets in this grouping may take longer than a year to convert to cash. You might be able to sell a building sooner than a year if you offered it at a drastically discounted price, for example. However, the understanding is that you would sell items in this category for a reasonable market price, which may take some time.

Items in this category depreciate over time under schedules appropriate for each item. This depreciation lowers the value of the asset by an amount each year. That yearly depreciation charge appears on the income statement, as you'll see in the next chapter, reducing your company's taxable income.

Financial Aid

There are five different ways to calculate depreciation. Some items can use one or more schedules at your choice, while others must follow a particular schedule. Your accountant will help you decide the proper schedule for each item.

In my example, I only show a building, however you could break that down farther to show building and land. Buildings are significant assets that may carry a corresponding mortgage, which will show up in the liabilities section. Buildings (but not land) depreciate over time based on a schedule.

Equipment is the machinery used in your business. It could be manufacturing equipment or computers, and it depreciates, although over a shorter period than buildings. This category also includes your office equipment such as copiers and so on. The furniture and fixtures category contains your office equipment and, in the case of retail businesses, the store fixtures. These assets depreciate as well.

Accumulated depreciation is the sum of the depreciation for all the items in the Property and Equipment section. Some balance sheet formats list depreciation for each item, however that detail is available elsewhere in your books and clutters the report, in my opinion.

Other Assets

This category, which may not apply in all situations, is a place for assets that you can't logically place into one of the other two groupings. In my example, I used a deposit, which could be for lease or for a future purchase. You can also put intangible assets such as patents, trademarks, and copyrights in this area.

Limiting Your Liabilities

Your business, like your household, runs in part on credit. You obligate the company to short and long-term commitments to pay for the resources it needs to function. Some of these obligations are day-to-day bills, while others can be long-term mortgages or loans. The balance sheet format requires you to list the short-term and long-term obligations separately, roughly in the same manner as assets were divided by current and long-term.

Current Liabilities

As the name suggests, your company's current liabilities are due soon. The general rule is within a year, however most of the items in this category usually have shorter fuses than that. Many of these payments are the day-to-day operating expenses of running your business.

Your accounts payable account represents bills you owe, but haven't paid. Your company will pay most of these within 30 to 60 days, although there may be some such as quarterly insurance payments that stretch out longer. This is obviously an account you want to watch closely.

Sales tax collected and accrued payroll taxes represent deposits to respective taxing authorities that your company has not yet made. There could be other tax deposit accounts, too, that are unique to your situation. It is in these situations where cash management is critical. With money accumulating in your account over a quarter, it is easy to spend it on more pressing needs. Don't do it! Having the cash to make the tax deposit on time is critical. Don't find yourself short when a deposit is due.

Financial Aid

The matching of current and long-term assets and liabilities is not by accident. Current assets retire current liabilities and long-term assets secure long-term liabilities. This matching, although not precise, lets you see the effect actions on one side of the balance sheet have on the other.

In the Red

If you miss a timely deposit of taxes, the IRS may slap you with a fine and interest. Some businesses set up a separate bank account for tax deposits. This way there's no chance you'll spend the money before it is time to make a payment.

Bank notes represent short-term lending from the bank that is due in fewer than 12 months. This may be a line of credit you draw on from time to time to cover cash shortages or to purchase supplies, but pay back quickly.

The current portion of the long-term debt is your monthly note payment due over the next 12 months. This may be a little confusing, but if you have a long-term note, say on your building for 15 years, that portion of the note that is due in the current year shows up under current liabilities just like any short-term obligation.

Long-Term Liabilities

Long-term liabilities represent obligations that extend beyond one year. This would include notes on buildings and land purchases as well as general long-term financing. For most small businesses, concerns such as bonds are not an issue, but they would go here, too.

What about leases? They are generally long-term commitments for building space or equipment and often run longer than one year. The general rule is leases do not show up on the balance sheet as an obligation—the payment falls into accounts payable.

However, there is a type of lease that you may need to put under long-term liabilities on the balance sheet. Often called capital leases, capital leases offer many of the benefits of regular leases, and typically you own the equipment at the end of the lease. In many ways, capital leases are just another form of financing a purchase. Your accountant will probably want a capital lease reflected on your balance sheet.

What You Own

The third part of the balance sheet is equity. This section details what your stake in the company is worth. It has several parts depending on how you organized your company. If you look at the balance sheet of a publicly traded company, you'll note that this section lists preferred and common stock among other categories. If your company has shareholders and issued stock, this section will look slightly different.

Retained Earnings

When your company makes a profit (I hope it does every year), you have several choices as to what to do with the money. Some of those choices depend on whether you have shareholders and/or a profit-sharing plan. Here are some of the common options you have when your company makes a profit:

- Pay all or part of it out in a dividend or profit sharing.

- Pay off a loan or buy something the company needs.

- Invest the money for the company.

Financial Aid

How you take money out of your business depends on the organization of your company. You may take a salary and dividends or rely on some other method. Your tax advisor can help you structure the best method for your particular situation.

There are others, but the main point is you can disperse the money to you and other shareholders or you can retain it in the company to finance growth. Retained earnings represent profits that stay in the company and increase its value. These retained earnings become part of your equity in the business, but don't look for the cash in a bank account. Unless that's where you put it, the money is at work building the business.

Paid in capital represents your start-up money that got the business off the ground. You may not have put it all in at one time, but this is the money that you used to "seed" the business and it remains part of your equity.

How It Balances

The three elements of the balance sheet work in unison to tell you how healthy your company is when you or your accountant created the report. A great deal of accounting work goes on before you can create this report, because it represents summary data pulled from your books. If any of that data is flawed, there will be problems with the report.

The balance sheet for your business may contain more or fewer items than my example, but it will roughly follow the same format. If there are items you don't understand, ask your accountant for an explanation so you don't miss any vital pieces of information. Later in this book, I'll spend considerable time with the balance sheet and the other financial reports, showing you how the information can help you manage your business. It's important that you understand what's behind the numbers on all of the financial reports so you can see how these tools work.

The Least You Need to Know

- Current assets can be converted into cash within one year.

- Long-term assets represent plants and equipment your business will use for longer than one year.

- Current liabilities are due sooner than one year.

- Long-term liabilities represent loans and other obligations lasting longer than one year.

- Retained earnings and paid in capital are your equity in the business.

4

The Income Statement

In This Chapter

◆ Defining Revenue

◆ Defining expenses

◆ Qualifying income and expenses

◆ Formatting income statements

The income statement, sometimes called the profit and loss statement, is where you monitor how well your company is doing. It is where you find the all-important bottom line, which tells you whether you made a profit for the period or lost your shirt.

On the surface, it is the easiest of the "big three" financial reports to understand because it follows a logic similar to our checkbooks—revenue and expenses. However, there is more information here than meets the eye.

If you have an income statement from your business out while reading this chapter, you'll see how the categories I discuss play out in your report. While not all the terms and categories may be the same, they will be close enough for you to see how your "real world" income statement is put together.

Measuring Revenue and Expenses

The primary purpose of the income statement is to capture in one report how much revenue you took in and how much you paid out for a defined period. That period could be a month, quarter, or year. This statement gives you a point-in-time reference of where your business is financially. In other words, are you making money or not? Although it may seem a simple question, it may be harder than you think to answer it, depending on the size and complexity of your business. A one-person consulting company's income statement will look much different from one for a manufacturing company employing 75 people.

What Flavor of Accounting?

When you or your accountant set up your books, you decided whether to use the *cash* or *accrual* method of accounting or a modified version of both. Each method has its strong points and works better for some businesses than others do. Which method you chose will drive, to some extent, how your income statement will look. This is not a book on accounting, but you need to know the basic difference between the two main methods of recording revenue and expenses. These explanations are very simplified versions of complex topics, but sufficient to get us pointed in the right direction when looking at income statements.

Cash Accounting

Cash accounting is the simplest form of accounting, but doesn't do a good job of matching expenses and revenue. With cash accounting, you record revenue when you receive it, regardless of when you did the work. For example, if you did a job for a customer in September, but weren't paid until October, that's when you record the revenue. Of course, you probably had expenses that you paid out in cash to produce the job in September so those would go on the books in September.

Money Talk

Cash accounting is a method of accounting that records an expense when it is paid and revenue when it is received.

Accrual accounting is a method of accounting that ties the expense and revenue of a transaction together, regardless of whether cash has changed hands or not.

The result is your September might look terrible with all the expenses to produce the work and none of the revenue, while your October might look terrific with all the revenue and none of the expenses associated with the job. You don't get a clear picture of what actually happened.

Cash accounting works fine for simple, small businesses without inventories. One-person operations, pure cash businesses, for example might do just fine. This method keeps you close to what is actually in the bank and is really a sophisticated checkbook register.

Accrual Accounting

With *accrual accounting*, you would book the revenue as earned but not necessarily as cash is received and book expenses as incurred but not necessarily as paid. This marrying of revenue and expenses gives you an accurate picture of what is going on in the business, but not necessarily your bank balance.

Although you can more easily tell if your efforts are paying off, you may not be able to tell if you are about to run out of cash. You'll need to train yourself to understand the income statement and the bank statement are two very different things that you must monitor separately. More precisely, you will need to monitor not only the income statement, but also the balance sheet (Chapter 3) and the statement of cash flows (Chapter 5). Only when you use all three together do you get the complete picture.

The best choice for your business is a decision you should make with your accountant, however, many small businesses find a version of accrual accounting works best. If you carry inventory or have sales over a certain dollar amount, the IRS will require you to use accrual accounting.

Notes and News
You may hear the income statement also called the profit and loss statement, or P&L for short.

The Formula

The formula for the income statement is simple:

Revenue - Expenses = Income or (Loss)

There is a variation on this formula, which I'll discuss in Part 2 of this book as we look at how financial reports can become powerful tools to make your business stronger. For now, let's stick with the basic formula, because that's how the income statement flows from top to bottom.

There are three major elements to the income statement that correspond to the income statement formula: revenues, expenses, and net income. Each area has its own set of subcategories and definitions, again depending on the type and size of business.

Income Statement Formats

Income statements come in several formats. The income statements you see in annual reports for publicly traded companies probably do not look like your income statement. Those statements conform to certain standards and contain less detail than the income statement for your business.

One way to think of the difference is that big companies must produce "reporting" income statements, whereas you should be more interested in "operational" statements. This doesn't mean you don't have reporting responsibilities. You may have a small number of stockholders and very likely have a bank or other creditors that will periodically review your financial statements.

Two common formats for the income statement are the single stage and the multistage. Each has its strengths and weaknesses. Here's what they look like in a simplified format.

> **Notes and News**
>
> Big companies also produce detailed income statements, but those are for internal use only and are usually not available to the public, since they may contain information that competitors could exploit.

Single Stage Income Statement

Notice that this format groups all the revenue and all the expenses into two tidy categories. This format works fine for very small businesses, especially service businesses with few employees and no inventory or real manufacturing process or equipment.

Revenues	**Expenses**
Sales	Cost of Goods Sold
Other revenue	Depreciation
Total Revenue	Salaries
	Advertising
	Administrative Expenses
	Interest Expense
	Income Tax
	Total Expenses
	Net Income

Multistage Income Statement

The multistage income statement separates operating income and expenses from other income and expenses. It also puts income taxes in a separate category. This format has the advantage of clearly defining income and expenses that directly relate to the primary business. Other income, interest from investments in this case, not directly related to the business along with expenses such as interest and depreciation get their own categories.

Revenues	**Other Income**
Sales	Interest Income
Cost of Goods	
GROSS PROFIT	**Other Expenses**
	Interest Expenses
Operating Expenses	Depreciation
Salaries	**INCOME BEFORE TAXES**
Advertising	
Administrative Expenses	Income Taxes
TOTAL EXPENSES	**NET INCOME**
OPERATING INCOME	

Formats are window dressing and their only function is to make the information easier to look at and absorb. Which format you choose is more a matter of what works for you rather than what's "right or wrong."

The Reality

An income statement for a small business will have a lot of detail, especially in the expense category. You may even have two income statements, which I'll explain in more detail later, that serve both the reporting and operational functions.

Many small business people focus most of their attention on the income side of this report, which is a mistake and often a fatal one. Let's look at a small business income statement and how it details the expenses in particular. Oddly enough, many income statements produced for small businesses don't detail the Cost of Goods Sold section, which can be the biggest chunk of your expenses. You may have to ask your accountant or tweak your computer program to get more detail here. The income statement process is one that begins with total sales and subtracts expenses to arrive at a profit or loss figure at the end.

Small Business Income Statement

Revenue	
Sales	$3,800,000
Cost of Goods Sold	
Purchases	$1,988,000
Shipping	$400,000
Equipment	$230,000
Total:	$2,618,000
Gross Profit	$1,182,000
Expenses	
Accounting & Legal	$2,000
Advertising	$431,350
Bank Charges	$150
Insurance	$12,500
Administrative Expense	$230,000
Payroll Taxes	$15,000
Rent	$25,000
Salaries	$50,000
Supplies	$25,000
Telephone	$25,000
Utilities	$20,000
Total Expenses	**$836,000**
EBITDA	$346,000
Other Expenses	
Depreciation	$5,800
Interest Expenses	$12,500
Net Income before Taxes	**$327,700**
Income Taxes	$10,000
Net Income	**$317,700**

Money Talk _____

EBITDA stands for Earnings Before Interest, Taxes, Depreciation, and Amortization. EBITDA is considered an accurate picture of how profitable a business is, because all non-business expenses are not considered in figuring earnings.

Income is what you keep after you pay all the expenses—in other words, profits or earnings.

Revenue is a specific dollar amount of sales. It is what you are paid for your product or service.

Revenues

Revenues are the dollars you receive for your product or services. When you record them on your income statement depends on the accounting method you choose. It is not uncommon to hear people use the terms *income* and *revenue* interchangeably. They are not synonyms. Revenues and sales can mean the same thing, but you can generate tremendous sales or revenues, and still lose money.

Income, earnings, and profit generally mean the same thing. So when we talk about the top of the income statement, we are always referring to revenues (that's why you will sometimes hear about a company's top line growth). Income, specifically net income, is the opposite, or bottom line.

If you or a member of your staff keeps the books, be certain the entries are consistent with the accounting method you and your accountant chose. The old cliché of "garbage in, garbage out" can be your worst nightmare (there's another cliché) if you don't follow the standards.

Every business has sales—if not it won't be a business for long. Even service companies that provide intangible products such as consulting or financial advice have sales for accounting purposes. For some businesses, it is easy to define a sale. A customer walks up to the checkout and pays for an item—a sale has occurred.

For other businesses, the definition is not quite so easy. A sale may occur when you sign a contract or when you receive a purchase order. However you account for sales, make sure you record them the same way all the time. This consistency is necessary to make reports and analysis meaningful.

Some income statements call sales *net sales*, because discounts and deductions for returns and allowances have been deducted from the amount in other areas of the books. Sales taxes, which you might collect from customers, are also allocated to another account.

Cost of Goods Sold

The cost of goods sold section includes everything that went into the purchasing or manufacturing of you products or services. It also covers the direct cost of any marketing or sales expenses for these products.

These expenses include:

- The wages of the direct labor involved in producing the product or services

- The material used in producing the product

- Any parts or components purchased

- Utilities

- Repairs to equipment and/or facilities

The idea is to tie expenses directly related to the product or service together with sales. Service businesses will often have a simple cost of goods sold calculation, while manufacturing companies may find this is a detailed section.

If your income statement doesn't provide you with the detail you need to understand the cost of goods sold category, ask your accountant to provide the details, especially if you have several product lines. You should be able to develop a gross profit figure for each product line if you know the sales and cost of goods sold.

Gross Profit

Gross profit, also called gross margin, is simply the cost of goods sold subtracted from sales. For many companies, this is a measure of how efficient they are at producing their product or service. In Part 2 of this book, I'll discuss ways to benchmark performance and this number plays an important role in those exercises.

If your company has several product lines, your accounting system should be sufficiently robust to calculate this number for each one. This will give you a way to measure not only efficiency and profitability of each line, but also a way to measure the performance of line managers.

Expenses

Expenses under this heading refer to the general costs of operating the company rather than the specific costs associated with producing the product or service.

Although these expenses may affect sales, they aren't directly tied to the production of the product. The exception may be utilities, which I'll expand on in that section.

Accounting and legal professional services typically fall under the general administrative functions of the business and belong in the expenses category. For some companies, this number will be relatively modest, while others may find it otherwise.

Advertising and marketing can be a significant portion of a small company's budget. Even

> **CAUTION**
>
> **In the Red** _____
>
> It is not unusual for small business owners to focus on generating sales with the belief that if they can bring in enough cash, they can cover their expenses. Unfortunately, many businesses fail, not because they couldn't generate sales, but because they couldn't control costs.

though these dollars may influence sales, they don't contribute to the actual production of the product or service, so they generally belong in this area instead of the cost of goods sold slot.

Bank charges refer to those fees associated with your accounts at the bank and any other services you buy from financial institutions. This is not the area for interest expense.

If you are in business, you should have insurance coverage including fire, theft, and property damage. You might also have life insurance on key executives and special insurance for your particular industry as needed. This is not the category where employee health insurance goes.

Interest expense is what you pay on your debt, both long and short-term.

In most businesses, your office expense includes all the costs necessary to run the administrative portion of your business, including office equipment, supplies, security, and so on.

You are required to collect payroll taxes (state and federal income tax withholding, Social Security, and Medicare) from all eligible employees each pay check and deposit those funds according to the appropriate IRS schedule. This is one bill you do not ever want to overlook. The IRS has zero tolerance with companies that fail to make deposits, since part of the deposit is employees' money.

In most cases, your rent falls in the general expense category. However, if you rent a facility just to produce a product, your accountant may want you to categorize that expense as a cost of goods sold. Likewise, service companies that operate out of a suite of offices may include rent in the cost of goods sold.

You should make these decisions with your accountant, who will know how similar businesses have categorized the expense. The idea is to make the income statement a useful document to you, and that goal should drive where you place expense items, within reason.

Financial Aid

Allocating manager's salaries is an item to discuss with your accountant. If their (or your) responsibilities cross several product areas, you may want to split their costs over those areas rather than dumping the total in administration.

Salaries of office and support personnel not directly tied to the production of the product or service fall in general administrative expenses. Some small businesses allocate a portion of the senior executive's salary to cost of goods sold, because it is likely he or she is intimately involved in product or service production.

General office supplies are those products needed to run the business that aren't part of the production process.

Telephones, in most cases, will fall under the general expense category. An example of an exception would be a call center, where telephones are the primary equipment used to deliver the service and would then fall in the cost of goods sold category.

Utility bills fall into a grey area. They could be either general expense or cost of goods sold, depending on your business. Here, common sense is the rule. For example, if you owned a small commercial printing business in a 10,000 sq. ft. facility, you might only have 500 sq. ft. of office space and the rest production area. Clearly, utilities belong in cost of goods sold in this case because most of the area is production.

It is worth repeating that you want an income statement that is accurate and reflects your true costs. If the cost of utilities play a significant role in the production of your product, it is important to tie those expenses to sales.

Total Expenses

Many income statements end here with a sum of the total expenses. I have included another step for those companies that use these additional categories. The format may be different, however, the information will be the same.

Other Expenses

Other expenses include items that are either noncash items or expenses that don't relate directly to the business itself.

Depreciation is a noncash charge for the declining value of an asset taken over a period of years. It attempts to match the value of the asset with the income it produces. For example, if you bought a machine for $10,000 and it had a useful life of five years, each year for five years, you would take a $2,000 deduction off expenses.

> **Money Talk**
>
> **Depreciation** is a way to charge off an asset over a period of years using a variety of schedules. The charge is an expense that reduces current earnings, but does not involve cash.

There are various depreciation schedules for different types of equipment and different methods for computing how much to deduct each year. My example above used the straight-line method.

If you do not have many depreciable assets, you may only want to make an adjustment once a year for tax purposes. On the other hand, if you have a significant investment in equipment, buildings, and other assets, you may want to consider taking a monthly write off.

Other expenses could include such items as a lawsuit settlement, or any nonoperating expense that doesn't fit any category above.

Net Income Before Taxes

Subtract expenses and other expense categories from gross profit and you will have your net income before taxes. If the number is positive, the company has made a profit, although a negative number shows a loss.

Income Taxes

Federal and state income taxes fall under income taxes. If your company did not make a profit, you may not have a tax liability for this item.

Net Income

This is what you've been waiting for—the bottom line. Net income is gross profit minus expenses minus other expenses (if any) including taxes. This is what you get to distribute as a dividend or retain within the company (see Chapter 3 on retained earnings).

Gross Profit - All Expenses = Net Income

Reporting vs. Operational Reports

As I noted earlier in the chapter, there is a big difference in the income statements you see for publicly traded companies and small businesses that are not subject to the same regulatory requirements. This doesn't mean you can do anything you want with your income statement, because there still are many other people and institutions who will want to see your financial statements, and they have to be able to make sense of them. The point is, your income statement is an important tool in running your business, and tweaking it with your accountant's help can make it a powerful ally.

Frequency of Reports

Most businesses see an income statement monthly, although a one-person business might not need it more frequently than quarterly. It is imperative that you have an annual income statement for tax purposes. Depending on how you handle depreciation (see above), you may have an annual income statement that differs from your monthly statements. Including depreciation reduces earnings, which can have an effect on your income tax liability. Your accountant is your best advisor on these matters because he or she knows your business situation.

Financial Aid

Creditors, including your bank and suppliers, will want to see current financial statements before extending credit or as part of their periodic review of your account.

Format of Report

You can use a variety of formats for income statements depending on what you find meaningful as a business tool. Here are some options:

- The current month can be presented in contrast to the same month last year.
- Each month can be added to a consecutive list of months in the year, so you can compare current activity with all previous months.
- The current month can be presented in relation to the budget for that month, a year to date actual, and budget figure. This format shows how your income and expenses line up next to the budget by month and cumulatively.

Sample Income Statement

Let's look at a sample income statement from a small business I hope to start some day. This will be my ticket to riches, if not fame and glory.

Income Statement Amalgamated Kumquats

	Jan. 2006		Jan. 2005	
Sales	$18,500	100.0%	$17,000	100.0%
Cost of Goods Sold	($12,230)	66.1%	($10,240)	60.2%
Gross Profit	**$6,270**	**33.9%**	**$6,760**	**39.7%**
Expenses				
Accounting & Legal	$750	4.1%	$750	4.4%
Advertising	$500	2.7%	$500	2.9%
Bank Charges	$45	0.2%	$45	0.3%
Insurance	$150	0.8%	$125	0.7%
Interest Expense	$30	0.2%	$30	0.2%
Office Expense	$500	2.7%	$450	2.6%
Payroll Taxes	$335	1.8%	$330	1.9%
Postage	$125	0.7%	$125	0.7%
Rent	$500	2.7%	$500	2.9%
Salaries	$2,800	15.1%	$2,600	15.3%
Telephone	$100	0.5%	$100	0.6%
Utilities	$200	1.0%	$200	1.2%
Total Expenses	**$6,035**	**32.6%**	**$5,755**	**33.8%**
Net Income	**$235**	**1.3%**	**$1,005**	**5.9%**

Sample Focus

Don't get hung up on the numbers—they're just for illustration. (Although you can see at a glance that my dreams of wealth are quite a ways off, based on this income statement.)

This format of comparing the current month to last year has some benefits in that it gives you a historical perspective. However, if your business is still young, this may not mean much. Young businesses tend to evolve rapidly, so comparing current operations to those of a year ago may not be very helpful. I'll discuss this more in Part 2 of this book.

For now, let's focus on how the report is constructed and worry about which comparisons work best later.

Statement Detail

Regardless of which period you choose to compare, your income statement will likely look like my sample in its format. There may be more or fewer categories and your accountant may want you to include depreciation, which I did not in this illustration. Most income statements use the percentage format to help you see the relationship of each category to sales.

Financial Aid

Why use percentages? Percentages let you easily compare period to period and see when items are out of the norm. The numbers will change, but the relationships to sales (if they are where you want them) should not.

Sales are always 100 percent and all other numbers on the income statement are percentages of sales. You find the percentage by dividing any number on the statement by the sales figure. My illustration carries the answer to one decimal point. You may want two for more accuracy, but one is the minimum because some numbers will likely be fractions of a percent.

Your accountant and/or software package can be tweaked (did you ever want to tweak your accountant?) to provide the level of detail that works for you. For example, some people find that reporting cents is distracting and would rather see the report with whole numbers. Others may not be satisfied until they see every penny.

Working Document

When we get to those chapters later in the book that focus on using financial reports, including the income statement, as strategic tools, you should be comfortable with the format and have a good idea of what is behind the numbers. All of your financial reports are primarily working documents to help you run your business better. Like any tool, it will help you best when you make it yours by finding the format that works best for you.

The Least You Need to Know

- ◆ There are different formats for income statements.

- ◆ Income statements for small businesses are rich in detail about the business.

- ◆ Cost of goods sold must accurately reflect the expenses necessary to produce your product or service.

- ◆ Depreciation is an expense you may take monthly or annually depending on your circumstances.

- ◆ Income statements are working documents that will help you run your business.

5

Show Me the Cash

In This Chapter

♦ Methods of reporting

♦ Sources of funds

♦ Uses of funds

♦ Changes in cash balance

It is not overstating matters to compare cash to blood for a company's health. Cut off or restrict cash and you have a sick company. The statement of cash flows identifies the source of cash flows needed to fund your company's various activities and calculates the effect of business decisions on your company's cash position. Thanks to the noncash items that appear on the income statement and balance sheet, you don't always know the correct cash situation. This chapter focuses on the report that clears the air on where your cash is coming from and where it is going.

Use of the Report

The statement of cash flows, which is required for publicly traded companies, can be very beneficial to small businesses, but not all will need it. If

CAUTION

In the Red

Managing your company's cash is one of the most important jobs you have as an owner. Even if your business is big enough for an accounting staff, stay on top of your cash position.

you have a very small business in the service area (consultant, for example), this report will be of minimal help. On the other hand, if you employ 15 consultants who all work on different projects, the report may prove very valuable.

One of the big benefits of the statement of cash flows is seeing your company's true cash position without all the noncash items, such as depreciation, clouding the income statement and balance sheet.

Where You Find the Numbers

The numbers for the statement of cash flows come from the balance sheet and income statement. In an attempt to clarify certain parts of a company's operations by matching expenses with income, accounting standards cause confusion about the cash position. The statement of cash flows clarifies the cash position, but by itself does not give you a complete picture of your company's health. This is why you have three financial reports—each tells you something different about your company.

Questions Answered

The statement of cash flows answers several important questions for the small business owner:

- Where did the cash for operations come from during the period?
- How much cash did the company spend during the period?
- How much did the cash balance change over the covered period?

There are other questions the statement of cash flows will help you answer, but I'll cover those when I discuss how to use financial reports in Part 2 to help you run your business better.

To find the answers to these questions, the statement of cash flows tracks cash coming into and moving out of your company. You build the report by taking all of the noncash items out of the income statement and balance sheet. You then make adjustments in various income and expense categories to distinguish between actual cash transactions and credit or paper transactions. As I walk you through the report, you'll see how this is basically an addition and subtraction exercise.

The report itself calculates changes in expense and income items from the previous period to the current period. These changes either add to cash or subtract from it, depending on whether the change was positive or negative.

Financial Aid

A statement of cash flows, like the other financial reports, requires a point of reference to be fully useful.

Timing

How frequently you or your accountant generate a statement of cash flows is up to you. For companies with a small workforce and few credit sales, quarterly may work just fine. Larger companies need this report monthly along with their balance sheet and income statement. Every business needs an annual statement of cash flows, no matter the size.

Three Parts

The statement of cash flows breaks transactions down into three groups:

- Operations
- Investing
- Financing

Of these three areas, operations are the most important and should be the source and use of most of your company's cash under normal circumstances.

Operations

This part of the statement of cash flows identifies cash transactions involved in the daily operations of your company. Revenue from sales and the expenses related to generating those sales fall into this area. This is the most important part of the statement of cash flows because it describes the heart of your business. There may be occasions when big numbers show up in the

Financial Aid

If you use some of the popular accounting software packages such as QuickBooks, you can "look inside" parts of the statement of cash flows to see the underlying transactions. This is helpful if some number doesn't look right or make sense to you.

other two areas, but in most cases, you can find the bulk of the cash that flows through your business in this area.

Investments

This part of the report focuses on investments in your company, such as buying or selling a building, land, or even a part of the company. Any capital investment in the business falls into this category. Under these circumstances, you would see a large plus or minus to cash, however these are usually not frequent transactions, so accountants consider the change to cash a one-time event, unlike the ongoing nature of operations.

Investments in marketable securities such as stocks or bonds, either buying or selling, also fall in this area.

Financing

If you borrow money or issue stock, you add to the cash position. This report is not about balancing, it is about cash and it doesn't matter whether you have to pay it back at some point or not—that's a concern of the balance sheet. One hundred dollars borrowed, raised by selling stock, or paid in by the owner is $100 cash on the statement of cash flows, and you should add it to the cash position. Likewise, debts repaid, stock repurchased, and dividends paid all come off the cash position. A large loan or stock issue would drive this number up, while the repayment would drive it down. However, like investments, it's normally not a frequent occurrence.

Formats

There are several formats for the statement of cash flows report. As with the other key financial reports, the format you use should be the one that offers the most information and is easiest to understand. Your small business report will not look like the ones produced for publicly held companies. You are more interested in functionality, and can structure the report to provide you the information in a format that meets that goal.

Sources and Uses of Funds

For many years, accountants called the cash flow statement a "sources and uses of funds" report. You may still see the report presented in that manner, with sources of funds on top and uses of funds on the bottom. The first figure is net income and all the sources of funds are added to it. This is followed by a listing of the uses of funds, which is totaled at the end. The uses of funds, also known as expenditures, are subtracted from the sources to give you a change in the cash balance for the period. This change, whether it is positive or negative, is added to the previous period's cash balance to give you the current cash balance.

Categories

The more current format is to group the sources of funds by the three categories: operations, investing, and financing. I believe this format is the most useful because it gives you a clear picture of the operations side of the business, and that's usually the most important area of the report.

This format of the cash flow statement gives you a clear picture of the changes in cash coming in and going out through the actual operations of your business so that investments made for equipment and buildings, as well as cash raised or dispersed via financing, don't muddy the waters.

Sample Report

The statement of cash flows is not a report you will have to file with any regulatory agency unless you decide to take your company public. A bank may ask you to submit it along with a balance sheet and income statement as part of a loan package or for some other business purpose. However, its main purpose is to be a working report to help you run your business better. To that end, work with your accountant to find the format that gives you the information you need. If you use a software package, see if you can tweak the report format to fit your needs. Many will let you customize reports.

Financial Aid

The statement of cash flows may be the simplest of the major financial reports to produce. You need the income statement and balance sheet from the previous period and a current income statement. Once you have identified the categories that add to or subtract from cash, the rest is simple math.

The increases and decreases on the report represent changes from the previous period—in this case the previous fiscal year. For example, the 2005 increase in accounts payable figure of $5,000 represents a change in that amount from 2004— not the total accounts payable expense. The 2004 accounts payable figure of $1,000 represents a change in that amount from 2003, and so on for all those categories labeled increase or decrease.

Statement of Cash Flows

Fiscal Year Ended Dec. 31, 2005

Cash Flow from Operations

	FY 2005	FY 2004
Net Earnings	$327,700	$302,000
Added to Cash		
Depreciation	$10,000	$9,000
Increase in Accounts Payable	$5,000	$1,000
Increase in Taxes Payable	$5,000	
Subtractions from Cash		
Increase in Accounts Receivable	$(2,000)	$(5,000)
Increase in Inventory	$(5,000)	$(3,000)
Net Cash from Operations:	$340,700	$305,000
Cash Flow from Investments		
Capital Expenditures	$(230,000)	$(25,000)
Cash Flow from Financing		
Bank Note	$(50,000)	$(200,000)
Cash Flow from Fiscal Year:	**$60,700**	**$80,000**
Change in Cash Position		
Cash at Beginning of Year:	**$83,000**	**$3,000**
Cash at End of Year:	$143,700	$83,000

Start at the Beginning

The statement of cash flows begins with the net income or the earnings figure from the income statement under accrual accounting (see Chapter 4). Because this figure is tainted with noncash items, the cash flow statement works though your financial reports, adds back noncash deductions, and subtracts changes that artificially inflate your cash position. You'll see how this works as I walk you through the sample report.

The first item you want to add back to cash is depreciation. Remember from earlier chapters that depreciation is an expense you take over time against the life of an asset such as a piece of equipment or building. Depreciation lowers your income tax liability by reducing your current net income, however it does not represent real money. So when it comes to figuring out cash flow, you add depreciation back in as cash.

Financial Aid

All this adding and subtracting of changes in numbers may seem confusing at first. However, looking at changes from one period to the next makes sense. Your company will always have accounts payable, so as that number rises and falls according to the balance sheets you are comparing, the difference between the two is the amount of cash available to the business.

Another way a company adds cash is to increase the time it takes to pay its bills. Increases in accounts payable indicate the company is using credit more in its purchases, or in some cases, running short of cash and unable to make timely payments. In either case, the company has more cash available for other uses. The same logic applies to increases in taxes payable. Taking more time to pay bills of any type leaves your company more cash, if only temporarily. You measure these increases from one accounting period to another.

Cash Goes Out

In addition to finding sources of cash to add back in to the books, the cash flow statement records areas where cash goes out. An increase in accounts receivable is one of those areas that you must subtract from cash. This is the mirror of the increase in accounts payable notation above, however, in this case your company is financing purchases for your customers. As you extend more credit or your customers are slower to pay, cash drains out of your business.

Financial Aid

Your credit policy is a tricky issue. For many businesses, selling on some type of credit is a market necessity. Loose credit policies may generate more sales, but higher losses to bad debts. When you increase accounts receivable with no change in total revenue, you take cash out of the business.

An increase in inventory means your company has paid for materials to up your on-hand supply. Assuming you paid cash for the materials, this increase indicates a decline in cash for the company and you subtract it from cash.

Net Cash from Operations

Once you make all of the additions and subtractions of cash from the net income figure, you have the net cash from operations. This is an important figure and you will see it in later chapters when we discuss analysis of your business.

Cash Flow from Investments

My sample report shows a subtraction from cash for capital expenditures. This could be for new equipment or some other asset your company purchased. If your company sold a large asset such as a building or land, this number would be positive and you would add the figure to cash.

Cash Flow from Financing

If you increase a bank note or take out a new note, you add cash to your business and it shows up as a positive on the statement of cash flows. This number also could be negative if you paid down or off a note, indicating a reduction in available cash. Remember, these numbers represent changes from the previous period.

Summing It Up

Net cash from operations (+/-) cash flows from investments and financing = net cash flow.

If you add or subtract the cash flows from investments and financing (depending on whether they are positive or negative numbers) from net cash from operations, you have the net cash flow for fiscal year 2005. If we had the cash flow statement for fiscal year 2004, we could calculate the change in cash position for the 2005 fiscal year, which is very helpful information.

Change in Cash Position

To begin a new report, you use the ending cash position from the previous period's report as the beginning cash balance for the current report. Add in the net cash flow (or subtract if it is a negative number) and you have the ending cash balance.

Financial Aid _____

Later in the book, I'll discuss some analysis tools, but you can look at several years' of cash flow statements and quickly tell if your company is improving its cash position, holding its own, or declining.

Other Items

My sample report is a simple representation of a cash flow statement. For many small businesses, it will work just fine, however you may find your company's report has other categories listed that I didn't include. Here are some of the more common additions and subtractions to cash that might appear on your cash flow statement.

Sources of Cash

Some of the other areas that may contribute to cash include:

- **Increase in Current Liabilities.** You have postponed paying for something or an expense is accruing, providing a source of cash.

- **Decrease in Investments.** A decrease in investments indicates the company sold a marketable security of some type and generated cash.

- **Decrease in Accounts Receivable.** A decrease in this item means your company is collecting more from its customers, and that is money in the bank.

- **Decrease in Inventory.** If your inventory is dropping, your company is investing less in supplies and has more free cash.

Notes and News

Unlike my sample report above, your statement of cash flows may contain several more categories sources and uses of cash.

Uses of Cash

Other areas where you must subtract cash include:

 ◆ **Payment of Cash Dividend.** If you paid shareholders a cash dividend this is obviously a draw on cash.

 ◆ **Decrease in Current Liabilities.** A drop in current liabilities indicates your company is paying off these items, which reduces cash.

 ◆ **Increase in Investing Activities.** If your company purchases marketable securities or makes capital expenditures, it reduces cash.

Others

There may be other items in your company that would be additions or subtractions to cash. Your accountant can help you identify those areas. If your company has foreign operations or receives payments in foreign currency, you will need to make some adjustment for exchange rates that may affect cash.

The Least You Need to Know

 ◆ The statement of cash flows draws information from the income statement and balance sheet.

 ◆ The net income figure is the starting point for figuring cash flow.

 ◆ Noncash items, such as depreciation, are added back to cash.

 ◆ Changes in certain balance sheet amounts indicate a change in the cash position.

Part 2

Make the Numbers Work

Your company's financial reports are just the beginning—consider them raw material. Once you have an idea of what they are all about, you can put them to work for you by applying some analysis. Don't worry, it's not that tough. This part walks you through some common financial analysis tools that will bring you a deeper understanding of your business. This is where the real payoff comes. Using your financial statements and a few ratios, you can look at how well or poorly your company is performing in a number of key areas.

Chapter 6

How Are Your Assets Working?

In This Chapter

- ◆ Working with ratios
- ◆ Two different kinds of ratios
- ◆ Meaningful information for investors and lenders
- ◆ Using ratios to monitor your business

It's back to the balance sheet. Time to put it to work calculating ratios and returns that will provide you with a check on your company's health. Potential lenders and investors look at these numbers, too, so it's in your interest to understand what they mean. However, their value goes beyond that—these ratios serve as benchmarks to gauge how well your assets work for you. This chapter gives you some easy tools to use that will tell you volumes about your business.

Using Your Balance Sheet

Your company's balance sheet is like a physical exam (or, more appropriately, a fiscal exam) given at a certain point in time. The report tells you many things about your business and specifically your assets, which don't appear on any other regular financial report.

For this discussion of assets, we'll use the same sample balance sheet found in Chapter 3.

Assets

Current Assets	
Cash	$15,000
Marketable Securities	$10,000
Accounts Receivable	$367,000
Inventory	$125,000
Prepaid Expenses	$10,500
Total Current Assets	$527,500
Property and Equipment	
Building	$2,021,500
Equipment	$200,000
Furniture and Fixtures	$5,000
Accumulated Depreciation	($58,500)
Total Property and Equipment	$2,168,000
Other Assets	
Deposits	$1,000
Total Other Deposits	$1,000
Total Assets	$2,696,500

Liabilities and Equity

Current Liabilities	
Accounts Payable	$215,000
Sales Tax Collected	$10,000
Accrued Payroll Taxes	$10,000

Bank Notes	$10,000
Current Portion of Long-Term Debt	$75,000
Total Current Liabilities	$320,000
Long-Term Liabilities	
Loans Payable	$2,284,000
Total Long-Term Liabilities	$2,284,000
Total Liabilities	$2,604,000
Equity	
Retained Earnings	$62,500
Paid in Capital	$30,000
Total Stockholder's Equity	$92,500
Total Liabilities and Stockholder's Equity	$2,696,500

This typical small business balance sheet will help us walk through the key financial ratios on assets that are important to your business. Working with your balance sheet will become easier with practice. If you have a current balance sheet from your business, keep it handy as you go through this section.

Working With Ratios

You need to get comfortable with ratios before we move forward. If you are mathematically challenged, not to worry, you already know and use many ratios every day. A ratio is a mathematical calculation that compares two numbers. For example, when you figure the mileage your car gets in miles per gallon (mpg) of gas, you calculate the ratio between miles driven and gas used. If you have driven 300 miles and put 15 gallons of gas in your tank, the mpg is 20—to state this as a ratio, you would say 20 miles driven to 1 gallon of gas, or 20:1. When working with financial ratios, we drop the second part, as you do and simply say 20 miles per gallon. Financial ratios let you compare current and past performance and help you predict future performance.

You may not feel comfortable reducing your business to a set of numbers and I'm not suggesting that you manage it strictly on numbers alone. However, without some quantifiable benchmarks, it will be impossible for you to know how well or how poorly your business is doing. Lenders and investors will know because they use these ratios. They shouldn't know more about your business than you do.

Key Financial Ratios and Returns

You can use financial ratios to monitor your company's health, measure productivity, compare your company's performance to industry standards and peers, and for internal controls. There are also others that want to see your ratios, including lenders, potential investors, suppliers, and, in some cases, regulators. Subsequent chapters will look at key ratios for the income statement and statement of cash flows. In some cases, you will need numbers from one of the other reports for a particular ratio.

Ratios can stand on their own, but may be more effective when compared to a previous period. This comparison gives you the opportunity to see movement for good or ill and make corrections if necessary.

Financial Aid

If you find a particular ratio or ratios helpful, begin charting them, either on a spreadsheet or with a pen and paper, to watch their movement. You may notice over time some seasonality in the way they change due to fluctuations in business conditions.

Liquidity Ratios

Liquidity is your company's ability to pay its bills in a timely manner. It measures the resources on hand to accomplish this task. This is one of the most important tests for lenders. It tells them if your company can repay a loan. It also tells you whether the company is heading for trouble if there is a significant decline in these numbers. In addition, you can use these tests to make some strategic decisions about your business. There are two main liquidity ratios: the current ratio and the quick ratio.

Current Ratio

The current ratio is a simple test that compares you company's current assets with its current liabilities. Your accountant can easily provide this to you if you are not receiving it on a regular basis already. Most popular software packages include this and the other major ratios.

The basic formula for the current ratio is:

Current assets ÷ Current liabilities = Current ratio

The formula most analysts follow is the following for current assets: cash + marketable securities + accounts receivable + inventory + other current assets.

For current liabilities: accounts payable + short-term notes + accrued liabilities + other current liabilities.

This test looks at the relationship between current assets, which, you remember from Chapter 3, can be converted into cash within one year, and current liabilities, which are due within one year.

A current ratio below 1.0 means current assets are less than current liabilities and the company may have a difficult time meeting its obligations in the near future. A current ratio above 1.0 suggests the company may have the resources to meet its short-term obligations.

> **Financial Aid**
>
> Current ratio numbers are guidelines that work for most businesses, but are not hard and fast rules. If there is a compelling reason for your company's ratio to be below 1.0, discuss it with your banker.

Quick Ratio or Acid Test

The quick ratio, also known as the acid test, is the same liquidity test as the current ratio, but measures your company's ability to meet immediate commitments. To do this, the quick ratio eliminates inventory from the current assets portion of the equation.

Here's the logic. Inventory is a broad term that includes finished goods and work in progress. Some parts of inventory may not be ready for sale and may require further investment of labor and parts to complete. It fits in current assets because you can generally sell it within one year, however, it is not as liquid as the other components of current assets.

For this reason, lenders view the quick ratio as a test of your company's ability to meet obligations in the very near term. A high level of inventory might distort the current ratio, but the quick ratio eliminates that problem.

Clearly, the quick ratio will be lower than the current ratio, but how much lower depends on the type of business. A service business should have the same current and quick ratio because service businesses don't typically carry inventory.

Using Liquidity Ratios

The current ratio and quick ratio have value beyond their quick check of your liquidity. You can use them to benchmark your company's compliance with key indicators. Here's how you might use these ratios.

Value of Current Ratio

What is the correct current ratio? More important, what is the best current ratio for your company? Let's walk through an exercise to see how you might get to this answer.

Using the sample balance sheet from above, this company's current ratio is 1.65. Here's how I got that number. The current assets are $527,500 and current liabilities are $320,000. Applying the current ratio formula: $527,500 ÷ $320,000 = 1.65.

With a current ratio of 1.65, the company appears in good shape to meet its day-to-day obligations. A ratio above 1.0 means the company has more current assets than current liabilities. Can you conclude that a company with a current ratio over 1.0 is in a good liquidity situation? The answer is no. One of the most important lessons in financial analysis is that no one number tells the whole story. A company could have a huge inventory or accounts receivable, which would make the ratio high. A company that has too much cash in the bank may think that it is a smart move, but it is poor asset management. Cash should be working for you in your business, not earning a few percentage points in a bank account (or worse, not earning any interest at all).

> **CAUTION**
>
> **In the Red** _____
>
> Don't fall into the trap of focusing on a single ratio or return. Every financial indicator has a flaw and only tells part of the picture. Use several to get a complete story.

If all parts of current assets and current liabilities look reasonable, then the current ratio is meaningful and you can use it to watch you company's liquidity. You can bet your banker keeps a close eye on it.

What Is the Best Current Ratio?

Once you see the components of the current ratio and how they affect the outcome, you can use that information to help you think about a number of questions. The first question you should address is, "What is the appropriate current ratio for my company?" This is where you put the tool to use and the current ratio becomes something more than a static number that your company either hits or misses.

We know that if the components of the current ratio are under- or overstated, it affects the ratio. This opens the door to examining each component as a business function and measuring the effect changes may have on the current ratio.

For example, if accounts receivable goes way up, it will likely pull up the current ratio. The question you need to ask here is how much credit the company needs to extend to remain competitive in its market. Asking yourself the following questions will help you determine what needs to be done.

- ◆ Should we change credit policies to tighten or loosen credit and what affect will that have?

- ◆ What level of inventory is necessary to serve our customers in the most cost efficient manner?

- ◆ Are we using our cash in the best way?

- ◆ What about our accounts payable? Could we earn some discounts for early payment?

- ◆ Where are we on our short-term debt and other liabilities?

Obviously, you don't make these decisions to hit a number; you make the decisions that are in the best interest of your business. When you have thought through all the components of the current ratio and established an acceptable level for each, you then have a current ratio target that is right for your company. If your business has a seasonal nature to it, your current ratio target may be a range that takes into account changing business patterns.

> **Notes and News**
>
> Want to see what other companies in your industry are doing? Check out BizStats.com for benchmark information on a number of different industries that use financial indicators.

Establishing Targets

In later chapters, I cover planning and goal setting in more detail, but for the purpose of this discussion, let's assume you have set a low and high target for each of the components of the current ratio calculation.

Current Assets

	Target A	Target B
Cash	$15,000	$20,000
Marketable Securities	$10,000	$15,000

continues

continued

Accounts Receivable	$367,000	385,000
Inventory	$125,000	145,000
Prepaid Expenses	$10,500	15,000
Total Current Assets	**$527,500**	**$580,000**
Current Liabilities		
Accounts Payable	$215,000	225,000
Sales Tax Collected	$10,000	13,000
Accrued Payroll Taxes	$10,000	14,000
Bank Notes	$10,000	15,000
Current Portion of Long-Term Debt	$75,000	90,000
Total Current Liabilities	**$320,000**	**$357,000**
Current Ratio:	**1.65**	**1.62**
Quick Ratio:	**1.26**	**1.22**
Worst Case Scenario		
Current Ratio:	**1.48 ($527,500 ÷ $357,000 = 1.48)**	
Quick Ratio:	**1.13 ($402,500 ÷ $357,000 = 1.13)**	

The Worst Case Scenario assumes you hit the low target for current assets, but the high target for current liabilities. This squeezes your liquidity, although the business is still above the danger stage.

There are tools to help you manage many of the individual components of the current ratio calculation; however, after you have these goals in place, your business has the beginnings of an operational plan.

When you get your financial reports and the current ratio is not within the target range, you instantly know some component is not where it should be. Although you should always look at each component, this early warning system can tip you off to a problem that may cause reviewing financial reports to move the top of your to-do list.

Return on Assets

Return on assets (ROA) measures how well your business is using its assets. You calculate ROA by dividing net income by total assets. This gives you a percentage return.

Net Income ÷ Total Assets = Return on Assets

High or Low

A high ROA means the company is making good use of the assets, while a low ROA suggests needed improvement. What is high and low depends a great deal on the industry. Manufacturers with heavy investments in equipment and so on tend to have ROAs in the single digits, while a service company's ROA will be much higher, at 20 or above.

Financial Aid _____

Return on assets is one of the most valuable indicators you can use, because it takes in all of your company's assets. However, even ROA has its flaws. Certain leases may not appear on the balance sheet and could affect your company's future.

What It Means

A simple way to look at ROA is that a small amount of assets should help you earn a large amount of net income. This indicates those assets are working hard for your company. On the other hand, a large amount of assets that produce a small amount of net income (or a loss) may not be working as hard as they should. Sometimes this calculation is called the return on investment (ROI), because the assets represent the owner's investment in the business. You can also use the ROI calculation on smaller projects.

Other Uses

While ROA can tell you something about how well your company is using its assets, you can also use a version of the formula on a smaller scale to determine if a new project is worth pursuing. In this case, ROI is more appropriate because you want to look at the investment in a specific project or item rather than all of the company's assets. Say you are thinking about a new product line or opening a new store. There will be a cost associated with the project and you should expect a return on that investment. You can use the ROA calculation to help you decide if the project is viable.

In Chapter 10, I'll discuss strategic planning in detail, but for now let's assume that you have a strategic goal that states any new project must achieve an ROI of 10 percent in a reasonable period or it is rejected. Using the simplified formula, you estimate the net income the project will generate and divide that by the total investment (assets) required to make the project happen. You may need to project the numbers out for several years if there is a start-up phase. If the ROI hits the 10 percent or higher mark within a reasonable period, you have a go. If not, you modify the plan to make it work or drop the project.

Companies use this method to manage profit centers or product lines independently. It allows you to manage a profit center, which could be an individual store, a product line, or even a sales territory. Small businesses can use this method with equal effectiveness as large companies.

Other Ratios

Several other ratios can help you manage your business more effectively. These ratios tell you whether your business is making the most of its resources or falling short in some areas.

Debt to Shareholders' Equity

Debt to equity is a way of measuring a company's risk of default on new or existing loans. Some loans require a certain ratio and if the company slips below that ratio, the lender may raise the interest rate or call the note. The formula is:

Debt to Equity Ratio = Long-Term Debt ÷ Equity

Some lenders require that short-term debt be included in the calculation as well. The idea behind this ratio is that note payments are fixed costs and must be paid even if business declines. Lenders want some comfort that the company has enough equity to ride out slow times and still make note payments.

> **Financial Aid**
>
> Some industries use more debt than others do. This is neither bad nor good; it's just the nature of the business. That's why you should only compare your company to other companies in the same industry.

A debt to equity ratio of 1 means the company used an equal amount of debt and equity to fund its operations. For many companies, this is where they want to be, however, discuss this with your accountant and banker to find the right level for your company in your industry.

Return On Equity

Return on equity tells you how the company is performing for its investors, even if that's just you. It measures how much in profits your equity is returning and is best looked at over a period to get a sense of direction. The formula is:

Return on Equity = Net Income ÷ Shareholders' Equity

You find net income on the income statement and shareholders' equity on the balance sheet. Use yearend numbers to get a more comprehensive picture and compare them to several previous years.

Unfortunately, you'll hear much about ROE as a measurement tool. The reason for this is ROE makes companies look better than they are because ROE doesn't measure the effect of a company's debt on future earnings. Net income only includes the current portion of the note payment in its calculation, so you don't get the total impact of the whole note. The result is that the return calculated by ROE is overly optimistic. You are better off using return on assets, which does a better job for small businesses of giving owners a real number to use in decision making.

The Least You Need to Know

- Lenders and investors look at ratios to help them make decisions about your company.

- The current ratio tells you whether your company can meet its short-term obligations or not.

- The quick ratio focuses on immediate obligations and your company's ability to meet those.

- Return on assets is a valuable tool that can help you manage your business more effectively.

- Debt to equity is another measure of a company's ability to repay loans. Lenders may require a certain level be maintained as a condition of a loan.

- Return on equity is a way to measure how hard stockholders' investment in the company is working—how much in profits is the investment generating.

Inside the Income Statement

In This Chapter

- Using margins and ratios
- Measuring efficiencies
- Gross and operating margins
- Cash ratios

Are your expenses and income where they should be? How do you know? Look inside the income statement for the answers and spot trends as they develop. Margins and ratios from the income statement and what they tell you about your business are the topics of this chapter.

Using Your Income Statement

Every business owner knows that a positive bottom line on your income statement is a good thing, and the bigger, the better. However, if that's as far as you go with your company's income statement, you're missing some valuable tools that can help you fatten up the bottom line even more (or turn it positive if you're losing money).

It's difficult to describe the look on a self-satisfied business owner's face when you show him or her how the $50,000 profit the company made last year should really have been a $100,000 profit. If you have a viable business and are not using the tools in these chapters to manage your business, there's a very good chance the company is not making the profits it should.

Working With the Numbers

You didn't start your business to be an accountant (unless of course you are an accountant). If you are worried about the math side of this and other chapters, put your mind at ease. The math is simple and I'll give you all the formulas you'll need. Just plug in your numbers and the rest is basic math—no algebra or anything beyond adding, subtracting, multiplying, and dividing. You'll be working with ratios, which I explained in the previous chapter, and returns, which are percentages.

Financial Aid _____

You don't have to commit these ratios to memory. When you find the ones that are the most helpful in your situation, integrate them into your financial reports so they become part of your monthly review. After you work with them for a while, these ratios and returns will seem like old friends.

Most important, I give you some guidance on how to use the numbers and make them work for you. Where it is applicable, I give you a target or a range for you to shoot for with your company's numbers. This way you'll know whether your company's numbers are on target or in need of corrections. Remember, you're not the only one looking at these numbers. Bankers, potential investors, suppliers, and other parties may look at your financial statements. They can calculate all of these ratios and returns for themselves. Even if you don't use the numbers on a regular basis, you need to know what they are and what's behind them for conversations with outside parties.

Income Statement Numbers

Most of the following calculations come from the income statement. You will have to borrow an occasional number from one of the other major financial reports, but most of the ratios and returns focus on the income statement. For this discussion, we use the income statement from Chapter 4 for reference:

Small Business Income Statement

Revenue	
Sales	$3,800,000
Cost of Goods Sold	
Purchases	$1,988,000
Shipping	$400,000
Equipment	$230,000
Total:	$2,618,000
Gross Profit	$1,182,000
Expenses	
Accounting & Legal	$2,000
Advertising	$431,350
Bank Charges	$150
Insurance	$12,500
Administrative Expense	$230,000
Payroll Taxes	$15,000
Rent	$25,000
Salaries	$50,000
Supplies	$25,000
Telephone	$25,000
Utilities	$20,000
Total Expenses	**$836,000**
EBITDA	$346,000
Other Expenses	
Depreciation	$5,800
Interest Expenses	$12,500
Net Income before Taxes	**$327,700**
Income Taxes	($10,000)
Net Income	$317,700

Sales Numbers

Raw sales numbers don't mean much. What your company does with those sales dollars is the telling story. Ultimately, how well your company turns sales into profits is the measure of your management effectiveness.

Financial Aid _____

There are two sales calculations that give you an idea about the efficiency of your sales revenue. One measures the overall efficiency of the company and the other looks at how well sales generate cash by looking at profitability from a cash perspective. Accrual accounting conventions, which introduce noncash items into your income statement (Chapter 4), distorts net income and may not give you an accurate picture of the profits your sales generate. Using some simple calculations, you can see how profitable your sales truly are.

Return on Sales

Return on sales (ROS) is a way to measure how well your company functions by calculating the profit produced by each dollar of sales. This is an important number because it tells you the efficiency of your company's operations, whether it's a manufacturing operation or a service business. The more profit you can squeeze out of every dollar of sales, the healthier your company. Here's the formula:

Net Income ÷ Revenue = Return on Sales

You'll find the net income figure on the bottom line and the revenue (sales) figure at the top of the income statement. Using our example, we find the return on sales is:

$327,700 ÷ $3,800,000 = 0.086 or 8.6%

For every $100 in sales, the company earns $8.60 in profits. The math is simple, but the answer may not be. How do you know whether this is the right number for your business? Your accountant and sources such as trade organizations may have information about what your industry norms are for businesses in the same size range as yours.

The benefit of tracking ROS is that you know what it will take in terms of increased sales to improve profits. As you improve the efficiency of your company, the ROS will rise and you can draw more profits out of the same level of sales.

Cash Return on Sales Ratio

Another way to check out how hard your sales dollars are working is to see how much cash they are generating. To do this, you use the cash return on sales ratio, which avoids the accrual accounting traps of the income statement and looks to the statement of cash flows for the cash number.

From the statement of cash flows (Chapter 5), we get the net cash provided by operations and use that number rather than the net income from the income statement. Here's the formula:

Net Cash Provided by Operations ÷ Revenue = Cash Return on Sales

Plugging in the numbers:

$340,700 ÷ $3,800,000 = 0.089 or 8.9%

Some businesses are naturally more efficient at converting sales into cash. Retail businesses, for example, convert most of their sales within a few days to cash; just long enough for checks to clear and credit cards to be processed.

When you run this calculation, you look at how much cash sales have put in the bank up to a given point in time. The return on sales formula relies on net income, which may include cash that the company has not received yet, thanks to accrual accounting conventions. This second measurement is strictly "in the bank."

Like all financial numbers, you need to exercise some caution when using this number. You should look at it over several periods to gain perspective and you shouldn't compare your business to other companies in different industries.

> **In the Red**
>
> Some businesses are too efficient in converting their sales into cash and the sales never register on the books. Don't be tempted to keep sales off your books to avoid taxes. When you are caught, the penalty can be severe.

Margins

Generally, when you hear the term margin, it is referring to the difference between the sales price of a product or service and what it cost to produce the product or service. There are several margins that you should be aware of, because the greater the margin, the better your bottom line will look.

Gross Margin

This is one of the more important numbers because you can use it for both your whole company and for individual product lines—stores or any other sub-units. Gross margin is the percentage profit after deducting all the direct costs of producing the product or service. If this sounds like cost of goods sold on the income statement from Chapter 4, you are exactly right. The formula for figuring gross margin is:

Gross Profit ÷ Revenue (Sales) = Gross Margin

Using our income statement above, here's the gross margin for my example:

$1,192,000 ÷ $3,800,000 = 0.31 or 31%

For certain businesses, this is not a bad gross margin. Many manufacturers won't come close to a gross margin this high, while high-end professional services may be higher. The correct gross margin for your business depends on the industry and size of your company.

> ## Notes and News
>
> Trade and industry associations are good sources for information on general margins and ratios. You can often find averages in trade publications that will give you an idea of where your company's targets should be.

Once you have an idea of where your company's gross margin should fall, it is easy to see where you need to make adjustments. You need to either increase sales without a proportional increase in costs or reduce expenses without losing sales—or both.

The additional benefit of using gross margin as a management tool is monitoring different operating units within your company, such as individual stores or product lines. You can hold individual business units and managers responsible for their numbers without burdening the operations with corporate overhead. It also allows you to judge each business unit or profit center on its own merits. A new store that recently opened may have different gross margin goals than an existing store with an operating history.

In later chapters, we look at strategic planning, which figures into how you might develop a plan that sets realistic goals for different profit centers, but uses a common set of measurements to check results. For example, your business has three profit centers in related, but different lines of business. You could set three different gross margin goals for each profit center that would be equally challenging for each unit, but recognizing the different business models of each. The low growth profit center might have a gross margin target of 25 percent, while the high end profit center would be expected to hit 55 percent gross margin and the third profit center could fall somewhere in between. The manager of each profit center would have the same degree of challenge to meet their goal and you could reward them on that basis fairly.

Operating Margin

The operating margin is a corporate number that looks at how well the company controls costs and is a step closer to the bottom line than gross profit margin. It looks at the relationship between the operating profit and sales. Operating profit is that number that includes all expenses except interest and taxes. It is also known as net income before taxes on some income statements.

This is a less important number and only helpful in comparing your company with others in the same industry. The formula is:

> Operating Profit ÷ Revenue (Sales)
> = Operating Margin
>
> or
>
> $337,700 ÷ $3,800,000 = 0.088 or 8.8%

Financial Aid

There are many ratios and returns available for you to use in analyzing your company. Many of these tools were designed to help people considering investing in a company, so they may not be helpful in managing the company.

The one thing this number tells you is how efficient your company is in holding down costs, especially those unrelated to the actual production of the product or service. If you have access to operating margins for other companies in your industry, it may be interesting to see where you fall.

Net Profit Margin

Net profit margin looks at your bottom line and is the relationship between your company's net income and revenue. This is the ultimate "top line—bottom line" comparison because you start with revenue (sales) and end with net income. What is left is your net profit margin.

The percentage tells you how well your company converted sales into profits (net income). Here is the formula:

> Net Income ÷ Revenue (Sales) = Net Profit Margin

Using our sample income statement, we find the net profit margin is:

> $327,700 ÷ $3,800,000 = 0.086 or 8.6%

This is as good a single number as there is for calculating how efficiently you manage your business. When all is said and done, what percentage of sales were you able to convert to profits? The net income margin answers that question. It doesn't tell you if that is the right margin for your business or not, however. You need to decide that for yourself.

Financial Aid

Net profit margin describes your ability as a manager to convert sales into profits. You can use it to track your efforts over time to improve the efficiency of your company.

If you get caught up in the numbers game, you can compare your gross profit margin and the net profit margin to see how well you are managing indirect costs such as administration, office expenses, and so on. Lenders and investors may have more interest in this number than you can find a practical use for, but it's worth knowing for that reason alone.

Does this formula look familiar? It should, because you just saw it as Return on Sales. The same calculation gives you two answers. Actually, it's the same answer just expressed two different ways. One way, we talked about the return sales generated and the other way looked at the overall efficiency of the business.

Interest Coverage Ratio

Interest coverage ratio definitely falls into the category of numbers a banker or investor will want to know. When we looked at the current and quick ratio, we talked about using assets to pay current and immediate obligations. The interest coverage ratio looks at whether the company's profits are sufficient to repay the interest obligations. This is why your banker will be interested in this ratio. Here is the formula:

EBITDA ÷ Interest Expense = Interest Coverage Ratio

EBITDA stands for earnings before interest, taxes, depreciation, and amortization.

Your income statement may have EBITA broken down or you may need to calculate it yourself. The number for interest coverage ratio should be higher than 1.5 and many bankers would want it even higher. At a 1.5 interest coverage ratio, your company pulls in $1.50 for each $1.00 it pays out in interest expense. You can see why banks would like a higher number.

Many lenders require a certain coverage ratio as part of the loan agreement. This gives them a degree of safety that your company has the ability of repay the debt. The coverage ratio is based on several factors, including the company's history of profitability, the assets involved, and other normal lending qualifications. If you fail to maintain the interest coverage ratio, the bank may raise your interest rate or call the note.

This number isn't much help in managing your business, but the people who extend you credit will be interested in it and you should be familiar with the mechanism behind it.

The Least You Need to Know

- Return on sales is a way to check the efficiency of your company's operations.

- Gross margin is the percentage left after deducting direct cost for producing the product or service.

- The net profit margin looks at your net income in relation to your sales.

- Interest coverage ratio calculates if your company is producing enough cash from sales to cover your interest expenses.

Chapter 8

Measuring Cash Flow

In This Chapter

- ◆ Free cash flow
- ◆ Cash flow coverage
- ◆ Current cash debt coverage
- ◆ Cash debt coverage

Cash is your company's most precious nonhuman asset. How you manage or don't manage it may make the difference between success and failure. As we observed in Chapter 5, accrual accounting practices often make it difficult to track actual cash in your business. Working with the statement of cash flows, you can get a handle on some key indicators for your business. This chapter zeros in on your cash—where it comes from and where it's going.

Using the Statement of Cash Flows

The statement of cash flows may be the most foreign of all the major financial reports to most small business owners. Yet, there is a wealth of information in the report that can help you manage your business more

Financial Aid _____

Cash management is one of your most important jobs. When it is time to talk to lenders or investors, you must be familiar with cash management terms and calculations.

effectively, especially if your company runs through a significant amount of cash on a regular basis (a retail business, for example). These measurements will help some businesses more than others will. You can be certain that lenders and potential investors will pay close attention to the calculations in this chapter. Companies with healthy cash flows can repay loans, fund more growth, and pay dividends to investors.

Working With Numbers

These calculations are not difficult and will help you make sense of your cash picture, which can become quite confusing if you have multiple business units or profit centers. Growing companies are in great danger of running low on cash if revenue lags behind expenses as it almost always does. Knowing where your company's cash position is will help you avoid outgrowing your bank account.

Calculating Free Cash Flow

Free cash flow is what your company has left at the end of the year for use at your discretion. It is cash left over after paying for equipment or other capital expenditures and reinvesting in your company's growth. It's cash you could put in a savings account. For most small businesses, achieving free cash flow is a major accomplishment and one that marks a top level of success. The formula for free cash flow is:

Cash from Operations – Capital Expenditures = Free Cash Flow

Let's look at our statement of cash flows from Chapter 5 and see how the calculation works.

Statement of Cash Flows

Fiscal Year Ended Dec. 31, 2005

Cash Flow from Operations

	FY 2005	FY 2004
Net Earnings	$327,700	$302,000
Added to Cash		
Depreciation	$10,000	$9,000

Increase in Accounts Payable	$5,000	$1,000
Increase in Taxes Payable	$5,000	
Subtractions from Cash		
Increase in Accounts Receivable	($2,000)	($5,000)
Increase in Inventory	($5,000)	($3,000)
Net Cash from Operations:	$340,700	$305,000
Cash Flow from Investments		
Capital Expenditures	($230,000)	($25,000)
Cash Flow from Financing		
Bank Note	($50,000)	($200,000)
Cash Flow from Fiscal Year:	**$60,700**	**$80,000**
Change in Cash Position		
Cash at Beginning of Year:	**$83,000**	**$3,000**
Cash at End of Year:	143,700	83,000

Cash from Operations - Capital Expenditures = Free Cash Flow

or

$340,700 - $230,000 = $110,700

If your company is consistently generating a strong free cash flow number, you have options. You can accelerate repayment of loans, make acquisitions, or pay dividends. Lenders and potential investors find companies with consistent records of growing free cash flow attractive partners.

Financial Aid

Free cash flow is particularly important in the investment community because it gives a business options to take advantage of opportunities.

Free cash flow is not a number that will necessarily help you in the day-to-day management of your business. However, lenders and potential investors will be very interested in these numbers and especially how they have changed over time. When we discuss preparing a loan package or investor material in later chapters, free cash flow numbers become very important.

Calculating Cash Flow Coverage

The cash flow coverage ratio is another of those numbers you will not use in the daily operation of your business, but it will come up when talking to lenders or potential investors. You don't have to worry about committing this one to memory, but you do need to know it exists and, when the time comes, refresh your memory so you can talk about it intelligently.

This ratio indicates your company's ability to generate enough cash to fund its growth in addition to paying the bills, and investors would like to see something left over for dividends if those are in the game plan. Calculating the cash flow coverage ratio is a two-step process:

1. First, you figure the cash requirements: you add capital expenditures + any dividends paid + interest expenses + the current portion of the long-term debt. All of these are found on the statement of cash flows except for interest expenses, which is on the income statement (Chapter 5). Here's what those numbers look like:

   $230,000 + $0 + $12,500 + $50,000 = $292,000

2. The second step is the actual calculation:

   Cash from Operations ÷ Cash Requirements = Cash Flow Coverage

Plug in the numbers:

$340,700 ÷ $292,000 = 1.16 or 116%

Any number above 100 percent is good. The higher the number, the better able the company is to cover the cash requirements. In my example, the company does not pay dividends, so that gives it some breathing room.

Cash Flow to Assets

Cash flow to assets is a measure that compares the cash your company generates relative to its size. This is another ratio better suited to lenders than managers, but you'll need to understand it. The formula is simple:

   Cash from Operations ÷ Total Assets = Cash Flow to Assets

Plugging in the numbers from the statement of cash flows above and the balance sheet (Chapter 3) we get:

$340,700 ÷ $2,696,500 = 0.13 or 13%

My sample company is on the borderline for this ratio. For its size, the company is not generating as much cash as some lenders might like to see. A score below 10 percent is a red flag. Lenders would like to see this higher and would be interested in how this number has changed over the past few years. If the trend is up, that may make them feel more comfortable, although a downward slope is a definite warning sign.

Financial Aid

Investors like to see companies that generate enough excess cash to fund some or all of its internal growth. This is a way the company reinvests in itself for a higher return than simply putting the money in some form of savings account.

Current Cash Debt Coverage Ratio

When we looked at ratios from the balance sheet, one of the most important was the current ratio. This ratio looked at whether your company has current assets sufficient to cover your current liabilities (current in both cases, meaning within a year or less.) That's a worst case scenario—you don't want to sell your assets to pay your bills.

What you want is your company generating enough cash to cover those current bills and then some, and of course, that's what lenders want, too. They feel comfortable with assets backing up your current liabilities, but hope you never come to that. What you'll want to show them is how your company can cover your current liabilities with the cash it normally generates.

The process of calculating the current cash debt coverage ratio has two steps. The first step is to calculate average current liabilities. Normally, you would average two or three years of current liabilities (from the balance sheet, Chapter 3) to get this number. I provided only one year's worth of numbers in my example balance sheet, so we'll pretend that's the two-year average.

The second step is to calculate the ratio for the current year, which is:

Cash from Operations ÷ Average Current Liabilities = Current Cash Debt Coverage Ratio

Plugging in the numbers:

$340,700 ÷ $120,000 = 2.84

Clearly, in my example the company is in excellent shape to meet its current liabilities with the cash it's generating. My example is probably more optimistic than most companies are. Anything close to and above 1.0 is acceptable, with a higher number always preferred.

Cash Debt Coverage Ratio

The cash debt coverage ratio is an expanded version of the current cash debt coverage ratio. (Are you totally confused with all these similar sounding names?) This ratio looks at how well your company generates cash relative to its total liabilities. In other words, does your company generate enough cash to cover all of your obligations, both short and long-term?

You use the same formula as above except you substitute total liabilities for current liabilities. This leads you to the formula:

Cash from Operations ÷ Average Total Liabilities = Cash Debt Coverage Ratio

Plugging in the numbers:

$340,700 ÷ $2,604,000 = .13

Financial Aid

If you know you are going to a lender in the near future, look at the numbers in this chapter and see if you can improve on them by making some adjustments. For example, you can reduce current liabilities if they are too high.

Given my example company carries a large long-term note, this low ratio is not surprising. Even so, it is still too much on the low side. However, most of the company's obligations are long-term (the very high current cash debt coverage ratio indicates more than enough cash to cover short-term liabilities). This number may mean more when compared with calculations over the past several years. Is the position improving, and if not, why? A large note for a building or expansion can dramatically drag down the ratio.

The Least You Need to Know

◆ Cash is vital to your company's health.

◆ Cash flow calculations measure how much cash your company generates to cover a variety of internal needs.

◆ Lenders and investors are interested in these numbers because they indicate your company's ability to repay loans and pay dividends.

◆ The calculations are important when preparing a financing or investment package for your business.

Chapter 9

Operational Analysis

In This Chapter

- ◆ Analyze your operations
- ◆ Numbers you can use everyday
- ◆ Calculations for assets, inventory, receivables, payables
- ◆ Work smarter, not harder

Look beyond the strictly financial numbers and you'll find a treasure of information on the operations side of your business. These hard numbers translate into dollars and sense. I have shared some operational ratios in the previous three chapters, along with other ratios that fall into the reporting category. You can put these numbers and ratios in this chapter to work for you every day. This chapter shows you how to monitor these key measurements and what to do if things go bad.

Operational Analysis Defined

I define operational analysis as the process of measuring the way your company does business. Once you have measurements, you can begin to manage the various parts of business. This concept holds true for every part of your business, however this book deals with finance, so I'll stick to that particular area even though it is broad. To repeat a cliché from earlier in the book, "if you can't measure it, you can't manage it," and operational analysis is about measuring.

Working With Numbers

The numbers in this chapter are important and you'll want to stay on top of most of them. Some will be more important than others depending on your business. Your accountant can help you decide which of these are key indicators and how often you need to monitor them. It is helpful to track these over time so you can get a feel for trends. Some software programs, such as QuickBooks or Peachtree will graph the results for you or you can build your own charts with a spreadsheet program. You can even hand-draw charts with some graph paper and colored pencils. However you do it, charts are great tools in illustrating trends over time.

Financial Aid

Operational analysis sounds much more academic than it is. It is about understanding the financial implications of your business to help you make better decisions.

Measuring Profit Centers

Return on assets (ROA) is one of the best tools you can use if you want to measure the management effectiveness (internal profitability) of a profit center. Your profit centers can be separate product lines, individual retail stores, production facilities, whatever you want them to be. What you need is a way to track each center's progress, which also gives you a way to measure the effectiveness of the center's management team. This use of ROA differs from our previous discussions in that it focuses on an individual product or project within your company so the calculation is somewhat more complicated.

The DuPont Formula

The DuPont Formula comes from the famous DuPont Chemical Company and is widely used as a management tool for measuring profit centers. The formula looks more complicated than it is, but it is very powerful. Here's what it looks like, and then I'll take it apart piece by piece:

$$ROA = (\text{After-tax Cash Flow} \div \text{Revenue}) \times (\text{Revenue} \div \text{Assets})$$

The ROA is the product of two ratios. The first ratio is after tax-cash flow, which is net income with taxes and depreciation added back in, divided by revenue for the profit center. The reason you use after-tax cash flow (you could use operating profit, EBITDA, also) is that profit centers usually don't have separate balance sheets. You are more concerned about actual performance and don't want to cloud numbers with noncash and nonoperating expenses.

The second ratio (revenue ÷ assets) is one we've already discussed—asset turnover. Let's see what the formula looks like when I plug in numbers from my sample company. I'll use the whole company's numbers, because I don't have any profit centers broken out, which is fine; the formula works just as well.

ROA = (After-tax Cash Flow ÷ Revenue) × (Revenue ÷ Assets)

ROA = ($333,500 ÷ $3,8000,000) × (Revenue ÷ Assets)

ROA = (0.088) × (Revenue ÷ Assets)

ROA = (0.088) × ($3,800,000 ÷ $2,696,500)

ROA = (0.088) × (1.41)

ROA = 0.1240 or 12.40%

After-tax cash flow comes from the income statement. Revenue also came from the income statement and assets came from the balance sheet.

The DuPont Formula is helpful in working with profit centers because many decisions pull the two component ratios in opposite directions. For example, adding new equipment allows you to expand your business, which improves your margin. However, the additional equipment may reduce your asset turnover. The DuPont formula will tell you if the additional investment will earn a sufficient ROA to justify the cost.

> **Notes and News**
>
> You can also use the DuPont Formula to evaluate a company you may want to buy or invest in. The formula lets you compare returns for companies in the same industry only.

Using the Formula as a Management Tool

The DuPont Formula gives you a tool to manage the performance of profit centers and assist you in making decisions. Using the formula, you can measure how individual profit centers perform to standards that apply just to that profit center.

You can hold the managers of each profit center accountable to numbers that are reasonable, yet challenging for that profit center. In a company with several profit centers, this avoids the "cookie cutter" approach that says each center must hit the same goal, which is usually unrealistic. Managers of high-margin profit centers shouldn't be judged to the same numbers as a start-up profit center. It's not fair to either one and your company will suffer for it.

The idea is not to compare profit centers in the normal sense, but to look at each and determine what a reasonable return on assets represents given the market, industry, competition, and so on. Once the ROA for the year is locked in to the strategic financial plan (Chapter 10), you can hold the manager accountable to that number. That number also rolls into your projections.

Making Decisions with the Formula

Should you open that new store or start a new product line? Small businesses face growth decisions with concern if they don't have the tools to make a reasonable decision. The DuPont Formula can help you make those decisions. You can use it to estimate the return on assets of a proposed new profit center.

It is a good idea to set some thresholds for considering new profit centers (more about this in Chapter 11). You can use the formula as a test for whether a proposed new line of business meets the threshold for consideration. This is extremely important because you're going to devote assets to a new profit center and most small businesses can't afford to be wrong too many times when launching a new business unit.

There may be times a proposed profit center falls below the ROA threshold, yet it still makes good business sense to move ahead.

If you are going to overrule the numbers, make sure there are legitimate business reasons to do so and that it is not your ego at work. Wanting something is not a legitimate business reason. Some legitimate business reasons are:

◆ Entering a new market that you know will be unprofitable the first few years, however, are confident there is a profit at the end of the tunnel.

◆ Starting a new product line that requires high volume to achieve profitability. What is your plan to generate the needed volume?

◆ Research and development. High tech or intelligence-based profit centers may need considerable time and resources before products or services are ready for the market.

In each of these cases and others you may think of, you need to have a plan for profitability. You are committing assets (personnel, equipment, cash, and so on) to a project and should have a clear plan and timeline for when the project becomes profitable. Set benchmarks for ROA along the way and hold managers accountable to meeting timelines and returns. If you don't, projects tend to become black holes, sucking in assets (cash in particular) that will drag your whole company down. You should be prepared to terminate projects that aren't meeting expectations and show no hope of coming around.

Financial Aid _____

You should never start a new product line or a new service without an exit strategy. If things go wrong, how are you going to get out with the least damage to your company?

Other Benchmarks

The following ratios track important numbers that you'll want to look at on a monthly basis. They are easy to figure and some software programs may calculate them for you. If not, they are simple math you can do yourself or on an Excel spreadsheet.

Calculating Inventory Turnover

The inventory turnover ratio tells you how well your company manages its inventory. The ratio looks at the relationship between what it cost to sell the product and the average inventory level maintained during the year. This particular ratio covers a year to get the best reading. The formula for inventory turnover is:

Average Cost of Goods Sold ÷ Average Inventory = Inventory Turnover

You'll need the cost of goods sold figure off of the income statement and the inventory figure off the balance sheet. Calculate the average inventory for the beginning and ending periods, then do the division. Plugging in the numbers from our sample company we get:

$2,608,000 ÷ $125,000 = 21

Here's how the answers come out:

- 12 means an average one month inventory on hand

- 24-25 means an average two weeks' inventory on hand

- 6 means an average two months of inventory on hand

If your calculation doesn't fall on a number that easily divides into 12 or by 12 (19 for example) you need to estimate. A score of 19 means you have an average of about 2.7 weeks of inventory on hand (52 weeks ÷ 19 = 2.7).

By this measurement, my sample company keeps very little inventory on hand, which for some businesses is a good thing. It means money is not tied up in inventory sitting in a warehouse for lengthy periods before it moves.

There is another step to this calculation that gives you the number of days it takes to for inventory to go through the system. You take the inventory turnover figure and divide it into 365, like this:

365 ÷ 21 (Inventory Turnover) = 17 days

This means that it would take about 17 days to sell your entire inventory, on average.

Doing these calculations is much easier than figuring out what the correct inventory level is for your company. Too much inventory and you sink a lot of cash into goods sitting in a warehouse for too long before they sell. Too little inventory and you run the risk of losing customers because you can't fill orders in a timely manner. Here are some factors to consider when deciding on a proper inventory level for your company:

- **Commodity or custom.** Are your products customized for particular clients or are they "one size fits all?" If every customer orders the same widget, that suggests you could build an inventory when it was to your advantage and be confident of moving the stock. On the other hand, you must handle customized work more cautiously. If only one customer can use the inventory, it is dangerous to sink too much money into product that you can't sell if that customer leaves.

- **Just in time customer.** Many manufacturers want their suppliers to ship parts just when they need them, which practically may translate into a week or two of supply at a time. They shift the inventory burden to you and count on consistent delivery schedules. Depending on the product, this may put a burden on your company to meet these short time tables, if the weekly order changes in size and composition. You may have to anticipate the customer's needs and stay ahead of their demand.

◆ **Sales predictions.** If your company is good at predicting sales, you can adjust inventory levels accordingly. However, if your business is volatile and/or seasonal, it may be difficult to predict inventory needs too far out.

These are a few of the considerations in deciding the right inventory levels for your business. Later in the book, I discuss strategic planning and ways to help you make these types of decisions.

Calculating Accounts Receivable Turnover

Most companies extend credit to their customers in some form. It's a part of doing business and figures into your marketing strategy. However, if you aren't careful, a loose credit policy can cost you dearly. A sale on credit is no sale if you never collect from your customer—it's a theft. Slow paying customers make you finance (unless you charge them interest) their business.

Credit policy decisions are important. If they are too strict, you may lose business, but if they are too loose, you may go out of business. Later in the book, I go over some strategic planning tips to help you figure out the best policy for your business.

In the Red

Poor credit and collection policies drain cash out of your business that in many cases is hard to recover. If you are not comfortable with your policy, get some expert help that can set up a system for extending credit and collecting late accounts. You can't afford to carry customers beyond a reasonable time.

You will want to stay on top of your accounts receivable, because it represents cash outstanding. One measure that you can use is the accounts receivable turnover ratio. This tool tells you how fast your customers are paying up. It is especially important to watch this number over time. Here's the formula:

Sales ÷ Accounts Receivable = Accounts Receivable Turnover Ratio

You find the sales figure on the income statement and the accounts receivable number on your balance sheet. Plugging in the numbers from our sample company:

$3,800,000 ÷ $367,000 = 10.35

To see how long it takes customers to pay their bills, use this formula:

52 weeks ÷ Accounts Receivable Turnover Ratio = Weeks Outstanding

or

52 ÷ 10.35 = 5 weeks

If you would like to see that figure in terms that are more precise, you can see it by days using this two-step formula:

1. First: Annual Sales ÷ 365 = Average Sales per Day

2. Second: Accounts Receivable ÷ Average Sales per Day = Days Outstanding

3. First: $3,800,000 ÷ 365 = 10,411

4. Second: $367,000 ÷ $10,411 = 35 days

The higher the accounts receivable turnover ratio, the faster your clients are paying their bills. The right accounts receivable turnover ratio for your company depends on many factors. Some industries operate on different pay schedules, for example, sub contractors in some construction trades may pay part up front, but not pay the balance until the job is finished and they are paid, which could stretch out for some time.

Financial Aid

Many small businesses won't cut late customers off because they are afraid of losing the business or offending a friend. What business? The free merchandise you are giving away?

It is extremely important to monitor this number on a monthly basis. If your days outstanding begin to stretch out beyond where you are comfortable, it's time to re-examine your credit policy and begin a collection process to bring in slow paying accounts.

Aging Schedule

An aging schedule is not a financial ratio, but a report that you should look at (or someone in your company should), at least once a week. This report lists your accounts receivable and categorizes customers' outstanding balances by how far back they go. It breaks down the receivables beginning at your first due date and stretches back in 15 to 30 day increments. The following table illustrates an aging schedule.

Customer	30-45 Days	46-60 Days	61-90 Days	Over 90 Days	Total
ABC	500	300			800
EFG	100	200	50	350	
HIJ		400			400
KLM	200	100	100	100	500
TOTAL:	800	1,000	150	100	2,050

Your report should be formatted to match your credit policy and to give you the most useful information. However, this example illustrates the importance of not only knowing the overall numbers and ratios of your accounts receivables, but also the details. The aging schedule gives you a blueprint for action by identifying customers that need immediate attention.

These outstanding accounts represent cash that is not in your company and if the situation gets out of control, you may find yourself in serious trouble.

Accounts Payable Turnover Ratio

The accounts payable turnover ratio is the flip side of the accounts receivable turnover ratio. You certainly want to pay your bills on time and maintain the credit rating of your company. However, bills represent cash leaving your company. Although you need to meet these obligations, choosing when to meet them can play into your cash management strategy.

The accounts payable turnover ratio tells you how fast you are paying your bills. This does two things. First, it lets you make sure you are not falling behind and endangering your credit rating—you especially don't want to be late with loan payments. Second, it tells you if you are paying your bills too fast. There's no harm in paying bills fast, in fact many people find that is emotionally more satisfying than having the bill hanging around unpaid.

However, unless the creditor offers a discount for early payment, you aren't helping yourself by paying any quicker than you need to pay. If the bill gives you 30 days to pay without

Financial Aid

If you have a bookkeeping person or department, set a policy on bill paying that considers timing, discounts, and size of bill. When money is going out of your business, you want to be in control of the process.

penalty, why not take it and hold on to your cash that much longer? Here's the formula for finding the accounts payable turnover ratio:

Cost of Goods Sold ÷ Average Accounts Payable = Accounts Payable Ratio

Cost of goods sold comes off the income statement. To find the average accounts payable, use the past two years and figure the average. Here's what it looks like using my sample company:

$1,988,000 ÷ $215,000 = 9.27

To see what this ratio means in terms of number of days in the accounts payable cycle, we use a similar formula to the one we used for the accounts receivable.

1. First: Cost of Goods Sold ÷ 365 = Owed per Day

2. Second: Average Accounts Receivable ÷ Owed per Day

3. $1,988,000 ÷ 365 = $5,447

4. $215,000 ÷ $5,447 = 39.5 days to pay

Based on this calculation, my sample company was taking slightly over 39 days to pay its bills. This seems too long, however in some industries it would not be out of line. You will need to establish you own guidelines for payments.

Discount Interest Rate

Many companies offer discounts for early payment—maybe your company does, too. The company may offer a 2 percent discount for payment within 10 days, for example. If you have the cash on hand, these decisions usually aren't difficult for you to make.

Good cash management dictates you should always ask what other opportunities you have for your cash before you make any major decision. For example, say you have a $50,000 bill that you can take a 3 percent discount on if you pay it in 10 days. The problem is you don't have that much cash on hand. To take advantage of this discount, you need to tap your line of credit with the bank for 30 days until you will be able to repay the bank. The bank is going to charge you interest for the 30 days, so is the discount still worth taking?

Here is a formula to help you figure out when a discount is a good deal if you have to borrow to take

Notes and News
Never spend cash lightly. Always consider every possible use for the money you have on hand or can borrow, before making a final decision.

advantage of it. This exercise assumes you are confident the business will have the cash to repay the credit line within the time you would normally pay the bill (30 days):

[(% discount) ÷ (100 − % discount)] × (360 ÷ Number of Days Paid Early) = Annual Interest Rate

If we look at a 3 percent discount for paying within 20 days, here's how the formula works:

[3(% discount) ÷ (100 − 3% discount =97)] × (360 ÷ 20 number of days paid early) = 36.73% Annual Interest Rate

Without the words:

[3 ÷ (100 − 3 = 97)] × (360 ÷20) = 36.73%

(3 ÷ 97 = .0306) × 18 = 36.73%

Clearly, this is a good deal because this formula is telling you that the annual percentage rate of this discount is worth almost 37 percent. That is higher than you are paying for the money you are borrowing on your line of credit (if not, find a new bank!). You can verify this by figuring how much it will cost you to borrow the money to take advantage of the discount. If you don't want to go to the trouble, pick up the phone and call your banker, he or she will be glad to tell you the exact costs.

My example is easy to see, but what if you couldn't repay the credit line for 60 or 90 days? At some point, you end up paying the bank as much interest as you gain in discount. That's why this formula is helpful. It's not one you need to use everyday, but it is handy when it comes time to make a decision. You can see your options in dollars and cents and make the best choice. This takes the guesswork out of management. You won't wake up in the middle of the night wondering if you made the right decision. The numbers will help you feel confident about the correctness of your decision.

Financial Aid

If you have a big bill headed your way from a vendor that doesn't offer a discount for early payment, call them, and offer one. Say you'll pay early for a reasonable discount. The worse that can happen is they'll say no.

Calculating Fixed Assets Turnover

The fixed asset turnover ratio is a way to look at how efficiently your company uses its fixed or long-term assets to create sales. Long-term assets include land, buildings, equipment, and other assets that would be difficult to sell for cash within 12 months. It may seem strange to look at sales and long-term assets in this manner, but there is a good reason for doing so. Maybe the old cliché, "expect the best, but plan for the worse," says it best.

You certainly hope things stay on track and there are no bumps in the road and the sailing is smooth. However, if the economy does slow down or you lose a major client, it is easier to reduce your variable costs than it is to get fixed assets off the books in a hurry. The fixed assets turnover ratio tells you how much in per dollar sales your company has tied up in fixed assets. The higher the fixed asset turnover ratio, the better your company will respond to slow downs. Here is the formula:

Net Sales ÷ Net Fixed Assets = Fixed Asset Turnover Ratio

We get the sales figure from the income statement (Chapter 4) and the asset figure from the balance sheet (Chapter 3). When I plug in the numbers from my sample company, here's what happens:

$3,800,000 ÷ $2,168,000 = 1.75

My sample company does not look too good in this department. Even though the ratio is above 1.0, it is still not high enough to show a real efficiency in using fixed assets to generate sales. Should this company get in trouble, the heavy dependence on fixed assets could make it difficult to weather the storm.

Financial Aid

Lenders love ratios that involve assets and cash, but they're not particularly helpful to you on a daily basis.

You should always look at what others in your industry are doing in this area. If your numbers are within industry norms, then there's not much to worry about. If your numbers are lower and are declining each year, that suggests your company is not getting the return from its assets it should.

Calculating Total Assets Turnover

This ratio is one more step back from the fixed asset turnover ratio. It looks at the same relationship to sales, but includes all assets, not just fixed assets. The ratio gives you an idea of how efficiently you are managing the company's assets. This number will be lower than the fixed asset turnover. The formula is:

Net Sales ÷ Total Assets = Total Asset Turnover

or

$3,8000,000 ÷ $2,696,500 = 1.41

This number confirms that the company is asset heavy and not producing the level of sales that one might expect. Although, different industries have different expectations for asset turnover ratios, it is important to note that low ratios suggest the company is not getting an acceptable return from its assets. Your accountant can help you determine the appropriate target for your company's ratios.

Recap of Operational Ratios

Operational ratios, returns, and formulas can help you run your business more efficiently and with greater confidence. They won't replace your common sense or knowledge of your industry. What they will do is give you some tools to help you see your company from several different financial angles. They will take much of the guesswork out of managing your business and help you answer questions about a variety of financial questions.

You don't have to be a math genius and you don't have to use all of these tools. The idea is to find those ratios that give you the key information you need to make decisions and integrate as many of them into your financial reporting systems as possible—even if that is as simple as charting paper and some colored pencils.

When I discuss strategic planning and budgeting, many of these tools will surface as measuring sticks or barometers for you to use. The following list includes ratios and returns from this and previous chapters that I believe are the most important. I have collected them here for your reference.

- ◆ **Current Ratio.** Chapter 6 gives you a snapshot of your company's ability to meet its current obligations.

- ◆ **Quick Ratio.** Chapter 6 is an even tougher test of your company's liquidity.

- ◆ **Return on Assets.** Chapter 6 measures how well your company uses its assets to make money.

- ◆ **Return on Sales.** Chapter 7 tells you how profitable your sales are.

◆ **Cash Return on Sales.** Chapter 7 measures how much cash your sales generate.

◆ **Gross Margin.** Chapter 7 is what remains after deducting the cost of goods sold from revenue.

◆ **Operating Margin.** Chapter 7 is the margin after deducting all the costs directly connected with the business.

◆ **Net Profit Margin.** Chapter 7 this number expressed as a percentage, tells you what your company made on each dollar of sales.

◆ **Free Cash Flow.** Chapter 8 how much cash is left over after all bills are paid.

◆ **Return on Assets using the Dupont Formula.** Chapter 9 this formula helps you determine whether a project or new product meets return on asset standards.

◆ **Inventory Turnover Ratio.** Chapter 9 tells you how often you turnover your inventory during a 12-month period.

◆ **Accounts Receivable Turnover Ratio.** Chapter 9 this tool tells you how long, on average, it takes to collect from your customers.

◆ **Accounts Payable Turnover Ratio.** Chapter 9 this ratio shows how long you take to pay your bills.

◆ **Discount Interest Rate.** Chapter 9 this formula helps you decide whether to take a discount and pay a bill early.

You won't use all of these formulas every day or even every month and this isn't high school, so you don't have to memorize them. However, you should know what they can do for you and how to read them if they show up on your financial statements. Use this book as a reference to refresh your memory about what these financial tools mean and how to use them, because they're powerful.

The Least You Need to Know

◆ Operational analysis is the process of measuring the way your company does business.

◆ Accounts receivable turnover ratio tells you how fast (or slow) your customers are paying their bills.

◆ Accounts payable turnover ratio tells you how fast you are paying your bills.

◆ Figuring the discount annual interest rate will tell you whether to borrow money to take advantage of a discount on a bill.

Part

Strategic Planning/ Budgeting

Adding 5 percent to last year's budget and calling it done is not the formula for success. Strategic budgeting is part of a financial planning process that looks at the strengths, weaknesses, challenges, and opportunities facing your business and creates a financial strategy. This part looks at the budgeting process as a portion of the overall financial strategy.

Chapter 10

The Strategic Planning Process

In This Chapter

- ◆ Defining a strategic financial plan
- ◆ Setting goals
- ◆ Measuring results
- ◆ Budgeting implications

Few business owners enjoy planning; they are "doers" by definition. However, to move your business to the next level, a strategic financial plan is necessary. Part budget, part operating philosophy, part planning document—this is your company's road map to success. This chapter discusses the process of setting financial goals before you begin planning and gives examples of how to measure progress.

Plan with a Purpose

If you were to take a random poll, most people would respond to the question, "what is the goal of a business?" with the answer, "to make a profit or make money." In fact, most business people would answer the question the same way. That answer would be correct as far as it goes. The problem is many "profitable" companies go out of business each year because they run out of cash. Thanks to accounting conventions, your company can show a profit and have no money in the bank.

The purpose of a strategic financial plan is to make sure that doesn't happen to your company. Your strategic financial plan accomplishes two important functions—it sets financial goals and defines measurements for success. When you develop a full business plan, the strategic financial plan rolls up into this document and serves as the backbone.

Setting Goals

Setting financial goals gives your company, managers, and employees something to target. Goals also provide a way to measure performance. Together, you create an atmosphere of accountability and focus that helps everyone know what they are doing and why. As you'll see in subsequent discussions, when you have a goal, you can measure all actions and proposed actions against that goal. Will this project get us closer to our profit goal? Will this marketing plan help us meet out new customer goal? You may be in a dynamic business that presents many opportunities. If you don't have a method of evaluating them, you may find your company going several directions at once. Goals keep you focused on what is important. If it doesn't help you achieve your goals, let it pass.

Financial Aid

Keeping your company focused can be a difficult task. A well-defined set of financial goals helps you stay on task.

The process of setting financial goals is not always precise, because you may not be able to predict the effect of external influences (the future economy, for example) on goals. However, you must do your best, working with the employees directly involved in the activity to come up with challenging but reasonably attainable goals.

Profitability Goals

There is an abundance of clichés about setting goals that I'll resist repeating. The importance of profitability goals is as much psychological as it is financial. The previous chapters introduced you to tools that will bring clarity to the financial health of your business. Setting goals brings clarity to where you want your business to go. If you are confident about where your company is financially, setting goals becomes an easier and more meaningful task.

New Thinking

Don't be satisfied with whatever is leftover after you pay all the bills. Set specific goals for what you want in profits (real profits, not accounting profits). I spend all of Chapter 11 talking about profits in more detail, but for this portion of the financial strategic plan, the important element is setting a specific goal.

To get to that point, we first have to undo some thinking that most of us grew up hearing. We learned the formula for calculating profit is:

Revenue − Expenses = Profit

This is the classic accounting formula and if you look at your income statement, that's exactly what you see. However, it is not a good operational statement, because it makes profit the passive result to two other active elements. As the owner of a small business, you want profit to be an active part of your business. To do that, you need to use this formula for profit:

Revenue − Profit = Expenses

Do you see the difference? There are two major differences beyond the obvious rearrangement of words:

- ◆ The first formula is an accounting tool that is concerned with what has already happened and how to report it. The second formula is forward looking and it directs future actions.

- ◆ The second formula places a limit on expenses (what is left after subtracting profit from revenue), while the first formula places a limit on profits.

This doesn't mean you can set a profit goal of 45 percent and everything will fall into place. Very few businesses make this much on the bottom line. You should set a realistic goal for your business. For some industries, the figure will be quite low, whereas other industries typically run

Financial Aid _____

Goals keep you active in those areas that are important to your company and make it easier to prioritize your time. "Does this activity move my company closer to a key goal?"

higher. Your accountant can help you set reasonable profit goals. Trade groups are another source of information on what similar businesses are earning. You can also check out www.bizstats.com, which offers profitability and other financial measures on a number of industries.

Choosing a Target

The number you use for your target is up to you, but many businesses use cash flow (net income + depreciation) as their goal for profit, because it represents cash available after depreciation is added back to net income. You can then express this as a percentage of sales. Here's how that looks:

$$\text{(Net Income + Depreciation)} \div \text{Revenue} = \text{Profit Margin or Percentage}$$

You know from the depreciation schedule your accountant provides what the depreciation will be for the next year, if that's your time frame. Unless you buy or retire assets, you can count on that number. What you will need next is a revenue projection and expense estimates. Planning is a dynamic function if done correctly with revisions, compromises, and recalculations as standard parts of the process. Here are some of the questions that go into the profit goal-setting discussion:

- Is our market expanding or decreasing?
- Do we sacrifice profit to build market share?
- Do we have the resources to sustain growth?
- Are there new markets we want to enter?

You set profit goals as part of a complete process that looks at revenue and expense goals, as well.

Revenue Goals

It all must start with revenue. Without that cash coming in the front door, nothing else matters too much. Setting revenue goals is a process of looking back and forward at the same time—this is where we were and this is where we want to be and what has to change to get us there.

Many years ago, a young entrepreneur met with his CPA to discuss the organization of the new business. The young man was very worried about taxes and wanted the company structured to take advantage of any and all tax breaks. The older CPA listened politely, and then pointed out that, "you have no products yet, no customers, and no revenue. Taxes should be the last thing on your list of problems."

Financial Aid

Building total revenue is imperative for most businesses. Without a growing revenue stream, there is only so much profit you can expect from your business.

The Buck Starts Here

The financial analysis tools you acquired in previous chapters should help you get a feel for how efficiently your company operates. If the numbers suggest that your company does not operate very efficiently, you may want to focus on productivity rather than increasing volume in an inefficient operation.

Revenue projections drive every other part of your financial plan. If you are just starting your business or it is still very young, it may be tough to make an accurate estimate. That shouldn't stop you from doing it with the understanding that revisions will be necessary.

If you are a manufacturer, increased revenue almost certainly means increased production, which affects labor, materials, equipment, shipping, and so on. The point is, you can't increase revenue without incurring increased costs elsewhere. Are you also going to raise prices and, if so, will the price increase offset some or all of the increased production costs?

For service businesses, increased revenue often means a larger staff and maybe new facilities. Retail businesses may open a new location. Again, the point is, increasing revenue will drive up costs in other areas of your business.

Here's where the work of the previous chapters pays off. If you have not been using the financial tools introduced in those chapters, you may not know in hard numbers how efficient or inefficient your business is. Building revenue in an inefficient business may only add to the problem and make it worse. The better decision is to fix the inefficiencies.

Your goal is to build a projected income statement that will detail what happens to expenses when revenue increases. With an understanding of your current ratios, you can make close estimates of the effect that increased production or services will have on your gross margin and operating income.

In the Red

Building revenue without maintaining your margin is like swimming upstream—you work harder, but don't get anywhere.

Expense Goals

Many small business owners don't even consider the possibility of setting goals for expenses. They assume expenses will follow revenue and there is not much they can do about it. Of course, that's partly true—when you increase revenue, you usually increase expenses to some degree. What business owners miss is the economic impact on their business of not setting expense goals.

Expenses represent cash leaving your company (if you think I dwell too much on cash, you're wrong and you've missed one of the most important points of this book so far—cash is your number one priority). You must pay expenses out of revenues and, ultimately out of your profits. If you didn't need the cash for the expense, it would go to your bottom line, so when you pay a bill it comes off your bottom line. Here's an example of what I mean:

> You had a good year and as a reward, you lease a nice SUV for a company car. It costs you $600 per month when you count the lease payment, gas, insurance, and so on. For the year, the car costs your company $7,200. That same year, your net income margin was a healthy 9.5 percent, meaning you made a $9.50 profit out of every $100 in sales.

Here's the question of the day: How much will sales have to increase so that your net income doesn't change to cover the cost of your new SUV, which, by the way, adds absolutely nothing to your company's bottom line. Here's the math:

($7,200 ÷ $9.50 = 758) × 100 = $75,800

Your company needs an extra $75,800 in sales (assuming you maintain the 9.5 percent margin) to pay for the annual $7,200 SUV tab and still achieve the same net income. Let's walk through the problem:

Revenues 1,000,000 × Margin 9.5% = $95,000 Net Income

When you buy the SUV, the $7,200 reduces your profit to $87,800. To return your net income to $95,000, you must increase revenue by $75,800.

($1,075,800 × 9.5% = $102,200) – $7,200 = $95,000 Net Income

But, wait, you say. This is not a valid example because the company can write off the lease (under the proper conditions) as a business expense, thus reducing income taxes. That may be true, but any benefit from a tax deduction will come in the future. In the present, your company is still out $7,200 in cash. Trading cash now for a deduction in the future is usually not a good deal, especially for a nonproductive expense. Do that too many times and your company will not have any taxable income and your deduction becomes worthless.

Tax deductions are valuable and they do reduce your bill, which means cash stays in your company. However, if the only benefit you can find to an expense is a tax deduction, that should raise a red flag. A new computer will also get you a tax deduction and may help to make your business more productive.

In the Red

Buying tax deductions is a waste of your precious cash unless you acquire something your company needs to meet one of its goals. Otherwise, you are draining cash out of your business for a future tax benefit. I'd take the cash any day.

Setting goals for expenses considers these issues and helps you make decisions about your valuable resources. Our new profit formula says expenses come after profits in how we view our business, which means figuring out ways to accomplish more with less.

I once took over the marketing department of a division of a large corporation. The group produced some visually stunning brochures and sales pieces; however, the department's costs were way out of line. The project managers were given free reign to hire the best graphic designers and other talent they needed, but were never given any strict budget guidelines. The first change I made was to put every project on a strict budget. The project managers complained that no one could produce quality material on such a budget. I dropped a stack of our competitors' brochures and sales materials on the table and pointed out that they seemed to find a way. Somehow, the marketing managers figured out a way to produce quality materials on a tight budget.

Set Specific Sales Numbers

Revenue goals should be quantified with hard numbers. "We want to grow a lot," doesn't quite get the job done. Look at all of your profit centers and set sales goals for each based on what is challenging and realistic for that unit. If you have multiple profit centers, don't give them all a blanket goal, because the single goal will be too low for some and too high for others in many cases.

Managers can break down specific sales numbers into sales territories, for example, so that salespeople work against a number they know will roll up to a bigger company-wide goal. If they do their part and everyone else does his or her part, the company will be successful.

Setting sales goals also means providing the means to achieve those goals. What does your company need to do in specific areas to achieve sales goals? More advertising? More salespeople? More distributors? Obviously, these have expense implications that you must be consider. Driving up revenue while driving down margins is not a formula for success.

Financial Aid

Break sales goals down as far as possible. If you have salespeople, each should have a goal. If you have profit centers, each should have a goal. Place the goal as close to the customer interaction as possible and it becomes much more than a number.

Marketing Goals

Marketing and sales belong together, but I have chosen to separate them for the purposes of understanding the financial implications of each. Marketing involves any activity in the company that relates to acquiring and maintaining a relationship with a customer. Selling certainly falls under that umbrella, but so do many other activities such as advertising, public relations, package design, pricing, promotion, and so on.

The Buzz

The buzzword in marketing is branding, which means building an identity for your company and/or its products in your consumer's mind, so that when they think of a particular product or service, they think of your company. Name a company associated with hamburgers. If you didn't think of McDonald's first, you are in the minority. The company spends millions of dollars each year making sure you think of them and they aren't alone. Virtually, every big name company spends a small or large fortune on positioning themselves in the market.

Can you directly tie sales to branding? You better believe McDonald's can or they wouldn't be spending millions doing it. Will you be able to tie sales to your marketing efforts? That may be slightly more difficult. Most small businesses don't have the resources to mount campaigns on the scale of McDonald's, nor do they have the sophisticated systems in place to track results. Of course you can track advertising results, which I discuss in the next section, but you may also benefit from the services of a marketing/public relations expert to help create some buzz for your company, if that is appropriate. It may be money well spent.

Advertising Dollars

Most businesses need to advertise, and depending on the industry, advertise extensively. No matter what business you are in, you need some advertising. Even if your company is a "business to business" supplier, you need to advertise. The question is, where and how much?

Advertising seldom works as a "do-it-yourself" project. If your company needs an advertising program, go to a professional for help. Advertising dollars may seem like wasted money, and they will be if you don't have two things:

- ◆ **Research.** Who is your target and what is the best way to reach this audience? Are you more focused on generating leads to potential new customers or driving business in the door? Be sure you know the market before launching a campaign that misses key parts of your customer base.

- ◆ **Follow up.** Always have a plan for tracking advertising results. Advertising professionals can help you design campaigns with this in mind. Even if all you do is have the person answering your phone ask each new contact, "How did you hear about us?" and keep track of the results, this information can help focus advertising dollars.

If you find an advertising approach isn't working, try something different. Advertising is sometimes difficult to hang numbers on and feel confident that you can see a clear line from the advertising to sales. However, that's no reason not to keep doing it. On a regular basis, you must ask the question, "what is the company getting for its investment in advertising?"

Financial Aid _____

Push for results in your advertising. Issue a call to action and encourage customers to do something (contact you, come in, phone, and so on).

Get a Website

You must have a website. This is not optional—every business needs a presence on the Internet. How far you go with your site will depend on your business and budget. Regardless of the type of business, you still need a website, and not one designed by your brother-in-law's teenager. Spend the money to get a site that reflects your company done by professionals.

A law firm isn't going to win many clients with a site that looks better suited to MTV and blares loud music at each visitor (however, a retail shop for teens might find that's just what they need). Regardless of how big or small your site is, it must look professional and fit your business, and you should update it regularly.

Other Opportunities

There are many other ways your company can improve its brands and raise awareness in the community without spending a great deal of money. Small business owners never seem to have enough time in their day, but giving some of your time to the community is one way to let people know about your company. There are many opportunities in your community for you to give something back.

Whether it's your favorite charity, the chamber of commerce, one of the service clubs, or some activity or organization involved with youth or youth sports, there's always more work to do than there are people willing to do it. This works best if it's something you really believe in, rather than just a way to do business. Find a way to contribute to your community by involving yourself and your company in something you support and people will notice.

Generating New Customers

Marketing may be the softest of the goals you have to set, but don't let that stop you from being specific. Your marketing, revenue, and profit goals all must fit together.

For example, you can't set a 15 percent increase in revenue goal without some way to get those additional dollars. Even if you plan to get most of the new dollars from existing customers, you need a mechanism.

Most businesses can't rely on exactly the same customer base from year to year. You will lose some customers no matter what you do and the best plan is to have a system in place to generate new customers. You know how quickly your company converts prospects to customers (or first-time shoppers to

CAUTION

In the Red

If you know it takes several months for a prospect to convert to a customer, you'd best have that "pipeline" full so there are customers flowing out on a regular basis. If you have to start from scratch, it could be a long couple of months without much new business.

repeat business). In many situations, the marketing you do today may not produce customers for weeks or months.

Think of your marketing as a pipeline with prospects going in one end and customers coming out the other. How long is your pipeline—in other words how long does it take you to convert a prospect to a customer? How big does your pipeline need to be—how many prospects do you have to put in to get one customer out the other end? How much does your pipeline cost—what do you have to pay to get a customer out the other end?

Be Specific

In many small businesses, the owner is the chief marketing officer. He or she is the face of the company and should devote time each week to marketing activities. Setting specific goals for your marketing program will save you time over the course of a year because you will have specific tasks to accomplish.

Here are some examples of specific marketing goals:

- ◆ Call five new prospects and five inactive customers each week.

- ◆ Involve the company and myself in one civic project (or charitable, and so on) each quarter.

- ◆ Begin an advertising campaign targeted at acquiring new customers (or whatever your target).

- ◆ Make sure each employee can accurately describe what the company does in less than 15 seconds and in their own words.

- ◆ Have a new graphic look designed for the company.

- ◆ Join a local business group (chamber of commerce, and so on).

These goals range from the easy and inexpensive to the more involved. You probably want a mix of both, however you should have some form of marketing activity each week. Don't hesitate to involve professional help; you aren't an expert at everything and the money spent with a solid marketing professional will come back to you many times over.

Budget to Goals

I cover budgeting in more detail in Chapter 15, however I want to introduce the topic here because it ties up the discussion of setting financial goals. The profit, revenue, expense, and marketing goals give your company a sense of purpose—here is what we will accomplish this year. Too often, this process ends right here and goals become filler in a file cabinet. If you are going to accomplish your goals, you must have the resources to do so and that's where the budget plays its role.

Work Together

Your goals must work with your budget and your budget must make your goals possible. One of the ways to accomplish this coordination is to make sure every goal has a budget or at least a line in your budget. These are working budgets that you and your key employees, if that is appropriate, hammer out before your begin the main budgeting process.

How is your company going to meet its revenue goal? Part of that answer is in the marketing goal, but part may be in an investment in new equipment to produce another product for existing customers. It may be in training dollars to make your employees more productive. You may need to spend money to reduce expenses by adding equipment that will let you do work you previously had to send out. For example, you may want to consider investing in a color laser printer that will let you produce custom brochures and marketing pieces.

In the Red

Without goals, your company is always reacting to what happens rather than proactively attacking your market.

Every goal must relate to resources that can make the goal happen—if not, what's the point? When you have specific goals with a budget attached to them, they begin to integrate into the life of your business.

The Goal Standard

When we look at budgets as a strategic tool, you'll see how this shifts from what could be an academic exercise to real life. One of the ways this happens is by using your goals as a road map. When you look at expenditures that don't further your goals, you've gotten off the track.

The other way of saying this is that every dollar you put in your budget and spend throughout the year should advance your company closer to one of its goals. If money is proposed for efforts that do not advance a goal, in the words of a former first lady, "just say no." There is danger here, especially in larger companies, that managers who want a pet project funded will wrap it in one of your goals whether it fits or not. However, I'm sure you're clever enough to see through these schemes. However, if you have been specific with your goals, playing games will be harder.

The Least You Need to Know

- ◆ Your strategic financial plan should set out financial goals that are challenging, yet possible.
- ◆ The purpose of a financial plan is to be proactive with your finances.
- ◆ Set specific goals for profits, revenue, expenses, and marketing.
- ◆ Your budget should reflect your goals.

Chapter 11

Shooting for Profit

In This Chapter

- ◆ Work your plan
- ◆ Reasonable profits
- ◆ Opportunities and threats
- ◆ Making it happen

Too many small businesses settle for whatever they can get—they're happy to still have the doors open at the end of the year. If you don't plan to make money, it'll probably be an accident if you do. Most small businesses would say they plan to make a profit each year; however, if you asked the owner to show you his or her plan or even to just state it clearly, there might be a problem.

Planning for a profit gives you a chance, but doesn't guarantee it is going to happen. If you take specific steps in line with what we've covered so far, your company can create a plan for profits. This chapter details how to begin doing that.

Work Your Plan

Your profit plan works only if you work it. The beauty of a well-thought-out plan is that it blueprints your work for you. When you share it with your employees, they understand what needs to happen to make the company successful. Does this lead to complete peace and harmony in your company? Not by a long shot, but it does answer a very basic question that every employee has: What are we doing and why?

Setting Your Goal

In Chapter 10, we discussed setting goals and touched on the importance of being specific in the process. There is no correct profit goal for every company. Some businesses naturally have higher margins than others do. However, there are some guidelines to consider when you set your targets, and these may be helpful as you begin to construct your plan.

The Minimum Goal

One way to look at setting profit goals is to use a variation of the same thinking that investors use when considering buying a stock or other investment. After all, you are investing your money and time in the business; you should have some minimum expectations in terms of return. The process of finding that minimum can take many forms; however, it usually ends up in the form of questions.

Financial Aid _____

Setting goals is not pulling numbers out of the air. It is about applying what you know and where you want to go.

The very first question is: What is the return on the safest investment I can make? Most investors consider the return on the 10-year Treasury Note the benchmark for the safest investment you can make. This is because Treasury notes are backed by the full faith and credit of the United States Government.

At the time of this writing, that rate was around 4 percent. This is where you start. If you can make 4 percent on your money with zero risk, why would you put money into a business that didn't return that and more?

The Risk Factor

Once you have a base rate, or "safe" rate, the next question is: How much more return do I need to compensate for the risk of investing in the business? This is a very subjective answer that will be different for each individual. In the investment business, this is known as the *risk premium*. What is your time and energy worth? What is the potential for this business? Where do I want to be financially in 20 years?

Come up with a number that makes sense for you and is realistic for the industry. If those two numbers are close, you are ready to move to the next step of setting profit goals. If the two numbers are far apart, now is the time to ask yourself if this is the best situation for you at this point in your life. There are many ways to reach your personal financial goals, so don't feel you are locked into a situation. An obvious conclusion you can reach is that you've selected the wrong business as a vehicle for achieving your personal financial goals. You need to decide if you want to operate a business because you really love the business or because you want to make a lot of money. Many people work at small businesses with no plans to get rich—they love what they do and they want to be their own boss. Others approach small business ownership with the idea of building something bigger and better. In the best of all worlds, you find yourself doing something you really love that makes you a lot of money.

Money Talk

Risk premium is the return over a "safe" investment you expect for the risk you take when investing. The riskier the investment is, the higher the premium.

The Caveats

There are have several issues to consider with the process I just described that may be obvious. First, small businesses are inherently risky and most investors would place a very high risk premium on any investment—so high that it would be impossible for most companies to achieve. Especially if you are just starting out, the risk premium is tremendous. To make the process meaningful, you need to be realistic about the risk you are taking by owning a small business. If you don't think you can handle the anxiety of small business ownership, look for other ways to invest your money that are less risky and may still offer some of the same rewards.

Don't let the risk of owning a small business become a burden. If you find that the uncertainty is too painful, consider an alternative use of your time and talent.

Those "other rewards" are the other caveat. Many people become small business owners not to get rich, but to satisfy a deeper need. The idea of being your own boss is tremendously appealing and people will sacrifice much to achieve that satisfaction. The process of creating and operating a successful small business is one way many people express their creativity and can be just as valid as art or music.

However, you still need to eat and you may have a family to consider, so don't let this need to create overwhelm your common sense—even an emotionally satisfying venture should provide you with financial rewards also.

If you are just starting out or your business is very young, it may take several years for the company to mature to the point that setting a minimum return expectation makes sense. That shouldn't dissuade you from setting expectations, even if in some of the early years you project a loss and that's what you shoot for with your planning.

What Is Reasonable?

What you need and expect in the way of a return from your business is one part of the equation. The other part is a realistic assessment of whether the business is capable of providing that return.

Where Are You?

If you have been operating the business for some time and it is not meeting your goals or you want to increase the profit (or decrease the loss), you need to use the financial tools from previous chapters and come to a firm understanding of where the company is financially. Without this basis, it will not be possible to set realistic goals. Pay particular attention to your gross margin, which you remember is:

> Gross Margin = Revenue – Cost of Goods Sold

This number tells you whether your company is operating efficiently or not. The lower this number, the less likely your company will make its profit goals. Your cost of goods sold number is everything required to produce your product or service. Think of them as variable costs since they change with revenue growth or decline.

What remains can be thought of as fixed costs (even though they may vary from month to month). These costs are not directly tied to revenue and don't necessarily change as it goes up or down. When you subtract these costs from your gross margin, what remains is close to your bottom line. (Review Chapter 4 for more details on this process.) Although it is very important to control your fixed costs, it is extremely important that you control your variable costs.

Financial Aid _____

Having a firm grasp on your financial picture is imperative in the goal-setting process. How will you know where to go if you don't know where you are?

Where You Want to Be

Setting profit goals is about focusing on a target in the future. When you have a good understanding of where you are today, looking to the future becomes somewhat easier. Unless you plan a major investment in the business or some other big change, moving your profit (net income) up in big increments is usually not reasonable.

Because your profit goal will drive your other goals, I recommend setting it first. This gives you a clear vision of where you want the company to go; what remains is how you make that happen.

Where Are Opportunities?

Opportunities take many forms. For example, an opportunity can be:

- A new client(s)
- A new piece of equipment that improves efficiency or opens new product lines
- The acquisition of another company
- A new marketing thrust
- A new key employee

You may see other possibilities in your own company. Each one potentially leads to more profits. The danger for many small businesses is that there are too many opportunities, not too few. Sorting through the possibilities takes time and focus; however, the financial tools from previous chapters can help.

One of the ways to gauge whether an opportunity is right for your company is to use the return on assets tool discussed in Chapter 9. This tool lets you measure the potential return of an opportunity and judge whether it meets your criteria. If you can't put together a realistic set of numbers for an opportunity, that is usually a red flag that you might want to pass on this one. Too many opportunities sound great until you put the numbers together and realize what sounded like a great deal is probably not in your company's best interest. Be careful that you don't let your eagerness get the best of your common sense. With the right assumptions, almost any deal will work. What you want are the correct assumptions so that you base your decision on solid numbers and not wishful thinking. Small businesses owners are people who make things happen. This is a great attribute; however, if you force the wrong opportunity, you may regret making it happen.

In the Red _____

Spreadsheet programs, such as Microsoft Excel, are great tools for plugging in assumptions and watching the effect on the answer. However, be careful that the assumptions you use make sense. A spreadsheet can make any project look good if you keep changing the numbers until you get the answer you want.

What Are the Threats?

Your small business faces many threats. This book is about one of the most common, which is a lack of understanding of how small business finances work. Most small businesses fail through self-inflicted wounds:

♦ Inadequate investment

♦ Poor management

♦ Lack of financial controls

There are others, but the point is, like the famous quote from the comic strip *Pogo* says, "We have seen the enemy, and he is us."

Your business faces other threats. Bigger fish tend to eat smaller fish. If you compete in a market with much larger companies, you are going to be at a disadvantage in many areas. A number of years ago I knew a woman who inherited a small hardware store from her father. When he started the store it served a growing neighborhood, but the community changed. Large "big box" retailers such as Home Depot and others moved into the market. Because this woman was a family friend, I went to her store to buy an electric drill. Unfortunately, her price was about $20 more than I would pay for the same drill at one of the discount centers. Her comment was that the wholesale price she paid for the drill was more than the big store's retail price. Needless to say, she was not able to keep the store, which paid her nothing as a salary, open much longer.

Technology changes and some businesses find that keeping up with those changes and staying competitive is very difficult. Digital color printing and copying centers have put a dent in the market for small commercial print shops, and franchise operations that offer a wide variety of services beyond printing and copying (think Kinko's) have better business systems and the support of corporate advertising in major markets.

You need a thorough look at your market to identify these external threats to your profit goals. Make a list of the most dangerous threats and what their effect would be on your company if one or more of them happened.

Financial Aid _____

Change is one constant in business. You either roll with it or it rolls over you.

Putting It Together

You now have four pieces of the puzzle and it's time to put it together and set your profit goals. This process can become very complicated, especially if you try to do it alone. In the best of all worlds, you would have your managers participate in the exercise so that more than one point of view is considered. If that's not possible, find a trusted colleague or friend who will give up the better part of their day to work through this with you.

The Pieces

Now you know where you are and where you want to go financially with your company. You've identified realistic opportunities and acknowledged the threats. The next step is putting the pieces together and setting your goals. Questions are always a good way to begin a process like setting goals. Here are some to get your discussion started:

- Is our current financial position strong enough to build on, or should the company focus on those goals and opportunities that will shore up our financial statements?

- Are there threats in the opportunities—does a change open the company to threats that previously didn't exist?

♦ Are there opportunities in the threats—can we partner with a competitor or take advantage of a change in the market?

Financial Aid

The goals you set for your company are not carved in stone; they are targets. If conditions change radically, you may have to rethink your goals.

♦ Does it make more sense to get smaller rather than grow—can we make a more predictable profit by narrowing the company's focus?

More questions will occur as you work through the goal-setting exercise. Use these to broaden or narrow your thinking as appropriate.

What Has to Change

It is almost certain that for you to reach your profit goals, something about your business must change. Moving from where your company is to where you want it to be will probably require that something different happen. Change is never an easy process, and, depending on decisions you make in the next chapters, may involve some pain for you or your employees. The parts of your business requiring change are covered in the next chapters. Opening new markets or introducing new products can be exciting. However, you may discover through this process that parts of your business will have to change in ways that are not always positive.

A small commercial printing business worked hard to make a go of it in a tough urban market. One of the big parts of the business was printing business cards for several large car dealers. Every week the customers added new salespeople who needed business cards. The shop had many other customers, but the business card trade kept them busy. However, after several years of this business, the owner took a hard look at his books and discovered that these "good" customers were costing him a fortune. Not only was the business barely making any money for the printing firm, it tied up employees and equipment that should have been devoted to much higher-margin business.

In the Red

Holding on to the past is often the easiest decision, but it may not be the right one. When you can look at customers or products and know the numbers tell you to let go, it makes the change easier.

When you use the financial tools from previous chapters, you may discover that your best customer (and perhaps, a friend) is costing you too much to keep. Letting go of this business that has been steady and paying on time for some new customers can be a tough call. However, the numbers don't lie. If you have too many good customers that barely contribute anything to your bottom line, your company won't go very far beyond where it is and potentially faces an early demise. Leaving the known and comfortable, no matter how unprofitable, is difficult—it will also be difficult on your employees.

Share with the Company

For many years the line between "labor and management" was very distinct. Now, many business owners choose to share company information with employees. If you are so inclined, consider sharing financial information with your employees as you feel comfortable. At the very least, you should strongly consider sharing your profit goals and the other goals that will follow. This is not a book about human resources, however getting all your employees on the same page with profit, revenue, expense, and marketing goals can pay significant dividends.

Employees who know and share the company goals are more likely to make daily decisions that reflect and support these goals. Small daily decisions that are closest to where work occurs pay off over time, and in most companies add up to significant contributions to the overall goals.

Many grocery stores operate on very thin margins, particularly in food items. A profit of 2 percent is not uncommon in larger stores. When employees understand that it takes an additional $100 in sales to replace $2 of groceries that spoil, are damaged, or are stolen, it makes a powerful impact.

Standards When Considering Projects

Profit goals, shared by the whole company, become standards that employees can hold up when considering even the smallest project or decision. When employees understand what the profit goal is for the company, it makes sense to think about the consequences of actions. This will become abundantly clear in Chapter 12 when I discuss how expense goals support profit goals. When your employees draw the line between decisions they make every day and your profit goals, their decisions become supportive.

Financial Aid

Every employee should be accountable for the profit goal. Some will directly address the profit goal by meeting revenue goals, while others can keep a lid on expenses. Show your employees how their jobs relate to profit and it will make their jobs more important.

Real World

A reality check: no matter what you do or how much you share about profit (or other) goals, some employees will never get it or just not care enough to feel a part of the program. Sharing goals and information with employees is not a cure for poor morale by itself and it will never convince the malcontents on your staff. The best you can hope for is that most of your employees, and certainly those in key positions, buy into the goals and what it will take the company to get there. Of course, sweetening the pot with a profit sharing program of some type makes this process easier. In a small company, a bad employee can do significant damage both real and psychological. Don't let a troublemaker spoil your efforts—remove them if necessary.

The Least You Need to Know

- Reasonable profit goals consist of several components, and you can figure out what makes sense for you using some easy tools.

- Before setting goals, you must know where you are financially.

- Knowing where you are and where you want to go is the first step of setting profit goals.

- Identifying opportunities and threats gives you the chance to consider what your company's future may look like.

- Deciding what has to change can be a difficult and painful process.

Holding Down Expenses

In This Chapter

- ◆ Setting expense goals
- ◆ Operational expenses
- ◆ Sales expenses
- ◆ Marketing expenses
- ◆ Administrative expenses

Holding down expenses is an important function, although it gets no respect. Everyone is excited when sales climb 5 percent, but there's no party if expenses hold or decline. That's unfortunate, because holding or reducing expenses can be profitable. This chapter looks at the expense side of the income statement and how you can plan and budget to increase profits if you lower expenses.

The Hole in the Bucket

Everyone in your company must be accountable for holding or reducing expenses. It is that simple. If you don't keep expenses in check, increasing revenue does not help your net profit. Out-of-control expenses is one of the top reasons small businesses fail, so this is not about being "cheap"; it's about survival. You will never keep your profit bucket full if it has an expense hole in it.

Setting Expense Goals

Set expense goals on several levels. The top level is a total expense figure that includes everything. This number works with top-level revenue and profit goals. The second level is at the operational unit level with breakouts for each product or service. A final level is at the line-item, where each expense is targeted.

At the Top

The goal for total expenses for the year is the easiest one to set because we are using our new formula, which makes profits more important than expenses. That formula makes expenses the difference between revenue and profit:

Revenues – Profit = Expenses

If you decide that your profit goal is 10 percent, and project revenues of $500,000, total expenses can be no more than $450,000. That $450,000 becomes your "expense pie" that must pay for everything. If revenues fall short, the expense pie shrinks and you make do with less. Should revenues exceed projections, make sure expenses still hold within the formula and don't rise out of proportion.

Firmly sticking to this discipline gives your company a profit every year. Accounting conventions, such as depreciation, may eat into your net income and it might fall short of 10 percent. However, that's fine—it just means you pay less in income tax, which is a good thing. The important numbers, your operating margin and your cash flow, will show a consistent, positive growth.

> **Financial Aid**
>
> Getting the job done with less is a great culture for your small business and it starts with your example. Don't ask something of your employees you're not willing to do. Redecorating your office with expensive furniture and artwork, while telling workers they have to work with substandard equipment, sends the wrong message.

The Operating Unit

Setting expense goals at the operational unit level is important because typically the highest expenses are there. This is the cost-of-goods section on your income statement and includes all items and expenses directly related to producing the product or service.

Established businesses with mature product lines or services should have a good handle on the expenses. The expense components and numbers are easy to find and project from year to year, taking into account product or service changes.

However, there is a real danger in familiarity. When you do something the same way for several years, it's easy to keep doing it that way rather than look for other possibilities. Years ago, I took over a corporate marketing department that published a large full-color magazine four times a year. One of my first decisions was to get new bids to print the magazine. The printer who was doing the work had the contract for the past five years, and each year he increased the price. When the bids came back in, I found a new printer who would do the job for nearly $300,000 less per year. This $300,000 went directly to the company's bottom line, which even for a large company was valuable.

The point for small businesses is to not keep doing things the same way with the same vendors just because it's easy. You might cost your company money.

Financial Aid

The biggest challenge you may face is "we've always done it this way." Avoid that problem and constantly ask your employees if there is a better, less expensive way.

The Nitty Gritty

The final level of setting goals is at the line-item level, which is closest to the person directly responsible for the expense. Here is where a good challenge to hold or reduce expenses in small areas pays off in the larger picture. Many employees can and will contribute to reducing expenses if they understand why it is important and are shown how even their small actions contribute to the company's success.

Many years ago, before computers revolutionized the insurance industry, a company I know did most of its business by mail. Employees filled in countless forms, mainly in pencil, for the company records. If an employee wanted a new pencil, he or she had to go down to the basement supply room, where the attendant measured the person's pencil stub. If the stub was too long, the attendant sent the person back to their desk with orders not to come back until he or she really needed a new pencil. Every expense came under the same scrutiny and that culture helped the company grow into a multibillion dollar financial services company that is a leader in its industry.

Operational Expenses

Operational expenses, or cost of goods sold (COGS) to use the income statement term, are usually the largest chunk of costs for a company. The expenses, which cover all the direct costs necessary to produce the products or services, must be watched constantly to avoid "expense creep."

Start from Zero

A common way to budget is to take last year's figures and add an estimated increase to them. Maybe vendors have alerted you to price increases, or you anticipate certain costs will rise because they always have in the past. This is not setting expense goals. A better way is to start over and look at every expense that goes into your products or services.

If this is an existing product or service and you use the financial tools from previous chapters, you know the gross margin (revenue – cost of goods sold = gross margin). If the gross margin is too small, now is the time to look at cutting costs (and perhaps raising prices, but more about that in the revenue section). Even if the gross margin is where you think it should be, you must hold expenses to keep that margin right.

Here are some questions to ask about your operational expenses to help you set goals:

- Are there steps in the process that can be eliminated or reduced?

- Does technology offer a cheaper way to do parts of the process?

- Would it be cheaper to contract some parts of the process to outside vendors or contractors?

- Can we bring work in-house that traditionally has gone to outside contractors?

- Are there other vendors/suppliers who will work for less?

- Is there a better/cheaper delivery method?

CAUTION

In the Red _____

Constantly looking for a better way doesn't mean jumping at every shiny trick that comes your way. Just because something is new doesn't mean it's better.

These will get you started, but there are undoubtedly questions that are unique to your business. The object is to question everything you do in the process of creating products or services with an eye to find a better, less expensive way of accomplishing the task.

Clear Policies

You want your employees on board with any program of cost reduction, but just telling them to hold down costs is not enough. You must give specific examples and in some cases, set out written policies so everyone knows the expectations. This is especially true when it comes to:

- Company computers
- Copiers
- Telephones
- Other office equipment
- Office supplies
- Production equipment
- Supplies used in production

Not only will these policies help keep costs down, they also clear the air of any misunderstandings about company policy on these issues.

Marketing Expenses

Setting financial goals for marketing expenses might seem like trying to nail Jell-O to the wall. Because it might be difficult to directly tie revenue to marketing expenditures, how do you know where and how much to spend on marketing? The answer varies from industry to industry. Retail businesses need more intense marketing than wholesale or manufacturing companies typically need. Your total marketing budget will be a piece of the total expense budget and must relate to the revenue and profit goals. Marketing includes advertising, which will be the largest expense for most companies, as well as other efforts such as public relations and building brand awareness.

Advertising Expenses

Expense goals for advertising depend on how heavily your company advertises and whether you use a professional agency. In most cases, I would recommend using a professional advertising agency to help you increase the effectiveness of your advertising expenses.

These agencies are comfortable working with strict budgets and adhere to them. Give the agency a number as their budget for your advertising and hold them to it. The budget includes actual advertising placement as well as creative time to design ads and administration of your account. If the agency provides the service, some type of tracking of the advertising's results is important.

Financial Aid _____

Advertising is not an exact science, but that's no reason to let poor results continue. If you're not getting a reasonable response, try something else.

If you have a substantial advertising budget, don't hesitate to ask for concessions from your advertising agency. There are ways an agency can stretch your dollars and will do so to retain a good client. Likewise, if your advertising dollars aren't producing the results you expected, consider letting another agency have a shot at your account.

Other Marketing Expenses

Maybe your company has had success with a catalog or other direct mail programs in the past. Before you continue with a past program, make sure you are getting the best return for your investment. There are two components to this analysis.

The first check you'll want to make is to examine the costs associated with the production and distribution of the marketing materials. Use the same questions I mentioned in the operational expenses section of this chapter to review printing and other production costs. Reducing costs of your marketing programs increases the return on investment and boosts your bottom line.

The second check is to determine how well the marketing is working—in other words, is it bringing in enough leads that convert to customers to justify the expense? Marketing must always have a goal. The ultimate goal is to generate revenue; however, some businesses initially seek leads for salespeople, while others want a request for a proposal of some sort or a sample of the product.

Marketing expense should equal revenue growth. If this is not happening, something is amiss with your marketing plan or execution. It will not work well to generate a number of new customer leads if no one in the organization follows up on them. If you can't convert leads to revenue, is it because the leads expected something you can't deliver (your marketing message is wrong), or is it because your follow-through is flawed and potential customers are turned off?

Sales Expenses

Setting financial goals for sales expenses can meet with some resistance from your sales staff if they are used to liberal expense accounts and support. This can be a touchy issue for employees that are mainly commission-based in their compensation. However, runaway sales expenses negate any gains in revenue.

Direct Sales Expenses

Direct sales expenses include those costs your company must pay to secure sales of your product or service. Although these costs come off your bottom line for tax purposes, they are a drain on cash. If you have salespeople, these costs include commissions, travel, and other expenses associated with securing sales.

You want to be smart about spending sales expense dollars, so when you set financial goals for sales expenses, one of the tasks is to set some priorities. For example, using the financial tools from previous chapters, take a hard look at existing customers, especially if selling to them involves travel or other expense. I suggest you rank customers on a profitability scale of your own devising. For example, you might have A, B, C, and D customers with A customers being the most profitable and D customers just barely profitable.

Given that you have a fixed amount of sales dollars to spend, which customers get the most attention? Would you spend the same amount of sales dollars on a D customer as you would on an A customer? Of course not; you must protect your best customers as your top priority. You might spend more on a B customer if you felt the customer would move up to A status with an extra push.

> **CAUTION**
>
> **In the Red**
>
> You make an investment in your salespeople and you should expect a return. Even if they work on full commission, they have direct contact with your customers, and if they operate at only 80 percent efficiency, they are leaving revenue your business needs on the table.

You can use the DuPont formula we discussed in Chapter 9 to track how well salespeople are doing. This formula allows you to see the effect of expenses on the gross margin of each sales territory. You can also account for differences in territories that might mean separate goals are needed for each territory. For example, a territory that covers a large geographic area may have more travel expenses than another territory in an urban setting.

Indirect Sales Expenses

Indirect sales expenses include those items such as collateral material (brochures, proposals, and so on) that are part of the sales process. These could also fall under the marketing umbrella of expenses if you wish.

If your company produces proposals or bids as part of the sales process, you should seriously consider using technology not only to reduce costs, but also to raise the quality of your printed material. High-quality color laser and inkjet printers are affordable and add a professional touch to presentations.

If you don't have the expertise on staff, hire a professional to design a proposal or bid template in Microsoft Word or some easy-to-use software. Use this template to produce high-quality bids or proposals—add digital photographs, if appropriate. Just make sure it is done right. Color printing won't help a poorly constructed bid or proposal.

> **Financial Aid**
>
> A properly equipped laptop computer can produce top-notch proposals. Many hotels now offer broadband Internet access, which would let your salespeople tap into any data they need for a proposal. With a professionally designed template, the proposal could be created and delivered the next day via e-mail or CD/DVD.

Salespeople, properly equipped and trained, can produce quality presentations, bids, and proposals on the road, and deliver them to customers or prospective customers either on the spot or the next morning. This immediacy saves time and money because you do not need a staff person back at the home office to produce the report and ship it off to the client.

Working smarter can reduce the number of support personnel salespeople in the field need, and that translates into a considerable cost savings.

Administrative Expenses

Your father wasn't wrong when he yelled at you because you left every light in the house on. The cost of keeping the lights on in any business can be significant, and that makes administrative expense goals important. Administrative expenses fall into three categories: equipment and services, supplies, and personnel.

Equipment and Services

Most offices can't function very well without some basic office equipment including telephones, copy machines, fax machines, computers, printers, and so on. Depending on your business, these might be bare bones or quite extensive. Your telephones and copier(s) can be leased or owned, although most businesses own the rest of their office equipment.

Your telephones and telephone service can be complicated to evaluate; however, you should get new bids for your phone service periodically, especially if your business is a heavy user of phone services. Whether you own or lease the equipment is a financial decision that you and your accountant can make based on what makes the most sense. No one answer is right for every business.

If your business makes many photocopies, you should reexamine your copier service periodically, but more importantly, you should look at the reasons you are making copies. A thorough audit of the copies you make and why they are being made may reveal a better way. With DVD burners available on most new computers, you might find that it makes more sense to burn copies of documents to this digital media rather than make paper copies, which must be filed.

Insurance is another key service that you should review on a regular basis for cost savings, especially if you provide health coverage to employees as a benefit. With costs rising every year, an annual review is not out of the question. Other insurance, such as workman's compensation and unemployment insurance, both of which are based on experience, should be reviewed for lower premiums when appropriate.

Supplies

Office supplies, especially in a large office, can run into some serious money. Centralizing purchasing can help you keep control of costs and know what is being spent on supplies. Printed guidelines for office supply use and requisition go a long way toward impressing on employees the importance of being careful with these resources. Set a policy for buying office supplies and follow it yourself.

Years ago at a large company, I was asked to investigate why the in-house print shop ran so much overtime. In my investigation, I discovered that various parts of this large company had standing orders for over 100 different telephone message note pads (this was before voice mail). There were no controls in place, so when a department wanted a telephone message pad, they designed their own and sent it down for printing. Talk about inefficient! I told the print shop to throw out all the designs except one, and print up 5000 pads at a time for inventory. When a department needed 30 or 40 pads, they were there in inventory. When inventory got low, the print shop did another big run (which is efficient for the print shop). This was cheaper for the company—even cheaper than buying preprinted pads—although

Financial Aid

There are many ways to save money on supplies: buy in bulk, use a high-quality laser printer to create your own letterhead, recycle draft prints into note pads, and so on.

some of the departments were not happy. I told them the print shop would be glad to print their design, but a custom print job would be charged to their budget at cost about 100 times what the preprinted pads cost.

When employees understand the true costs of supplies and the impact on the bottom line, it is easier to get everyone to think conservatively about expenses.

Personnel

Administrative personnel are an expense—a necessary expense, but still an expense. The takeaway is you must be careful if you add personnel to the administrative function. Their salary and benefits come off the bottom line, so you need to see that without that person, your company would not function as efficiently. In other words, you should add a person only to prevent an erosion of efficiency and perhaps the loss of customers.

The management trick is to know when the existing staff is stretched too thin and another person must be added. That assessment comes with estimating revenue and general activity growth. If you are looking at a seasonal phenomenon, consider temporary help if that is a possible solution rather than adding a permanent person to the payroll.

Employees are not like pieces of equipment. You can't add and delete them easily. Hiring a new person in a small business is a serious financial commitment; however, it is also an emotional commitment to the existing employees. A good hire will fit in with the existing employees, not only in terms of skills, but also in terms of personality.

Share with Employees

Some small business owners find that an open book policy works well to motivate employees to reduce expenses. They share financial statements with their workers to show how important these expense goals are and the impact it has on the company when they meet these goals. However, other owners might not be as comfortable with being so open. There's not a right or wrong answer here, but a question of style. But if you can share at least some information with employees about expenses and profits, it helps them to understand what they can do, and that helps you and your business.

The Least You Need to Know

◆ Every employee should be accountable for holding down expenses.

◆ Operational expenses are the biggest chunk of the expense pie and must be closely watched.

◆ Marketing expenses should return an appropriate amount of revenue.

◆ Be smart about sales expenses.

◆ Carefully evaluate your needs before you hire any additional administrative personnel.

Chapter 13

Sales Targets

In This Chapter

- ◆ Value of existing customers
- ◆ Qualifying existing customers
- ◆ Qualifying new customers
- ◆ Setting sales goals

The market for your products or services is a dynamic place because of new competitors and changing customers. In earlier chapters, I discussed the importance of revenue, because without cash, your company cannot continue. This is another way of saying nothing happens until a sale is made.

All of your financial goals and projections depend on setting and meeting sales goals. This chapter explores the process of setting sales goals in a market that always wants to know, "What can you do for me today?"

A Moving Target

Setting sales goals might seem like trying to change a flat tire on a moving car—the darn thing won't hold still long enough to get the job done. Many small businesses find the process of planning and goal setting so time-consuming and frustrating that they simply don't formally do either one. Maybe that works for you, or at least you think it does. The problem is that without a process to set goals, you skip the opportunity to evaluate existing customers and determine the guidelines for accepting new customers.

Setting Your Goal

Setting a sales target or goal is not about picking a number or numbers out of the air. You must consider where you want your business to go, assess your existing customer base, and make a realistic evaluation of potential new customers. Most of your revenue comes from existing customers, and most of your new revenue will probably come from the same existing customers. A smaller percentage of new revenue comes from new customers. This relationship isn't true for every business, although it works for most small businesses that practice good customer service.

Existing Customers—Worth Their Weight in Gold

Your existing customer base is the heart of your revenue stream in most cases. If you have done a good job with customer service and stayed competitive in pricing and quality, most of your revenue will come from this base. The care of the customer base should be a top priority for the small business owner. Depending on the number of customers in the base, the owner should meet many, if not all of them, on a regular basis.

> **CAUTION**
> **In the Red** _____
> Don't ignore your existing customers while you prospect new business. Your existing customers keep the lights on and pay the bills—ignore them at your own peril.

Your personal attention to customers is important not only to customer service, but to help your sales force (which could be you) increase the amount of business from each customer. It is easier to sell to a satisfied customer than a complete stranger, so work with them to provide new solutions to their problems.

If you know your existing customers, you should have an idea of what additional business is possible from them. Some will be doing well and are candidates for additional products or services, although other customers may be in trouble and you should anticipate cutbacks or a total loss of business. This information goes into your goal-setting exercise.

Asking for New Business

The best way to ask for new business from an existing customer is to not ask for it—at least not directly. You and your business will be more welcome in a customer's office if you come bearing solutions and not price lists. Your customers have problems, just as your business has problems, and what they need are vendors with solutions. It's your job to discover what those problems are and what solutions your products or services can provide. When that happens, you have made a sale.

As you develop new products or services, find ways to present them as solutions for customers. For example, if your company has a floor cleaner, ask your customer if it would be all right if you brought a gallon of it by for the maintenance people to try. Don't just drop it off at the front desk, but take the time to work side by side with the maintenance crew cleaning a floor with your product. Explain the benefits of the cleaner to them and make sure they understand how it works and why it is superior to what they are currently using.

Leave a sales sheet that details the benefits of your product such as ease of cleaning, smells better, EPA approved, mixes quickly, and so on. If the maintenance crew chief is convinced that your product cleans better and quicker than what they currently use, he becomes your inside sales person (he might even be the one who makes the decision). The point is, you have brought a solution into the customer's business, not a price list and order form. New business will come if you know your customers and offer solutions. When you can see these solutions, you will have a better idea of how much more business you can expect from this customer.

This technique works just as well whether you sell 5 gallons of cleaner or 500,000 widgets. Your company size makes no difference; you want to stay close to your customers, so that you can see opportunities for new business.

Financial Aid

Customer relations is not just about "chewing the fat" with the owner. When it's appropriate, develop a relationship with your customer's employees, especially the ones who directly use your products or services. This is good customer relations, and you may get tips on how to improve your products or services.

You may also discover that you have reached the limit with a customer for whatever reason. That is important information, because it plays into your sales targets and tells you and your sales force how much time and attention you should spend on this customer.

What If You Just Don't Know?

Some customers are going to resist your every effort to establish a relationship. They will not give you any time and don't want to talk about their problems. They want a price or bid and you out of their office. There are alternative ways to get at them that might be more successful such as meeting them in nonbusiness settings, but in the meantime, you need to determine whether you can count on more revenue from them in the coming year.

Financial Aid

Don't give up trying to establish a relationship with reluctant customers. You might have to hear many "no's" before you hear a "yes," but persistence is a powerful persuasion tool.

A review of the customer's history can give you some insight—have they been steadily increasing or do their orders come in random bunches? With some customers, the best you can do is give it a good S.W.A.G. (scientific wild-a** guess).

Which Customers Are Not Worth Keeping?

If existing customers are so important to your sales goals, should you consider dropping any of them? The answer is a resounding yes. There are a number of reasons you may want to drop an existing customer or change the terms of your relationship. Here are some:

- Consistently late-paying customers rob you of cash as we saw in earlier chapters. They might consistently order, although if you finance their business, you lose money on every transaction. Either work with them to get payments current, begin charging interest on late payments, raise prices to cover your true costs, or tell them you cannot work with them until they meet your terms.

- Customers who demand special services or treatment, but don't pay for it, take the profit out of your product or service. Using the tools from earlier in the book, look at the cost of goods sold for the product or service and factor in the price for the additional demands. If the customer is unwilling to pay the extra charge, it is time to drop them.

- Customers who want changes to your products or services but don't want to pay for them are cutting out the profit. Stick to your agreements and insist on payment in full for change orders. If the customer is unwilling to compensate you, look for another customer.

◆ Customers that are not profitable or barely make you a profit tie up resources you could use on customers that are profitable. These companies are highly risky, and it's possible that they won't be in business for a long time.

◆ If customers are not paying enough for your products and services because you haven't raised prices enough and your expenses have caught up with revenue, you need to either change terms or drop them as a customer. Perhaps you have given in to their pleas to hold price hikes down too often and now your costs have risen to the point where the profit is squeezed out of the product or service. You do not make any money from this customer, and in fact, you might lose money because of them.

How do you know if a customer falls into the unprofitable category? You use the financial tools we discussed in earlier chapters; in particular, you want to develop an accurate cost of goods sold (COGS) figure for the products or services this customer purchases. After you have an accurate COGS, you want to add in the extra costs associated with this customer, if any. These might include the items above or others particular to your business.

When you have that figure, you can compute a gross margin for the customer by subtracting the COGS from the customer's sales numbers to get a gross margin for that customer. How does this gross margin compare to other customers or the gross margin on the income statement? You will know when a customer is more trouble than they are worth when you put the numbers to them.

CAUTION

In the Red

There is a huge difference between being busy with unprofitable work and making money. In earlier chapters, we looked at the financial tools that help you tell the difference between spinning your wheels and moving your business forward.

One of the hardest things a small business owner can do is turn down an order or tell a customer no more business. Yet many small businesses fold each year because they keep servicing unprofitable customers. These small business owners can't understand why they are broke when the shop is always so busy. If you understand your company's finances, you won't find your business in this situation.

Finding New Customers

Almost every business needs to generate new customers each year—some more than others do—but it's an important activity to all companies. For many small businesses, new customers might account for only a small percentage of increased sales each year, yet without those new customers the company would be in serious trouble. Despite your best intentions, you will lose customers each year. Some leave for no apparent reason, others get mad at something, others fold, some you might dismiss, but you lose customers regardless of the reason. New customers resupply your base and add new revenue.

Every small business hopes to land a big new customer. However, if you do get business from a new customer, realistically you first get a few small orders before the bigger jobs. You might find that you spend a disproportionate amount of time working on new customers for new revenue they bring in. Your marketing efforts help the process, although most small businesses grow through personal contact with the owner and senior staff.

The marketing goals we discussed in Chapter 10 should correlate with your new customer goals and tie in closely with the next chapter on expanding market share. The main pitfall that many small businesses fall into is expecting this process to happen overnight. Working your marketing plan and getting your company better known in the community will help you attract new customers, but this does not happen overnight. Consider new customer development an investment in the future—the time and energy you put in today pays dividends down the road when you convert some of your contacts into customers.

> **Financial Aid**
>
> Finding new customers can be time-consuming for some small business owners, but it is an investment in your company's future that you must make.

What About Retail Businesses?

You may be wondering if much of what I discussed in the previous sections applies to retail businesses where you may not know all of your customers. The answer is yes, for the most part. You still need to think about ways to sell more to repeat customers and you still need to think about ways to bring in new customers. Dealing with problem customers is somewhat less complicated, because most retail businesses don't directly issue credit. If you are burned with a bad check, you have some recourse and you can work with credit card companies on bad charges if that happens.

You are more interested in eliminating unprofitable product lines when you set sales goals. You also use the same basic process to calculate the COGS of the product and gross margin. Based on earlier discussions, you might have a minimum gross margin for each product that acts as a filter to eliminate unprofitable or low-profit products from your shelves.

Setting Specific Goals

First, look at your existing customer base to make projections about what you expect from this revenue source, and discuss any unprofitable customers. Then it's time to put hard numbers to your sales goals. Some business people find specific goals unnerving because they involve a commitment, whereas nonspecific goals allow much more wiggle room. If you say your goal is to increase sales next year, that doesn't commit you to much beyond a $1 increase over this year's revenue. If you say your goal is a 15 percent increase in revenue, broken up between existing and new customers, you commit your company to some specific targets.

> **Financial Aid**
>
> Specific goals—hard numbers—make everyone aware that this is serious business. As the owner, you set an example for your employees that you expect these specific goals to be met and intend to do everything you can to see that it happens.

A Sales Goal Worksheet

You might find this exercise helpful depending on your business—consider using some form of it to set specific sales goals. You must be specific because that focuses everyone in the company on targets and clarifies expectations for the coming year. Here is a sample sales goal worksheet that illustrates how you might begin thinking about the process:

Existing Customers	Last Year	Next Year	Confidence Factor	Goal Set
Customer A	$25,000	$30,000	95%	$28,500
Customer B	$15,000	$18,000	95%	$17,100
Customer C	$32,000	$32,000	100%	$32,000
Customer D	$26,000	$30,000	95%	$28,500

continues

continued

| Customer E | $17,000 | $15,000 | 90% | $13,500 |
| Total | $115,000 | $125,000 | 95.68% | $119,600 |

New Customers	Last Year	Next Year	Confidence Factor	Goal Set
Customer X	$0	$10,000	60%	$6,000
Customer Y	$0	$5,000	50%	$2,500
Customer Z	$0	$5,000	40%	$2,000
Total	$0	$20,000	50%	$10,500
Grand Totals:		$145,000		$130,100

The purpose of this exercise is to go through your customer base and assess the potential sales for the next year. My illustration is simple so you don't get hung up on the numbers and miss the point of the exercise.

Use this format, or one that you devise, to see what each customer contributed to revenue in the previous year. The next column is an estimate of what increase in sales you can expect for each customer in the coming year. I call the fourth column confidence factor, because your projection for the coming year is, in most cases, an estimate. How confident are you that your business can meet this goal? This is a "be honest" question, not a time to brag. If you know your customers well, the confidence factors should be high. Apply the confidence factor percentage to the projection for next year and you have a tempered goal.

There are several items of note in my illustration. The first is that only one customer (C) has a confidence factor of 100% for the projected sales. This might indicate a signed contract that covers work for the coming year. Customer E either looks as if it is finding other vendors or is in financial trouble, because its revenue is projected lower for the coming year.

Financial Aid

Whether you use this worksheet or devise one of your own, the important point is to get the process down on paper (or a computer spreadsheet) so you can work the numbers.

The worksheet shows three new customers for the coming year. The assumption is these are prospects you have been working for some time and believe you can convert in the coming year. Because you don't have any experience with them yet, the confidence factor should be lower than for existing customers, unless you have firm indications to the contrary.

What to Do with the Numbers

You now have some numbers to work with—the question is, what do they mean and how do you use them? The first set of numbers is from your existing customer base. These should be your most accurate projections; of course, you can't know the future, and bad things happen, but you try to account for the unexpected. In my simple example, I show a projection for next year of $125,000 and a confidence-adjusted total of $119,600. If you disregard the actual numbers, you have created a range of possibilities for next year's revenue from existing customers. It's not a "best case–worse case" scenario, because the low number is too high for that. However, based on your estimates and judgment, the revenue for next year will fall somewhere between these two numbers for existing customers.

You could set a sales goal for existing customers of $190,000, but that would fly in the face of reality. It is possible one of your existing customers could give you a huge increase, but it is just as likely (maybe more so) that one could fold. This is why simply pulling numbers out of the air without any thought is a waste of time.

Now you can set your goal for existing customers at something between your projection ($125,000) and the confidence factor adjusted goal ($119,600). Where you set it is up to you, but at least in this range you are making a rational choice based on a process.

You can use the same process with new customers, although the estimates are less accurate, because they are not as well known as your existing customers. If you have been in business for some time, you can see how your company has done in converting other prospects to customers and retaining those customers. Don't let your optimism overrule your good judgment.

Your Goal

For the sake of moving the discussion forward, let's say you decide that the confidence-adjusted goals for both existing and new customers were reasonable targets for next year. This gives you a sales (revenue) goal of $130,100 ($119,600 + $10,500). This represents a 13.1 percent increase over your sales of last year, which

Financial Aid

Setting your sales goal becomes a simple decision after you have done the projections for each customer, including projected new customers.

is an ambitious increase for most businesses. If you are just starting out, a large percent jump from one year to the next is not unusual; however, the larger your company gets, the harder it is to make big percentage jumps. Your actual numbers might be smaller than my hypothetical example.

Making It Happen

Setting sales (revenue) goals is only part of the equation. The next part is to make those goals reality. You are almost there because of the analysis you did on your customer base. Now, you just need a plan to achieve your goals. If you have a sales force, you should always include them when you analyze your customer base. They should have good insights into what their customers are doing and what solutions your company can offer to generate more business.

Getting from Here to There

Increasing your sales by 13 percent requires changes, because, in most cases, that extra business does not simply walk through the door. For each customer, you need to develop an action plan in concert with the salesperson assigned to that account, if you have one. The action plan doesn't have to be formal, but it does need to state in writing specifically what will change (add new product line, upsell services, add more quantity, and so on), so that you hit the sales goal for that customer. Include appropriate review dates (monthly, quarterly) so you can make any adjustments in a timely manner.

Small Bites

When you break your sales goals down into small account-by-account tasks, the job of raising revenue by 13 percent doesn't seem so overwhelming. Everyone knows his or her responsibility for each account, and the company can work together to make it happen. If you use commissioned salespeople, consider a laddered scale that pays a higher percentage for exceeding your goal.

However you run your sales function, shooting at a goal that comes from a thoughtful process makes more sense than pulling a number out of the air. Your employees will see the logic of the goals, especially if they participate in the process, and they will have an emotional stake in personally meeting their goals.

The Least You Need to Know

◆ Your existing customers account for most of your sales.

◆ It is better to drop unprofitable customers than have them drag your company down.

◆ You need new customers to replace other customers that leave for any number of reasons.

◆ Use a process for setting specific numbers for your sales goals.

Chapter 14

Expanding Market Share

In This Chapter

- ◆ Winners and losers
- ◆ Identify new markets
- ◆ Defensive marketing
- ◆ Setting your goals

Successful marketing increases immediate sales, and it also increases awareness of your company in the market to enhance future sales. Expanding your market share is not just for large companies. Small businesses also need to focus on this issue, because in many competitive markets the rule is "eat or be eaten." This chapter discusses expanding your presence in the market.

Moving Markets

Most small businesses compete in a market with other businesses of various sizes. The overall market for the products or services might be growing, flat, or shrinking. The number of competitors might be increasing, flat, or decreasing. In many cases the growth rates of the market and the number of competitors will match each other. If you want to grow your company's market share, it will be at the expense of your competitors, who will either lose a customer or not get a new customer who moves into the market.

Expanding Markets

If you are fortunate enough to work in an expanding market, you have the opportunity to grow your market share along with the general expansion of the whole market. This is the easiest way to grow market share, in most cases because there is usually enough new business to keep the whole market agitated. With new business opportunities for the taking, there will generally be some reshuffling of existing customers, which also gives you the opportunity to pick up market share. Just be sure you take care of your existing customer base. It doesn't help your market share to have new customers come in the front door and existing customers go out the back one.

> **In the Red**
>
> Expanding markets can be exciting; however they also can attract new competitors. When markets reach a certain size, larger companies may be willing to compete that weren't interested before.

Flat or Declining Markets

Flat or declining markets are difficult, especially for marginal businesses in your industry. Surprisingly, if your company is on sound financial footing, these can be just the times to pick up significant market share, as weaker players close shop and their customers become available. Although it is not a decision to enter into lightly, this might also be a good time to acquire a competitor who has a good customer base, although lacks the financial controls you put in place. Enter this decision with care and some professional guidance; however, it is a way to grab a chunk of market share.

The Market Size

If you have an idea of how fast the market is expanding and you know the size of the current market, you can estimate what your new market share will be based on your goals.

The reality is that few small businesses have the resources to identify their market this precisely. Most compete directly against other businesses that don't publicly report sales, so gathering information on total market size can be difficult.

When you consider market share goals, remember that you must be consistent with the reality of the market and your competition. If the market (customers) for your products or services is flat or shrinking, you can only project a large increase in market share if you replace one or more competitors.

Why Set a Goal

Your market share goal might be the softest of the goals you set because it does not lend itself to easily discovered numbers. However, market share is an important number because it measures your company's competitive standing. Although it can be difficult to see the "big picture" of your market, you can focus on specific products or services and how your company can achieve an advantage over its competitors.

Financial Aid

Just because a goal might be harder to define than others is no excuse to let it slide. Without some tangible target, expanding market share has no accountability.

Product or Service Share

If it is difficult to know the total market, it may be somewhat easier to narrow your focus and target specific products or services. You probably know most of the main competitors for your products or services. One way to expand market share is to set goals for particular products or services and aggressively go after business that competitors currently own.

This process walks close to setting revenue goals, but there is a distinction—revenue goals focus on customers, while market share focuses on products or services. There are several reasons that increasing market share through your product might be attractive to your company:

- **Economies of scale.** Depending on your product or service, there might be significant savings by increasing your volume. You might be able to purchase components in larger quantities at cheaper prices. Production costs per unit can drop and your gross margin rises.

- **Brand credibility.** If your product or service is the market leader or one of the market leaders, that conveys a level of credibility. It is easier to sell to new customers if you have a position of prominence in the market.

◆ **Economic stability.** If your market is subject to periodic contractions, market leaders can more easily weather the storm.

You may not desire to be the biggest fish in the pond, but you don't want to be the smallest, either.

What It Takes

Increasing your share of the market in a particular product or service requires your marketing and sales goals to coordinate. Most likely, you will also need to change some parts of how you conduct business. You might pick up some market share when new customers enter the market or when existing customers become dissatisfied with their present provider. However, to make a real difference in your market share, you have to take customers away from your competitors.

Financial Aid

You might think that your products and services are second to none. However, you need to detach yourself to see how they really stack up to your competitors.

To attract your competitor's customers, you have to differentiate yourself on some basis, such as:

◆ Price

◆ Service

◆ Quality

◆ Convenience

◆ Innovation

You might need more than one of these distinctions to lure a customer away from a competitor. And know that your competitor is probably not going to sit idle and watch you take bread off the table.

Big Fish, Little Fish

The definition of "small business" is broad enough that some larger businesses and smaller businesses fit under the umbrella. This complicates our discussion of market share somewhat; however, it also is an opportunity to consider where you want to position your company. Many small businesses survive and thrive because they fill niches that larger companies find too small to be profitable. Large companies have too much administrative overhead to support, so they can't afford small niche businesses. It would not be uncommon for large companies to have a threshold at say $50 million annual revenue before they would even consider a business worth acquiring or starting, and some have even higher requirements.

Even "larger" small businesses find that small niches aren't profitable if they don't generate a minimum amount of revenue. You should have those types of guidelines in place at your business as we discussed in previous chapters. With a firm understanding of your company's finances, you'll quickly see when an opportunity is too small to possibly work. However, you may decide that you want to keep your company small, so that you can take advantage of those opportunities that others can't afford.

Big Fish

Most small business people want to grow their business, and that means they must expand their market share. Depending on your industry and competition, you can have a shot as the top dog if you work hard. Of course, you might be competing with national chains or huge corporations that you'll never overcome, so you shoot for the highest number possible.

Competing with big corporations presents challenges and opportunities, which gives you the chance to position your company as an alternative based on some advantage your product or service has over the giants. You might pick up customers that the 800-pound gorilla in the market can't or won't service because the account is too small. Your job is to find those areas mentioned above that distinguish your company and work those into your marketing and sales plans. Giant companies are a challenge because they can bring so many resources to bear on problems and products, yet they are also notoriously slow to change with the market.

One of the oldest stories in management circles tracked the rise of IBM as the leader in computer technology (this was years before the personal computer). IBM owned the mainframe computer market. In addition, virtually every computer engineer and technician was trained on IBM equipment and software, so when they were in positions of responsibility, they recommended IBM products. The saying in the information systems industry was, "no one ever got fired for recommending IBM." The vast majority of computer installations in business and government were IBM. There was just one problem—the computer world was changing and IBM couldn't adapt fast enough. IBM is no longer the sole leader in every aspect of computer technology. Even though IBM gave legitimacy to the personal computer as a business tool, it couldn't keep up

Financial Aid _____

There are many ways to successfully compete with the giants; however, if you're selling commodity goods, price is probably not an area you are going to win. Find some other way to be better, possibly through service or support.

with market changes. IBM left the door open and small companies that no one ever heard of such as Compaq, Dell, and Apple soon ran IBM out of its leadership role. In 2005, IBM sold its personal computer division to a Chinese company.

Your company can compete with giants if you are nimble and can adapt to your customer's needs. Just make sure you don't become complacent also or some smaller company will beat you.

Little Fish

Of course, many small business owners prefer the word small in front of business. They want to keep their business small and manageable. Frequently, these are professional service providers that can make a comfortable living with a small staff (or alone) and don't want the headaches of large payrolls and big facilities to manage.

The Internet has opened the door to small companies operating on an international basis. Many companies that operate successfully on the Internet are one-person enterprises who work out of a spare bedroom.

Years ago (even before the Internet—known as the Dark Ages for younger readers), I operated a successful "virtual" company. I contracted with one company that would manufacture and ship my product. Another company answered my 1-800 number and took orders. I used another company to design my advertising and marketing pieces. I had no employees. My job was marketing the products and going to the post office to collect the mail, which included mail orders for the product and the credit card slips from my phone orders. Today, I could run that same business with even more ease over the Internet, as many small business owners have discovered.

The decision to stay small is not without peril, however. If you are the main (or only) income producer for the company and you get sick or injured, your income may slow dramatically or stop altogether. The small business owner who wants to remain small should talk to a qualified insurance professional about disability insurance protection to cover lost income in the event you are unable to work for an extended period.

Competition

It comes as no surprise that while you are expanding market share, your competition is, too. Depending on the industry and market, you may find that it's a fight just to hold position, much less gain ground. Even if it is not that obvious, you need to know what the other side is doing with its marketing plans. I'm not advocating "spying" on your competitors, although you should keep your eyes and ears open.

In the Red

Although I advocate openness with employees, be careful if you have a technology company or handle sensitive information for clients. A disgruntled or loud-mouthed employee can cost you dearly.

Gathering Information

I don't think it's generally a good idea to ask your customers about your competition. However, you'll probably hear things even without asking. I'm always a little cautious about "volunteered" information about a competitor, because I'm concerned about the motives behind it. I would try to independently verify any second-hand information before you act on it. For example, if a customer suggests a competitor is about to cut prices 10 percent, I would want to find a way to confirm that before I offered to match that cut. Customers are not above playing one vendor off another.

If your competitors have websites, check them frequently. If the competitor offers free e-mail updates, sign up using a personal e-mail or a web-based e-mail account, such as Yahoo! or Hotmail.com. For retail competitors, visit their stores or have employees or spouses visit. Order products, where appropriate, and check the quality. In other words, if it's possible, you should be a customer and note any changes in their pricing or product.

Be Defensive

In previous sections, I've talked about how to differentiate your company and position your company's product or service to build market share. Of course, your competitors can use the same technique on you. That is why it is important to know as much about your competitors as possible.

If you understand your company's financials, it also pays off in this area. When you have a good grasp of the true costs of producing your product or service, it is not that difficult to estimate your competitor's costs. If you have a manufacturing business, your competitor probably uses similar equipment to produce the same goods. They are likely to pay a similar wage scale, and so on. With some knowledge of each competitor's costs that might be unique to that business (this one owns their building, but that one rents, and so on), you can build a reasonably accurate cost of goods sold (COGS) and gross margin for the product. This information can help you decide if and how they might compete on price.

Perhaps your competitor's niche is quality or convenience. In each area, you need to explore where you are vulnerable and look for ways to defend your position. If you can't match or beat a competitor on a point, you need to prepare a defense that shows how you excel in other areas to compensate. Most customers understand that vendors who promise everything usually disappoint in some area eventually. Years ago, I had a sign in a business I owned (this wasn't original; I'd seen it somewhere else):

Financial Aid

Your financial reports guide you in what you can and cannot afford to do for clients. The numbers should set the boundaries, not your competitive drive.

"We offer the highest quality, the lowest prices, and the fastest service. Pick any two."

In the end, you have to decide how much you can bend to keep or win a client. In Chapter 13 I discussed when you should let customers go if they were unprofitable. Don't let your defense of market share turn profitable customers into money losers. At some point, you have to say I can't stay in business and cut my prices that much. It is time to take a hard look at how you can cut expenses (find new suppliers, for instance) or just say it's time to look at new product lines where you can make a profit.

The Economics of Market Share

You pay a price to gain market share, which you hope is an investment that returns itself many times over. However, you have to know how much you can afford to pay for market share—just like anything else you buy. If you pay too much, you might never recover your investment. There are several economic strategies you can use to gain market share that help mitigate the cost.

The Combo or Meal Deal

Walk into any fast-food restaurant and you'll see a menu featuring combos or meals, which usually include several items and a drink for one price. For example, most hamburger places offer a hamburger, french fries, and soft drink as one meal. You order a "Number One" or a "Happy Meal." If you look at the items priced separately, the meal is a "bargain" because it costs less than the sum of the items.

So are the fast-food places doing their customers a favor? Maybe; however, that's not the main reason for the "meal deals." The reason they offer food this way is that they sell more than if customers had to order each item separately. Rather than force customers to decide if they want fries and, if so, what size, and the same for a drink, the fast-food chains make it easy for the customer. Maybe you didn't particularly want the fries, although it is easier to order this way.

The lesson from this example is that one of the strategies you can use to increase market share is to package products or services in such a manner to make it easy for the customer to buy. Earlier, I told you about a business I had where a company manufactured my products and shipped them for me. The reason that particular company handled my product was because they offered the shipping option. They were not the lowest-cost provider; however, they offered a service that solved a problem for me and, because of that, they got my business. Other companies were willing to do the manufacturing, although they would not ship the product to my customers.

Financial Aid

Your best package of products or services solves problems for your customers. If you solve problems at a reasonable price, you win market share.

In packaging products or services, you might take a profit hit on one to gain market share on the other. If you understand the costs of everything involved, you can make an intelligent decision about how to bundle and price products and services in a way that makes an attractive package for your customer and still earns you the profit you need. If you don't understand the finances of your business, this is a recipe for disaster.

The Upsell or Loss Leader

Retailers might be familiar with the concept of the loss leader—offering an item, usually in an advertisement, at an extremely low price to get customers in the door in hopes they buy something else, too. The practice is not appropriate for every business;

however, some variation is an effective way to build market share. This strategy doesn't usually work well if you offer only a few products or services.

The concept is simple—offer a product or service at an attractive price and after the customer is on board, try to interest them in additional purchases. You need to handle this with some tact or you turn customers off and build a reputation as a greedy hack. Another word of caution: your initial product or service should be something of value and not a cheap gimmick. If you take your time and build a relationship with customers that come in through this method, it can be successful over time.

There are two important considerations for the loss leader plan to work. The first is you must know the cost of your product or service and decide if you want to sell at, below, or just above cost. This decision affects your bottom line, so think about it carefully. If you take a loss from each sale, that missed profit needs to be recovered somewhere else.

The second consideration is that you must have a plan in place to sell additional products or services to these newfound customers. Ideally, it would be something that goes along with the loss leader, and you might need to customize your approach with different customers to meet their individual needs. Regardless, a modifiable game plan is required.

For example, a commercial printer might offer an "identity" package to new customers consisting of letterhead, envelopes, and business cards all coordinated with matching paper, ink, and so on. After the customer is on board with this package, offer him business forms, marketing brochures, annual reports, and other high-end products as an upsell.

If you know your costs going in and have a solid game plan of products and services to sell, you have the financial key to paying for the loss leader strategy of increasing market share.

Your Costs

You can use one of these strategies or a completely different plan to gain market share that works for your industry. Regardless of what strategy you use, the important financial consideration is that you must always understand the financial implications. It is an acceptable strategy to take a loss or break even on a product or service to gain market share; however, it needs to be a conscious decision on your part and not an accident because you didn't understand the financial implications.

The Least You Need to Know

- Gaining market share usually means a competitor loses some.

- Becoming a leader in your market gives your product or service credibility.

- Protecting your market share from competition is as important as gaining market share.

- Understanding the economics of market share helps you shape strategies.

Chapter 15

The Strategic Planning Budget

In This Chapter

- Start from scratch
- Departments accountable
- Be goal-driven
- Stay stingy with cash

Now that you have worked through the main areas of your company and established some goals and priorities, it is time to translate those targets into a strategic budget. This process allocates resources according to the goals you established. This chapter shows you how to build a budget to fund those priorities, so you spend your cash wisely.

Change Your Perceptions

Many small business people cringe at the word "budget," because it reminds them of the corporate grind they left behind. They still do one, but they hold their nose at the same time. You, however, have let go of your negative perceptions and realize that a budget is a tool that helps you make money. I'll admit to not being fond of budgets for many years myself—they reminded me of being in a very small closet.

Financial Aid

Your strategic budget completes the loop of the financial reports we discussed at the beginning of the book. The budget defines your company's finances and the reports tell you how well or poorly the company is performing.

My thinking has changed over the years and now I see the budget as a means to accomplish goals; it's not an obstacle to creativity. If a mental image helps, think of a bright summer day. If you stay out in the sun too long, you can get sunburned. However, if you take a magnifying glass and focus the sunlight on a piece of paper, in a matter of seconds, the focused sunlight burns a hole through the paper and can set it on fire. Your budget is a magnifying glass that focuses your resources on specific areas rather than spreading them over wide expanses.

The Budgeting Process

The process for building a budget varies from company to company, and depends on size and your disposition. How many people are involved, the rules for budgets, and when the process occurs differ among companies, although there are some general guidelines you should follow. The first one details how to start the budgeting process.

Starting from Scratch

The first step to build a useful budget is to forget the old notion that the new budget is last year's budget plus 5 percent. That's the type of thinking that perpetuates mistakes and funds out-of-date ideas. Instead, clear out the entries from last year and start over. This type of budgeting (called zero-based budgeting) challenges every dollar the company spends and asks you (and your department heads) to justify the expenditure.

This gives you the opportunity to look at every expenditure to see how it relates to the goals you set about expenses, revenue, and profits. Those goals are your guides to decide whether an expense is justified or not.

Your Goals Decide

You have three main goals for your company: an expense goal, a sales (revenue) goal, and a profit goal. Other goals, such as marketing and market share, support one or more of these main goals. Of the three main goals, profit is obviously the one that is most important to most small businesses; however, you can't get to your profit goal if you don't meet your revenue and expense goals. The point is that most of your budget should address these three main goals and every item on your budget must either directly or indirectly support your top three goals.

For example, when you are doing the overhead portion of the budget (office supplies, rent, utilities, telephone service, and so on), which goal do these expenditures fall under? The answer for most small businesses is the expense goal. We know that most of these costs don't directly relate to the company's product or service (although in a pure service business, they might), so to help meet the expense goal, we examine each item to see how we can hold down costs without hurting the company. Some ways that can save you money include:

- Buy office supplies in bulk
- Buy, rather than lease, a copy machine
- Change telephone vendors

Don't be shy to ask for concessions from vendors, especially if you are a good customer—just be reasonable.

Hold up each item on your budget and ask what goal it belongs under and whether it advances or hinders that goal. Any cost savings advances your expense goal just as any items that can increase sales advance the revenue goal.

Financial Aid

When you base financial decisions on goals, they become easier to make. Does this expenditure advance our profit goal? Do we really need this full-color, duplex copier or will the single-sided, black and white do?

Conflicts

There will likely be some conflicts when establishing budgets. Based on profit, expense, and revenue goals previously established, you have defined the size of the pie (the total budget). When departments begin cutting up their slices, you might find the sum of the parts is greater than the whole, so you must make compromises and revisions. The bulk of the conflicts come on the expense goals. The marketing department typically wants more resources to meet its goals in support of the sales goals. Product managers want more money to tweak items, and so on. All of these conflicts should be worked out through negotiation; however, you should always stick to your final main (profit, expense, revenue) goals.

Building a Budget

In smaller companies, the owner typically does the budget alone, although in larger companies it might be a joint effort between the owner and department heads. More input from people and departments results in a better-constructed budget. In the best of worlds, your employees have an understanding of the budget construction and feel they played a role in shaping it.

Departments Work Under Established Goals

Although zero-based budgeting gives each department a clean slate, it doesn't give them a free hand to do whatever they want in terms of styling a budget for their area. Your goals have set out priorities that direct the actions of every department. Depending on those priorities, some departments might have a bigger budget than last year, although others could have a smaller budget. You need to be sensitive to your department heads that they don't take a reduced budget as a sign of failure on their part or a lack of confidence by you. If you feel they have failed and you do lack confidence in their abilities, the way to address that problem is not through the budget.

Timing

Building a budget under zero-based budgeting takes some time, so don't wait until the end of your fiscal year to begin. Time is one of the precious commodities small business owners find in short supply; however, this process is worth your investment. It is especially helpful to have your strategic budget completed before you start your new fiscal year. This gives an added psychological push of importance to it, whereas dragging it over to the new year makes the budget seem more of an afterthought.

> **Notes and News**
>
> Changing your fiscal year is not difficult; however it shouldn't be done without some forethought. You might end up with a year that is shorter or longer than 12 months, and that can be confusing.

For retailers or other businesses that are seasonal in nature, I suggest a fiscal year that ends one or two months past your busy season. This gives you a chance to get past that hectic time and move into a time when business is more relaxed and you can take some time to focus on the budget. You know best when that period is for your business. If your fiscal year-end doesn't fall at the right time, check with your accountant to change your year-end.

New Products or Services

If you plan to introduce a new product or service, the strategic budget is the place to fix development and marketing costs, along with a time frame for completing the project. New efforts without firm deadlines and budgets tend to grow in size and cost, and never seem to get finished. Zero-based budgeting helps focus resources on new projects in a way that holds people accountable for their on-time, on-budget completion. When new products or product enhancements slip, it hurts both revenues and expenses.

Years ago, I worked briefly for a company that published business reference books. They had a hard time meeting deadlines for publication dates. I asked how many deadlines they had missed and was told with a chuckle that they had never made a deadline. It was a running joke in the company that books never got out on time. The problem was this "joke" cost the company dearly, not only in money, but also in credibility with its customers who never received orders on time. Fortunately, technology rescued this company because it eventually dropped its book publishing and began putting all its information online. When the material was ready, it went online and the company didn't have to meet any deadlines.

Starting on the Right Foot

Many people find developing new products or services exciting and challenging. They thrive under the pressure to create something new or enhance an existing product. However, mention that they must work within a budget and they come crashing back to earth. Creativity without constraint might be fine in the art world, but it doesn't work in the world of business. There are guidelines, goals, and budgets, so that efforts are focused not on what the developer wants to do, but on what is important for the company. New product development that doesn't fit with existing product lines is a waste of resources. Imagine General Motors advertising an exciting line of new cars and trucks and, by the way, we also make a high-fiber cereal. You might come up

Financial Aid

Be careful about the temperament of the people working on new products (including you). There are people who get energized when they create something new, but as soon as it becomes an accepted product, they lose interest. It won't serve your company well to invest money in a new product or service and then have everyone lose interest in it.

with a great enhancement to your lead product; however, none of your customers want it or will pay for it. In both cases, the needs of the business were put secondary to the development process.

Right Foot

Even if you've done your research, introducing a new product or service is risky. What if it doesn't hit the revenue projections? What if the costs go over your projections? There are many things that can happen to new products and services—the majority of which are bad. You want to minimize the risks whenever possible, so you make sure the product or service is reasonable for your market in terms of price and quality.

However, to help a new product or service get off to a good start, make sure the launch is on-time and on-budget. This helps your creditability with customers and protects your bottom line because you stayed within the budget. From day one, the product starts with a good reputation, both externally and internally, which helps the company.

Stuff Happens

Despite our best planning and designs, sometimes things happen and a new product or service just won't come in on-time or on-budget. This is frustrating because if the problem is large, it can mess up your other goals and other areas of the strategic budget. Find out what went wrong and learn from it so it doesn't happen again.

In the meantime, what do you do? You must first determine the extent of the problem.

- Is this just a development problem that won't affect the implementation costs or profits?

- Is this a fundamental design flaw in the product or service that will take major dollars to fix?

- Will the fix change the product in such a way that it no longer fits what we wanted?

- How long will it take to fix the product, and how expensive is it to fix?

These questions and others you may think of need answers before you proceed further. Don't be concerned about dropping a product or service at the last minute if you can't get satisfactory answers to your important questions. There is no sense in throwing good money after bad.

Building Your Budget

The strategic budget should conform to your accounting system, so that you can get the reports you need on a regular basis. If you need to add line items for new projects, do so before the new fiscal year starts, so that you have a budget to compare with actual expenditures.

The Formula

Remember our operating formula from previous chapters:

Revenue – Profit = Expenses

Those three elements are also our main budget goals and will be reflected in the budget. As you work through the line items, keep this formula in mind, even though it does not show up on the income statement in this manner. Your first task is an overall budget for the company, which covers all revenue and expenses. This information rolls up into the monthly and annual income statement and then can be compared to the budget.

Most accounting software lets you look at your income statement several ways. One of the most important views is actual results versus budgeted results. This lets you know if you are on track or need a midcourse correction.

Entering Expenses, Income

Your budget is most useful if you can target income and expenses to periods rather than taking a total, dividing by 12, and putting the answer in each month. You should know expenses far enough in advance to slot them in the months they occur. For example, if you know you are going to have a three-month marketing push April through June that costs $12,000, it doesn't make any sense to put $1,000 per month in the budget for each month. It will come out right at the end of the year, but you won't be able to tell that until then. Instead, budget $4,000 per month for those three months (or however the money breaks down). You'll be able to see instantly whether you are under or over budget.

Financial Aid _____

Projecting revenue and expenses separately each month makes a budget pair up well with your income statement. It gives you a much clearer picture than if you simply take the average amount for each month.

The same goes for income. Some retailers have a seasonal business where the bulk of their income occurs during a specific period (the holidays beginning with Thanksgiving, for example). If your business has that seasonal nature, reflect that in the budget, so that your income is heaviest in the appropriate months and lighter other months. You want your budget to reflect your business, and few businesses have the same numbers each month.

Departmental or Profit Center Budgets

If your business is large enough to have departments or separate profit centers, you want to do those budgets next. The process is much the same as completing the budget for the company, except you look at an individual piece rather than the whole. Obviously, departmental or profit center budgets track with the company budget. If the department has a big expense in March, that should show up on the company budget in March also.

The benefit of doing budgets for departments and profit centers is that it brings the important numbers close to where decisions are made and action is taken. For example, if you owned a company with several retail stores, it might be hard for the managers and employees in those stores to grasp the total corporate budget. However, if they have a budget (with goals) for their store, it becomes personal and manageable.

With the proper education, training, and incentives, the employees can become engaged in meeting goals and budgets. Too often they are left in the dark and don't understand why decisions are made, some of which aggravate customers. For example, a vendor you use goes out of business. Unfortunately, this vendor carried a popular item in your store and you can't find any other source for it. It disappears off your shelves with no explanation and your employees must deal with disappointed customers. Now you've angered your customers and frustrated your employees. A better strategy would be to find something close, if possible, to the lost product. Tell your employees what happened and suggest they explain to the customer that the source for the item is no longer in business, but we've found this item, which many people enjoy.

Financial Aid _____

Getting employees on board with the budget, especially expenses, is a big step toward meeting your goal. Consider some incentives to reward participation.

If your employees relate to the budget and goals and you give them the training and information they need, most do their best to meet the challenge.

Stingy with Cash

One of the purposes of a strategic budget is to guard your cash. This is one of the more traditional functions of any budget, but it is a very important one nevertheless. No matter how flush you believe your company is today, tomorrow may be a different story. Small (and large) businesses that continue from one year to the next with some success are those that value their cash and spend it reluctantly. I'm not talking about being cheap. I'm talking about making sure every dollar you spend is necessary and does something to advance one of your goals.

The Filter

Your strategic budget is your filter that stops ad hoc projects and expenses, large and small, from consuming cash and other resources. There are many opportunities for small businesses to spend money—from new marketing and advertising possibilities to new product lines. Some of these opportunities may be worth pursuing, but not at the expense of dropping your well-thought-out plans and budget on a whim. Any opportunity that must be acted on immediately is usually one that you can safely pass on.

If it's not in the budget, don't add it at the last minute. You are better off passing on a good opportunity than hastily grabbing at a deal that will likely turn sour. Most small business owners need to understand there will always be another deal. If it is a legitimate opportunity, it won't need an answer tomorrow. Take the time to look it over and analyze the deal from all angles.

Revise with Caution

Even with the best of plans, things happen—both good and bad—that can throw your budget off on a permanent basis. What should you do? For example, halfway though the year you lose a major customer that provided a significant contribution to your revenue. Unless you can hustle up some new business in a hurry, you are going to be off budget for the rest of the year. Your revenues will be down and, depending on your business, your expenses may not drop enough to offset the loss. This means your profit goal is shot.

If you are just a few months from the end of your fiscal year, it is probably not worth revising your budget. Just tighten your belt and look for ways to cut a proportionate amount of expense from the budget. This will slide you in closer to your profit goal.

However, if you still have six months or more remaining and no real chance of replacing the lost business in a hurry, it might be wise to revise the budget. You do this for fiscal and psychological reasons. Revising the budget to reflect the lost revenue will bring the numbers into reality. No one will have to do mental math to calculate what the numbers should be absent the missing client. Besides, it won't do anyone's morale any good to look at dismal numbers for the rest of the year.

Financial Aid

Some small businesses find a quarterly review of the budget progress is important to refocus everyone's attention on important details, especially if there's slippage in certain areas.

These unusual circumstances call for revision. Revisions are not called for just because it is difficult to meet the numbers. That defeats the whole point of budgeting. When you wimp out just because it is not easy, you give your employees permission to not try very hard. It's like my grandfather used to say, "If it were easy, everybody would do it."

Eye on the Prize

The endgame is that if you stick to your budget and meet your goals, your company makes money—it's that simple. Assuming your business idea is reasonable, the odds are that you will fail not because you didn't generate enough business, but because you spent too much money. Your strategic budget keeps you, your employees, and your company focused on those goals that make your company successful and ensure that you don't spend any more than you need to achieve those goals.

The Least You Need to Know

- Start your strategic budget with zero balances in all items, and then justify every penny that goes into the budget against your goals.

- Make each department or profit center accountable for its own budget and its contribution to the overall budget.

- New products or services must meet your goals and start on-time and on-budget.

- Your strategic budget protects your cash because it makes sure every dollar you spend advances one or more of your main goals.

- Revise your budget only under extreme circumstances and not because it is difficult to meet.

Chapter **16**

Financing for Growth:
Debt vs. Equity

In This Chapter

◆ Differences between debt and equity

◆ Benefits and drawbacks of debt

◆ Benefits and drawbacks of equity

◆ Combining debt and equity

You have two basic choices to raise money for your business: Mortgage your soul or sell it. That's a little harsh, but there's nothing easy about financing a small business. Whether you are just starting out or trying to take your business to the next level, there's a good chance you need additional cash to make it happen. This chapter looks at the trade-offs between debt and equity financing and how you can decide which is best for your business.

Two Flavors of Money

After you have put your own money into a business, where do you go for more cash to expand your business? Most small businesses, especially those just getting off the ground, do not generate enough cash to finance all the growth they may want. You must look outside the business for this additional cash, and it is available it two primary forms: debt and equity financing.

Debt Financing

Debt financing is simply a loan. It can come from a bank, a governmental agency, an individual or group, or another source. Its main characteristics are that it must be paid back and interest is charged on the principal amount borrowed.

Financial Aid

If you are nervous about being in debt, you may want to reconsider being a small business owner. It is almost impossible to grow a small business without going into debt.

A loan is the most common first round of financing for most small businesses. It is frequently used to buy equipment or other hard assets. Banks are not fond of lending money to companies that need to borrow money to pay their ongoing bills. Debt financing is discussed in more detail shortly.

Equity Financing

Equity financing comes from selling ownership or shares of stock in your business. The people who buy the shares become part owners of the business and you have financial and legal obligations to them. However, you don't have to repay the money they invest, so you don't have any note payments. There are some rules about how many investors you can have before you fall under certain codes regarding publicly held companies, but for the most part, you can continue to operate as before.

Although equity financing certainly has benefits (not having to pay back the money is huge), not every small business will find it easy to attract investors. Even though you retain control of the company, any investor can claim access to your complete books and question your decisions—more about equity financing later in this chapter.

Benefits and Drawbacks of Debt

The next five chapters discuss the details of debt financing, but this section details the questions you should consider before you plunge into debt. First, realize that debt in and of itself is not a bad thing. Used wisely, it can propel your business ahead much faster than if you rely on internal cash flow. However, there is a "dark side" to debt that you should know.

Using Leverage

Leverage is a financial term that means, in nontechnical terms, to use borrowed money to increase your return. In the case of small businesses, when you borrow money you are leveraging the capital already invested in the company so that it can expand at a faster rate. A company might be considered highly leveraged if its borrowings exceeded invested capital. An equal mix of debt and invested capital is considered about right for most companies; however, there are many exceptions.

For example, you start a small business with $200,000 of capital. The business operates on this money, in addition to any profits that are reinvested in the company. If you borrow $500,000, you now have $700,000 to invest in the operations and the opportunity to grow much faster. If you invest the money wisely, the

Money Talk

Leverage is the amount of debt your company uses to finance its assets and operations.

expanded business repays the loan and you now own a business worth much more than your original $200,000 investment. Additionally, if the opportunities present themselves, you can repeat the process, borrowing $1,000,000 this time, and keep growing. It should be noted that this is an extreme example of a highly-leveraged business and not a recommended business plan.

Preserves Stockholder Equity

One of the important benefits of using debt is that it preserves your equity in the company, which increases it over time as you build the business and pay off loans. This makes sense if you remember our discussion of the balance sheet back in Chapter 3. To refresh your memory, the balance sheet formula is:

Assets – Liabilities = Equity

When you secure a loan, it goes in the long-term liabilities section of the balance sheet. Presumably, you bought an asset with the money, such as equipment, real estate, or maybe a competitor. In any case, it shows up under assets on your balance sheet. If you invested the money wisely, the asset side of your balance sheet should grow faster than the liabilities side declines with the bank note's retirement. When you finally pay off the note, your assets (through a combination of appreciation, cash, and so on) are significantly higher than before the loan. With the note off the liabilities side of the balance sheet, your equity is much higher than before.

Financial Aid

When you are able to borrow money, build your business, and have the expanded business pay off the debt, you are said to be using other people's money to run your business. The "other people's money" is the loan you obtained.

The value of your company has increased significantly; however, you have not taken any money out of your pocket to make that happen.

Leverage Can Work Against You

The picture I've painted is how it is supposed to work, but we all know that life has a bad habit of happening on its own terms, which are not always in our best interest. Leverage can be a powerful ally or a terrible enemy:

"Give me a place to stand and with a lever I will move the whole world." —Archimedes, Greek mathematician.

Archimedes knew the power of leverage. Unfortunately, some small business owners discover it only when leverage turns against them. Let's reconstruct the previous example and see what happens when the situation turns sour. You have $200,000 invested in your company and borrow $500,000 for expansion. Unfortunately, now your $700,000 company (with $500,000+ in debt) isn't working like you hoped. Despite your best efforts, sales have shown only modest increases—not even enough to cover the note payment.

You think another $100,000 would turn things around, but your banker says no. You find you are working harder than ever just to pay your regular bills plus the bank note. The assets you bought with the loan are depreciating faster than you can pay down the loan. Nevertheless, you are still hopeful of turning the situation around. In the meantime, you dread going to the office every day because you are, for all practical purposes, working for the bank.

How do you get out of this mess? That's another book and the answer varies greatly from company to company. However, in many cases you just buckle down and work your way though it, hoping you can build your business to overcome the dead weight of this note payment. Talk to your banker about the terms of the note—there may be some temporary relief. Your loan officer will work with you if she feels you are making every effort to work with her.

> **CAUTION**
>
> **In the Red** _____
>
> When things go south with a bank loan, your friendly loan officer might be replaced by a not-so-friendly recovery officer for the bank whose job is to salvage what they can from the mess. If your business is in real trouble, the bank can call the note and try to recover any assets attached to the loan.

Poorly Structured Debt Stifles Growth

Some need more financing than others do—it's a natural part of their business. Companies involved in real estate, manufacturing, or shipping, for example, tend to be capital intensive, which means they need to borrow money on a regular basis as part of their business.

If your business needs to borrow money on a regular basis to finance raw materials, inventory, acquisitions, and so on, make sure you have expert help in structuring the debt. A combination of short-term and long-term debt is usually the right ticket for many capital-intensive businesses, but finding that balance is not a do-it-yourself exercise unless you have the training and education to pull it off. For example, if you put too much short-term debt on your balance sheet you can find your company is not eligible for long-term financing when you need it.

Mistakes in this area can be costly, not only in interest expense, but in loss of flexibility to meet your business goals. If you borrow significant sums of money, seek the guidance of your accountant or loan officer to help you structure the loans in a manner that makes the most sense for your business.

Benefits and Drawbacks of Equity

Raising equity for your business means you take on shareholders. Their money becomes part of the capital structure of the company and shows up as cash on the balance sheet. Unless there were stipulations with the investment, you are free to use the money as you see fit, although you have an obligation to shareholders to act in the best interests of the company. The final four chapters of this book look at various forms and sources of equity financing.

You Don't Have to Pay It Back

The best feature of equity is you don't have to pay it back. There is no note and no interest payment. No liability shows up on your balance sheet—in fact, your company's net worth goes up by the amount of the investment; however, your net worth is no longer the same as the company's because you now have other owners.

Financial Aid _____

If you want to sell some of your business to raise money, don't think a simple handshake and a check will do. If your business is incorporated, there are legal documents to process and corporate minutes to take. Consult an attorney to make sure you follow all the correct procedures.

In the world of business, not all dollars are created equally. Although you want to guard each dollar in your possession carefully and spend each wisely, an invested dollar carries more weight than a borrowed dollar. Potential lenders and other potential investors find invested dollars on your books more impressive than borrowed dollars. Invested dollars indicate a level of confidence in your business that is above that usually shown by lenders.

Did I mention you don't have to pay it back?

Using Equity Financing

You can use equity financing for anything you want; however, you should have some project or special expense in mind. One way that some small business owners look at equity funding differently than debt funding has to do with how they use the cash. Because they don't have to repay equity funds, owners can choose to use that money for investments that don't have an immediate or quick payoff, but are vital to the long-term health of the company. For example, you might use equity funds for the overhaul of a major piece of computer software or the purchase of a new facility.

Financial Aid _____

After you get your business out of the garage and into the mainstream, casual relationships and the loose exchange of personal and corporate assets is a real no-no. Get some guidance from your tax advisor on the way to handle the separation of personal and corporate assets.

Your best use of equity funding is to take your business to the next level (whatever that is), rather than paying your day-to-day bills. However, some young businesses need an injection of equity to keep going while products or services develop. Unfortunately, if the company doesn't start moving, you can fritter away your invested equity and have nothing to show for it.

Start-Up Equity Financing

If you are just getting your business off the ground, coming up with money to invest in the company can be difficult. There are several sources:

- Personal savings
- Home equity
- Friends and family
- Credit cards

You may wonder how some of these end up in equity financing; for example, friends and family and credit cards sound more like debt financing. What often happens with friends and family is they make a personal loan to you, which becomes your seed capital in the company. From the company's perspective, the money is invested capital, although it is a loan on your personal financial statement. You can use credit cards to purchase equipment and supplies for the new business. If the business doesn't reimburse you, those purchases could be considered invested capital also.

Adds to Net Worth of Company

Adding equity financing increases the net worth of your company because there is no corresponding increase in liabilities. This is why it is important if possible to use the equity funds for assets that ultimately add more value to the company. Every dollar you spend should directly or indirectly be targeted at adding value to the company, and equity funds even more so.

Reduces Your Stake in Company

Equity financing is not a present—it comes with a price. That price is a piece of your business. When you sell shares of your company (or take on limited partners), you dilute your ownership. For example, if you sell 40 percent of your company to investors to raise $200,000 and five years later sell the company for $5 million net, you write those investors a check for $2 million.

Most small businesses won't hit that big a pot of gold; however, the point is valid. When it comes time to sell, whether you get a good offer, you are ready to retire, or your estate is being settled, those investors get 40 percent of the net proceeds. It is possible those investors contributed nothing to the business except their initial investment.

Between now and then, the new owners share in the profits of the business to the extent of their ownership. If you distribute profits to yourself, a proportionate amount must go to the other owners.

Stockholders to Answer To

A psychological factor to consider is equally valid. Some small business owners chafe at the notion that they have obligations to anyone. Although the laws vary from state to state, investors generally have rights of access to company books and reports and the state can require an annual meeting of all stockholders to conduct corporate business.

> **Financial Aid** _____
>
> Before you take on investors, ask yourself if you are ready for even a little criticism of how you run the business, because when someone invests in your company, they buy that right.

On the other hand, some investors can bring years of business expertise along with their money, and business owners who aren't hung up on their ego can benefit from their experience. You can choose your investors with care. You may not want retired Uncle Billy hanging around the business all day annoying the employees with tales of how it was in the good old days, even if he is willing to invest in your company.

Make Mine a Combo

Most small businesses use a combination of debt and equity to finance their growth, although debt is the more common route. Equity (not counting the owner's contribution) can be hard to come by for many small businesses. If your business is in a position to take advantage of both, you are indeed "sitting pretty."

It Takes Money to Borrow Money

If you have invested capital on your books, it can make it easier to borrow even more money. You might, for example, be able to refinance short-term notes with a single longer-term loan on better terms. Using the leverage discussed earlier, you can take a small sum of invested equity and combine it with borrowed funds to create a much larger capital package. Having cash in the bank (equity and loans), opens many options for your business.

Don't Try This at Home

Structuring your capital can be a complicated process. If you are not experienced or educated in equity and loans, it's time to get some expert help. There is a whole discipline of expertise that works on structuring companies' finances to take advantage of all the resources at their disposal. Talk to your accountant about helping you structure your equity and loans.

The Least You Need to Know

- Debt and equity financing are not the same, although they can accomplish the same goals.

- Debt financing preserves your stake in the company; however, it can turn against you if business is soft.

- You don't have to repay equity financing, although you give up some ownership in your company.

- Most small businesses use a combination of debt and equity to finance their activities.

Part 4

Financing Your Business with Debt

Almost every growing business needs financing to fund new projects, new markets, acquisitions, or a variety of other needs. There are several sources to draw on for financing, from short-term loans to long-term financing, including friends and family, banks, SBA programs, and other formal lending structures. You can also use other financing techniques such as factoring, inventory financing, and so on.

Chapter 17

Preparing Your Loan Package

In This Chapter

- ◆ Objective of your loan package
- ◆ Major pieces of your loan package
- ◆ Getting the best use of your loan
- ◆ A repayment plan for your loan

Before you go asking for a serious loan, you need to prepare a loan package. This document, which may later need some modifications, shows the lenders why it is a good idea to loan money to your company. Lenders expect this document to contain certain information—don't disappoint them. This chapter outlines what that package needs to contain.

Loan Package Objective

Your objective when you prepare a loan package is simple: you want to secure a loan. However, it goes beyond that. Although you won't present your loan package in your first meeting with the potential lender, you still

Financial Aid

Don't try to be something you're not. "I don't know, but I'll find out," is an acceptable answer to a financial question. Bankers don't know all the answers, either.

want to make the right impression and show him how seriously you take your business.

Lenders understand that not everyone is a wiz with finance. However, if you have taken the time and trouble to prepare a professional-looking loan package and can answer basic questions about the finances, it adds a great deal to your credibility.

The Big Questions

Your loan package must answer three major questions to the satisfaction of the bank before it considers your loan package. These questions actually have many components, although here is the summary form:

- Do you have the technical and managerial experience and competence to run this business?

- Does the business have a reasonable plan to access an existing and viable market?

- Does the business have the cash flow necessary to service the debt and sufficient collateral to secure the debt?

In a direct manner, your loan package addresses these questions and provides additional material that helps the lender understand your business and how you plan to use the loan.

Major Components

The major components of the loan package are designed to give the lender the most complete picture of you and your business. Securing a loan is not a one-conversation process, so expect to spend some time with your lender, especially if you haven't established a relationship before now. The loan package should document everything financial about you and your company, because the lender will ask if it's not included.

Who You Are

This portion of the loan package should include a complete resumé including your work history, military service (if applicable), and education. Be sure to include any special training, education, and so on. Also include any civic, church, or volunteer work you do, as well as any family information, hobbies, and outside interests. All this information helps the banker get to know you as a person. It is important to develop a trusting relationship with your banker.

Financial Aid

Bankers want to know the people they are considering for a loan. Although it may not feel that way, you are their customer.

Company History

Even if your company is young, include a company history. How did it get started? Who were your first clients? Was this the fulfillment of a dream? People like to hear about successes, and even if you aren't making a million dollars a year, you do something that many people wish they could do—you own a business. This doesn't have to go on for pages, but it is another opportunity to connect with your banker on a personal level.

The Beginning

Include a section on why and how you started the business. Don't go into detail here on the market you serve; there will be a separate section for that later. However, do cover what made you decide that this was a good business opportunity. Include a short summary of any research you did, whether it was formal or informal. Did you start part-time in your garage or basement and grow from there? What was your first facility or shop like? Be brief, but give your banker a sense of your roots.

How You Got Here

How did you grow the business? What challenges did you face along the way? This part can briefly describe the transition from start-up to full-time business and how you adapted to changing customers/ markets. Did you expand your advertising or marketing? Was this a period of rapid growth or did you build slowly? Your story gives the lender a sense of continuity with your past and helps her see how your company came to where it is today.

Financial Aid

Almost everyone likes a success story, and most small businesses that survive represent successes. Banks are more likely to lend money to companies that are on their way up.

Company Financials

It is important to connect with your banker; however, it is also important to make sure your financials are accurate. This is where you want to have it done right, even if it means you pay your accountant extra to prepare all of the financial documents in your loan package. As noted earlier, bankers don't expect everyone that comes in for a loan to be a financial genius, although they do respect those customers who make the effort to understand finances, even when they don't come from a financial background.

History

Your loan package should include at least three years of financial history (income statements, balance sheets, statements of cash flow) for the lender to review. You can explain problem areas with footnotes if needed, but don't try to cover up an obvious bad year. If you haven't been in business that long, include your complete history.

The numbers need to be accurate and formatted in a neat and readable manner. If you have software that formats the reports for you, use it. If not, have your account-ant either prepare the numbers or review them for you for accuracy and formatting. Here is a suggested format; however, your accountant may have a preferred format that works as well or better.

Small Business Income Statement (in Dollars)

	2003	2004	2005
Revenue			
Sales	$1,500,000	$2,500,000	$3,800,000
Cost of Goods Sold			
Purchases	$784,665	$1,307,700	$1,988,000
Shipping	$157,880	$263,120	$400,000
Equipment	$90,780	$151,295	$230,000
Total:	**$1,033,326**	**$1,722,115**	**$2,608,000**
Gross Profit	**$466,674**	**$777,885**	**$1,192,000**
Expenses			
Accounting & Legal	$1,500	$1,500	$2,000
Advertising	$224,275	$326,250	$431,350

Bank Charges	$150	$150	$150
Insurance	$10,000	$11,000	$12,500
Administrative Expenses	$185,000	$200,000	$230,000
Payroll Taxes	$11,000	$13,000	$15,000
Rent	$23,000	$24,000	$25,000
Salaries	$50,000	$50,000	$50,000
Supplies	$25,000	$25,000	$25,000
Telephone	$28,000	$26,000	$25,000
Utilities	$18,000	$19,000	$20,000
Total Expenses	**$390,925**	**$515,900**	**$836,000**
EBITDA	**$75,749**	**$261,985**	**$356,000**
Other Expenses			
Depreciation	$5,800	$5,800	$5,800
Interest Expenses	$12,500	$12,500	$12,500
Net Income Before Taxes	**$57,449**	**$243,685**	**$337,700**
Income Taxes	$10,000	$10,000	$10,000
Net Income	**$47,449**	**$242,685**	**$327,700**

You should use the same format for the balance sheet and statement of cash flows.

A short narrative pointing out significant highlights (major contracts, new products, and such) can accompany the historical financials.

Financial Aid

Some accountants like to use percent change columns in these types of reports. That's a matter of preference. If your accountant wants that format, go for it.

Financial Projections

Your package should also include financial projections for the current year and three years into the future. These projections should reflect how the loan flows through your company either in the purchase of assets, expanded facilities, or whatever your plans for the cash include.

The projections must show a reasonable scenario (no triple-digit growth) that makes sense and is supported by other parts of your package (market description, and so on).

Be sure to include in notes or narrative the underlying assumptions for the projections (market share increases, sales growth, and so on).

You should use the same format for projections that you used for the historical financial data. This makes it easier for your lender to follow what you're projecting and compare any items to historical data.

How You Use Your Loan

You need to state clearly and in some detail exactly how much you want to borrow and how you will use the loan. If you are buying equipment, state what you are going to buy, the model, the price, and how it will benefit your company. If it is new product development, describe what you want to accomplish. You may have several pieces that need funding—if so, break them out separately. Bankers want to see a well-thought-out and documented plan for the use of the loan.

This is an important piece of the package, so make sure you have done your homework and documented your needs. Be comfortable talking to your banker about how you will use the money. Make sure you borrow enough to cover your needs. You are not begging the bank to do you a favor—they are in business to make loans; that's how they make money. If anything, you are doing them a favor by giving them your business, so don't be shy about asking for everything that you need.

How You Repay Your Loan

Banks make money by making loans, however they don't make money unless the loans are repaid. Your lender will be keenly interested in your plan to repay the loan. This is where the future financial projections come into play. You might want to show your lender how you intend to draw down the note over a certain period and begin principal and interest payments.

For example, if you needed a total of $200,000, but used only $100,000 immediately and took the remaining $100,000 six months later, that would be reflected in your financial projections, as would your note payments. Show the banker how the loan will help grow the business and contribute to cash flow, making it easier to pay principal and interest on the note.

Financial Aid _____

Here's another preference issue. Some people feel the loan package should include a "worst-case scenario." In other words, what if all those rosy projections turn to ashes and the business doesn't come close to hitting its projections? How are you going to repay the loan? I think this is best handled verbally if it comes up as a question—and you'd better have a good, well-rehearsed answer.

How You Secure Your Loan

Your loan from the bank can be secured in two ways. Banks are not in the risk business—they avoid it whenever possible. When banks make loans, they want much more collateral than necessary to secure the loan. There are two primary methods of securing small business loans, and both are often used at the same time.

Company Assets

The bank wants a lien on every asset your company owns. They want security for their loan and tons of security to back it up. If you purchase an asset with the borrowed money, that goes on the bank's lien list automatically, meaning you can't sell or dispose of it without clearing it through the bank.

Personal Assets

If you have some idea that the company is solely liable for the loan, your banker will quickly dissuade you of that notion. The bank (or virtually any lender) wants your personal guarantee on the loan. This means your personal assets are also pledged as collateral for the note. If your company has tangible assets (real estate, marketable equipment, for example) that exceed the loan amount by a significant percentage, you may be able to negotiate some arrangement that excludes some of your personal assets.

For most small business owners, count on personally guaranteeing the loan. You will need to provide a personal financial statement—most banks have a form for this, which you can include in your loan package.

CAUTION   In the Red _____

You can't hide behind the corporate shield when it comes to loans. If really bad things happen, the bank looks to you personally to repay the loan and takes whatever they legally can of your personal assets.

Other Material to Include

Your loan package should include a number of important documents and summaries. This information is background and is provided as documentation for the lender. Here are the major documents and lists you need to provide:

◆ Details of all leases the company has for equipment or real estate

◆ A list of all assets such as real estate, equipment, and so on, including a fair market value of each

◆ Details of all insurance the company has in force

◆ Company tax returns for the past three years

◆ Personal tax returns for the past three years

◆ Your detailed resumé, which emphasizes education and work experience related to the business

◆ Personal and professional references

◆ Any additional information unique to your business or industry that is not covered elsewhere, which helps the lender understand your business

This information goes in the back of the package and is noted in the table of contents.

Professional Look

Take the time to make your loan package attractive and easy to read. This goes back to a previous point—demonstrate to your banker that you are serious about your business and this loan. When people come in with loan proposals scratched out on legal pads, bankers have to wonder how serious they are about their business. Appearance counts, so take the time and, if necessary, the money to make your loan package stand out.

Looking Good

Your final loan package will probably be 30 or 40 pages (or more), when you include all the attachments. If you are talented in formatting documents, you can do this yourself. However, if that is not your strong point, hire someone to do this for you. Your accountant may offer this service or you can use a designer/word processor to format everything in a professional manner.

The top-drawer packages are printed on color laser printers so you can use charts and graphs to illustrate your financial reports or other segments of the package. Do not use clip art or cute graphics. The only artwork should be professional-looking charts and graphs. If you want to include a limited number of pictures, have professional digital pictures taken that can be printed in the loan package at the appropriate places or included in the supplemental material at the end of the package.

Use Your Accountant

Your accountant should be involved in the process from the beginning. If he has experience with local lenders, he might suggest additions or deletions to the items mentioned that are accepted practice. Follow his lead. Your accountant should either prepare or review all of the financial data in the loan package, and especially the projections. Make certain you both are comfortable with the projections and underlying assumptions.

> **Financial Aid**
>
> It adds credibility if your accountant signs off on the financials in the loan package. He might be reluctant to certify the projections, but he might say he has reviewed them. Check with your CPA about what levels of attestation they would offer on your financial statements.

When it comes time to present your loan package, if you feel you are not comfortable with the numbers, ask your banker if your accountant can attend the meeting to answer financial questions. However, if at all possible, get your accountant to coach you until you can do the presentation by yourself.

Organization

There is no one way to put together a loan package. How you organize the material should make sense to you and flow logically for the lender. The package should follow in the order of how you plan to make the presentation. Here is a suggestion for an order that might be a good starting point. Feel free to modify it to fit your package and needs.

◆ **Executive summary.** This is a one- to two-page summary of what your business does, how much you want to borrow, what you will do with the funds, and how you will repay the loan. This is the "big picture," with few details, but presented in an exciting manner that conveys the opportunity the loan creates.

- **Company history.** A short history of the company from creation to present that highlights your success and discusses any challenges you overcame.

- **Your market.** A description of the market(s) your company serves and why you are uniquely positioned to succeed.

- **Your plan.** What you want the money for and how it will move your company to the next level or open new markets and so on.

- **Your finances past.** A brief review of where you have been financially. Include how you got started and the amount of invested capital you have in the company.

- **Financial projections.** How the loan will move your company forward with new products, markets, and so on, and how this will translate to your financial reports.

- **Repaying the loan.** How the company will repay the loan under the new structure. You need to show where the cash will come from.

- **Personal commitment.** Your personal commitment to make this work because you believe in your company and see this as a great opportunity.

- **Questions.** Ask for questions about your business or the projections presented in the package. Make the session a conversation about how you and the bank can work together.

Presentation

When you present your loan package, don't read it to the lender (they could read it for themselves and will after you leave). Instead, study the document enough that you can simply talk about it in a very organized manner. Don't open your copy—if you need notes to jog your memory, write them on index cards you can place on the desk and refer to when needed. Everything outlined in the previous list should be covered in 15 minutes or less, unless the banker interrupts you for questions, which is not a bad thing.

After you have talked through it and asked for questions, you can return to specific parts and go over those in more detail. That's the time to open your copy of the document and point out details where appropriate. If you don't get questions immediately, you can take the initiative and go back over certain points you think are important in more detail. Have several copies of the package, in case the banker wants an extra to share with others at the bank.

The Least You Need to Know

- Your loan package should address three questions: do you have the expertise to run the business; is there a market for your business; and how are you going to repay the loan?

- Bankers expect certain components in every loan package, including company and personal financial information.

- Your loan package must specifically address how your business will use the loan.

- The presentation and look of your loan package is important and tells the banker you are serious about your business and the loan.

Chapter

18

Traditional Debt Financing

In This Chapter

- ◆ Finding a banker
- ◆ Getting to know your banker
- ◆ Working with a banker
- ◆ When there are problems

For established businesses, there are several approaches to debt financing—some short term and others long term—however, the traditional source of financing for small businesses remains commercial banks. This chapter covers the traditional debt financing option that is generally available to small businesses, as well as how the relationship should work.

Sources of Traditional Debt Financing

The commercial bank continues its role as the lender of choice for established small businesses. Larger businesses have other choices, such as bond issues and commercial paper, that are not practical for small businesses. There are programs that work with banks such as the Small Business Administration (SBA), which I discuss in Chapter 20, and other nonbank lenders that are covered in the next three chapters. However, the bulk of small business loans come from commercial banks.

Not for Start-Ups

One area that banks do not like to serve is the start-up market. Most commercial banks do not lend money for you to start your business. This is not absolute. Banks do make loans to young companies, although they are often personal loans to the owner disguised as business loans, and these loans are heavily collateralized.

Financial Aid

Look to family and friends for start-up financing after you have tapped your personal assets. Banks don't lend 100 percent funds for start-up businesses.

If you have no business or personal assets, don't count on a bank loan to get your company off the ground. Look for start-up money elsewhere and when you are up and running, then go to the bank. Banks are not in the risk business, and businesses are at the most risk in the start-up phase. There are some industries banks avoid, such as adult entertainment; itinerant businesses such as carnivals; gambling, and other types of businesses that are borderline legal or would embarrass the bank.

Banks

Despite what you might have heard, banks want to lend your business money, because that is how banks make money. Well, maybe not your business—they have to check you out first—but they want to lend money to some business. Lending is not an act of charity on their part—it's their business. They may want you to think they are doing you a favor, but the truth is you are their customer and they need you as much as you need them.

How Bankers Think

The commercial banking business is very competitive, especially in larger urban areas. If you have a reasonably successful small business, it's quite possible you have banks calling on you for your business in some markets. If you belong to any civic groups such as a chamber of commerce, or a service organization such as the Rotary Club, you find bankers in attendance. If your community has small business groups, bankers are there.

Although bankers are hungry for loan business, they are also wary because the failure rate for small businesses is high. So although they are eager to get to know small business owners, they are not eager to lend to every small business. The longer your company has been in business with a solid record of growth and profits, the more likely you attract their attention.

Five Cs of Credit

Lenders often refer to the Five Cs of Credit when they make decisions on loans. These characteristics, in the form of questions, summarize the elements that a banker or any lender reviews before making a loan.

- **Character.** Does the person intend to pay off the loan as reflected by standing in the community and past behavior; are they serious about the business and the loan?

- **Capacity.** Does the borrower have the capacity to pay off the loan? Do they have the financial ability to pay?

- **Capital.** What is the general financial condition of the borrower as reflected in the financial statements, both business and personal?

- **Collateral.** What security or assets does the borrower offer for the loan?

- **Conditions.** What are the general economic conditions of the industry and geographic area? Do they lend themselves to growth or will they hinder the business?

Financial Aid

If you don't have one of the "five Cs" or there is a problem, think about how you can rectify the situation before you begin your talks with a bank.

Finding a Good Banker

How do you find a good banker? A "good" banker is one that approves your loan. However, you can't look at a room full and pick out the ones that will approve your loan (in fact, they all may look alike). The definition of a good banker is subjective; however, the following sections provide some direction on how to find a good banker.

Characteristics of a Good Banker

The first and most important trait of a good banker is his willingness to learn about your business. He should visit your facility and see what you do and how you do it. He should listen to your plans and see where you want the business to go. He should ask questions, and do much more listening than talking.

If you have had an account at a bank for several years and no bank officer has ever approached you about finding out more about your business, begin looking for another bank. This exploration of your business should begin even before you raise the question of a loan.

Know Your Banker Before You Need a Loan

The relationship with a good banker is just that, a relationship, which means you have an obligation also. Don't wait until you need a loan to get to know your loan officer. If he knows something about your business before the subject of a loan even comes up, you are ahead of the game. If you have invited the banker to your business, respect his time and let him know you would like an hour to walk him through your operation. Make sure you stick to that schedule. Prepare a packet of any promotional literature about your products or services, so that the officer can refer to these later.

Financial Aid

Most bankers are easy people to get to know. They are hired, in part, because of their people skills, and you shouldn't have any trouble building a relationship with a bank officer. However, if it's just not working between the two of you, try someone else that is easier to work with.

Even if you don't plan on asking for a loan anytime soon, make sure to send the banker copies of any new marketing materials or press releases you issue with a personal note from you. Should you land a big contract or win a large new client, let the banker know that, too. Before you ever ask for a loan, the banker has a sense of you and your company.

Where Are They Hiding?

If you don't have a good relationship with an officer at the bank where you currently have your commercial account, or you don't feel like this is where you'll get the best offer, begin your search for a new banker. The best place to start is with friends and colleagues that have had successful loan experiences. A referral is a good way to get started. Your accountant and attorney probably know several local bankers they might feel comfortable recommending.

Don't be hesitant to call these bankers and tell them you are looking for a bank to handle your company's financial services, including loans, and ask for a brief meeting to see if there is any interest. You are interviewing them for your business, so make it clear you want to know what services they could provide your company. Look for the chemistry between you and the loan officer that seems like it will make a good working relationship.

Don't Put All Your Bankers in One Basket

Do not submit loan proposals (see Chapter 17) to more than one banker at a time. Banks usually respond in a timely manner to your loan requests (if they don't, look for another bank). Although some might argue that you could play one bank against the other and get a better deal, the bad feelings aren't worth any savings you might squeeze out of the deal.

However, that doesn't mean you shouldn't have some backup plans. You might have a working relationship with one bank and banker; however, make sure you know other bankers. If your deal goes sour, you want to know you can call on another banker to begin working on another loan request.

> **In the Red**
>
> If you jump from bank to bank every time you think you can get a little break, you will soon get a reputation, and bank officers will be reluctant to work with you because they know you will take your business down the street at the first sign of something better.

Working With Your Banker

Every bank has their protocol and procedures for the loan approval process; however, they all follow roughly the same path. You need to understand how this works and the time frame, so you'll know what will happen when.

The First Step

The first step is usually a conversation with the loan officer when you express your interest in a loan for your business. This shouldn't be the first time you've spoken to this person, so the conversation can be rather informal. Explain that you are in the process of putting together a loan package and ask if there are any special forms the bank wants included.

You should also ask the loan officer to explain the loan approval process, including the steps involved and the approximate time each will take so you can estimate when you might have a funding decision. This is not to pin her down to a specific date, but to give you an idea of how long the process generally takes.

Next Step

The next step is for you to prepare the loan package as described in Chapter 17. Be sure to incorporate the special forms the loan officer gave you, even if they duplicate information you have covered in other parts of the loan package.

The Final Step

Make your presentation and let the bank process work. Don't ask the loan officer to shortcut the system on your behalf, and don't call every day for an answer. You know the time frame, so let the system work. If you appear desperate, it does not help your cause.

While you are biting your fingernails, the loan officer is reviewing your proposal. She might call if there are questions or missing information, but if you have done a good job with your proposal, the odds are that won't happen. The loan officer probably prepares a summary of your proposal for the loan committee (depending on the size of the loan) and a recommendation to fund. If she doesn't think the loan is a good deal for the bank, the loan committee probably never sees your proposal. Some banks give senior officers the authority to approve loans under a certain amount without loan committee approval. Your loan officer can tell you if your loan falls into this category.

> **Financial Aid**
>
> Waiting to hear if the bank will fund your loan can be a frustrating and nerve-wracking time, but you must let the bank do its job. If you haven't heard within the time frame specified by your loan officer, it is okay to call and ask the status of your application.

What If the Bank Says No?

If the bank turns you down, it is not unreasonable to ask why. That information can be helpful to restructure a new proposal or work on correcting problems with credit or other areas in your personal or business history. Sometimes banks say no because your loan doesn't fit their profile of the type of loan they want on their books (too small, term too long, and so on).

If there is something problematic with your loan proposal, such as a financial projection that doesn't make sense or market assumptions that seem outrageous, take that information and rethink your proposal. That feedback can save you from making a terrible mistake, and being turned down for the loan could be a blessing.

The Bank Says Yes

Oh, happy day! Your loan was funded, now the work begins. However, your relationship with the bank officer is even more important than ever. In a way, the bank is now your partner and you need to make every effort to communicate with that partner on a regular basis.

Progress Reports

Let the bank officer know what's going on with the business, both good and bad. If your loan was to purchase equipment, for example, invite the officer out to see it when the equipment is installed and operating. Let her see how you have used the loan proceeds as you said you would and explain the benefits to your business.

Your loan agreement probably requires periodic financial reports. Make certain those are on time and done correctly. If you have financial questions that the loan officer can help with, most are glad to help. Loan officers are also excellent resources for referrals if you need a particular service or supplier.

Financial Aid

It is almost impossible to give a bank too much information. Be cautious about sharing proprietary data with your loan officer in casual communications, and be careful not to bury him or her with spam, but the more information you share the better.

When Things Get Rough

As long as your business is doing well and those note payments keep being met, it is easy to let your relationship with the loan officer slide. However, if you hit some rough water, you'll regret you haven't talked to him or her in six months. Maybe business will continue smoothly for the term of the loan, but maybe it won't. If bad things happen, you'll want a sympathic ear at the bank, not one that hasn't heard from you in a very long time.

On the other hand, if you have followed my advice and communicated regularly with your loan officer through the good times, a call saying you are having some problems is easier to hear. If you have a setback, such as losing an important client or some other major loss, let your loan officer know right away. If you find the business squeezed for cash and it is difficult to make the note payment, don't wait until it is past due; call the bank officer beforehand. Explain the situation in detail—is this a temporary cash flow problem or a major revenue shortfall?

If it looks like you can't make the whole payment, ask if you can go on an "interest only" basis until you get things sorted out. Work out a plan to get the business back on track, take it down to the bank, and talk it over with the loan officer. Keep the lines of communication open. The last thing a bank wants is a failed loan, even if they can recover much of their money through seized assets. If you show that you are working as hard as you can to right the business and pay back the loan, banks can be extremely flexible. However, bank officers are also realists. If there is nothing left of your company and no way to generate cash, no matter how hard you work, it is unlikely the business comes back. At that point, the bank will cut its losses and move on to the next deal, and so should you.

> **CAUTION**
>
> **In the Red** _____
>
> Honesty is always the best policy, especially when things aren't going well. Any attempt to cover up or hide bad news makes it only seem worse and makes the banker suspicious.

What Bankers Want

Bankers want to see your business succeed. They want customers that grow and prosper and borrow (and repay) more loans. They want customers that use other financial services and pay the associated fees. Banks are willing to work with you to help your business succeed; however, they are not willing to take much of a risk to do it.

What Bankers Want to See

Bankers want to see hard working, honest small business owners who are committed to their companies and willing to back that commitment with their own capital. They want to see well-thought-out loan proposals and business plans that make sense and use real-world assumptions to achieve reasonable results.

They don't care that you are not a financial genius, although they do want to see that you are serious about your business and understand the basic financial reports. If your business involves complicated financial planning, they would like to be a part of that process along with your accountant.

What Bankers Want to Know

Bankers want to know that the financial information they see about you and your company is accurate and timely. If you are not comfortable with producing these numbers, hire an accountant to prepare them for you, but make sure you understand what they mean. Be able to answer basic questions about your company's finances and have the honesty to say, "I don't know, but I'll find out" when appropriate.

The Least You Need to Know

- Finding a good banker is a process of looking for a relationship that works both ways.

- Get to know your banker and introduce your business to him before you need a loan.

- Bankers have a process for handling loans—respect that process by following it and honoring its timeline.

- When there are problems with your business, communicate them immediately and honestly to your banker.

SBA Loan Programs

In This Chapter

The Small Business Administration (SBA) may be one of the few federal agencies that can really help your small business. The agency offers a variety of services for small businesses, including loan programs, that make funding possible where banks have said no. This chapter gives you an overview of the SBA's loan programs.

What Is the SBA?

The SBA was formed in 1953. It grew out of many predecessor agencies in the federal government that worked since the Great Depression to help businesses. The agency offers a wide variety of programs and services for small businesses beyond loans, including counseling, education, advocacy, and disaster assistance. The SBA website (www.sba.gov) lists ways to access the agency's services in your area.

What Is Small?

The SBA has specific definitions of small businesses that vary from industry to industry. These standards determine which companies are eligible for SBA services and programs. According to the SBA website, here are the most common size standards:

- Less than 500 employees for most manufacturing and mining industries
- Less than 100 employees for all wholesale trade industries
- Less than $6 million in sales for most retail and service industries
- Less than $28.5 million in sales for most general & heavy construction industries
- Less than $12 million in sales for all special trade contractors
- Less than $0.75 million in sales for most agricultural industries

About one-fourth of industries have a size standard that is different from these levels. They vary from $0.75 million to $28.5 million for size standards based on average annual revenues and from 100 to 1,500 employees for size standards based on number of employees. Some SBA programs have different standards. If you have a question about whether your business qualifies under the SBA definition, contact the nearest office and obtain a ruling. Later in the chapter, you see why this is important.

The vast majority of all companies fall into the category of "small," according to the SBA.

Financial Aid

Big companies, such as IBM and General Motors make the news, although most businesses in the U.S. fit within the SBA's definition of small.

SBA Programs

The SBA offers many programs that help small businesses in addition to the loan programs. The agency offers educational workshops and online assistance for small businesses on a variety of topics.

Nonloan Programs

The SBA offers a number of online and live educational workshops and classes on topics including starting your business, managing your business, marketing, planning, tax issues, government contracting, and so on. These courses range from purely educational to guidelines on using SBA programs designed for small businesses. For example, certain percentages of federal contracts are set aside for small businesses. Minority and women-owned businesses have special programs that assist them to grow. The SBA website is a rich resource if you want to find out how the agency can help.

> ### Notes and News
>
> The SBA has offices in many cities across the country. The SBA website has an interactive map. Click on your state, and it lists all the offices. You can then pull up a state-specific SBA site (www. sba.gov).

Loan Programs

The SBA has a variety of loan programs that cover different circumstances. This chapter covers the main programs as well as some of the more common special programs. Many people have an image of the SBA as a stereotypical government agency that takes forever to make decisions and buries you in meaningless paperwork. That may have been true in the past (and you still may find remnants of that thinking), however, the agency has undergone some radical changes over the last 15 plus years, and it is much more responsive to the needs of small businesses.

SBA Loan Programs

In most cases, the SBA doesn't make loans directly to businesses. Instead, it guarantees part of the loan, which takes much of the risk off the bank. Because banks don't like risk, this helps them make loans to small businesses that may be considered too risky without the guarantee.

SBA Loan Guarantees

Let's look at how the loan guarantee program works and how you can use it for your business, if appropriate. The idea behind the guarantee program is to let banks or other lenders make loans to businesses that were not quite qualified. The SBA loan programs are not for marginal businesses that are on the verge of failing or for poor credit risks.

How It Works

The SBA loan guarantee programs work through private lenders, so the agency becomes the third partner in the transaction. Not every lender works with the SBA, so if you want to consider the guarantee program, make sure the lender is certified to deal with the agency (more about this later in the chapter). Even though the SBA guarantees the loan, all of your contact is through the lender. You may never see or speak to an SBA employee.

Types of Loans

Although the SBA offers numerous types of loan programs, there are three main programs that small businesses deal with most frequently. The other programs cover special situations, such as disaster recovery or pollution control, and may target special segments of the small business community, such as minority or women-owned businesses. The three main loan programs that the SBA offers include:

- Basic 7(a) Loan Guaranty
- Certified Development Company (CDC), a 504 Loan Program
- MicroLoan, a 7(m) Loan Program

Of these three programs, the 7(a) Loan Guaranty program is the one most businesses find attractive because of its flexibility and ease of application.

Basic 7(a) Loan Guaranty

The 7(a) loan guaranty is the most frequently used of all SBA programs. It is strictly a loan guarantee and is offered only through commercial lenders—mainly banks, although some other lenders. If you're interested in obtaining an SBA loan guarantee, you need to understand how the process works and what role the bank plays.

Most Popular Loan Program

The 7(a) program is the SBA's most popular loan guarantee program because it offers very flexible terms ranging up to 25 years for fixed assets, such as real estate or machinery, and up to 10 years for working capital. You can use the funds for almost any valid business reason. The eligibility criteria are broad to accommodate a variety of small businesses into the program, according to the SBA website; however, your business still must meet certain criteria.

SBA Lenders

Most 7(a) lenders are commercial banks, and that's probably where you have your contact. Banks that participate in the program must structure their loans to accommodate SBA requirements. You apply to the bank for a loan and if the bank turns you down, even with the possibility of a 7(a) loan guaranty, there is no recourse to the SBA. The bank's decision is final. You can't appeal the decision to the SBA. At this point you should rethink your loan package and begin talks with another bank.

When you apply for a loan, the bank decides whether to fund the loan itself or whether to seek a 7(a) guarantee because of some weakness on your application. The bank will tell you if they are going to seek an SBA guarantee and you can refuse if you want, although there is no gain in that since the bank will not fund your loan without the SBA guarantee.

Financial Aid

Your first contact is only with the lender. The SBA is in the background and works with the lender. If the lender turns you down, there is no appeal to the SBA.

What Is Guaranteed

The 7(a) program does not guarantee the entire amount of the loan. The SBA guarantees a percentage of the loan and, in the event of default, it pays the bank up to that percentage after you have repaid all you can with business and personal assets pledged to the note. You always remain 100 percent obligated for the total amount of the note, regardless of the 7(a) guarantee. The owner of the business must personally guarantee SBA 7(a) loans. In the case of partners or shareholders, anyone owning 20 percent or more of the company must personally guarantee the loan.

Criteria for a 7(a) Loan Guarantee

The SBA has requirements you must meet in addition to the conditions the bank requires. They follow much the same range of "Five Cs" that were discussed in Chapter 18. The SBA places a primary emphasis on cash flow to repay the note. There are other criteria that the SBA follows for the 7(a) program, and you should familiarize yourself with what they are and how you rate.

Company Size

The SBA is strict about its role as a resource for small businesses. The beginning of this chapter listed some broad guidelines with what the SBA considers "small." There are numerous exceptions to those guidelines. A more definitive guideline can be found on the SBA website, which lists size limits by North American Industry Classification System Codes (NAICS). NAICS is a way to identify businesses by a six-digit code. For example, a Quick Printing company is 323114, although a Books Printing company is 323117. The SBA defines each industry classification as small either by an annual sales number or by number of employees. The SBA considers both Quick Printing and Book Printing companies small if they have 500 or fewer employees. On the other hand, an Electrical Contractor (238210) falls into the small category if it has less than $12 million in annual sales. If you fall near the guideline, check with the SBA for a ruling.

> **Money Talk**
>
> **North American Industry Classification System Codes** (NAICS) are six-digit numbers that uniquely identify different types of businesses. These numbers help distinguish businesses from one another.

Qualifying Companies

Almost all types of companies are eligible for 7(a) loan guarantees. As a rule, the business must be in the United States, and the owner must contribute a reasonable amount of equity and alternative sources of financing including owner equity, which must be used first, according to the SBA website. The site provides a complete list of businesses that are eligible with conditions and businesses that are not eligible at all. Most of the eligible businesses with conditions have other funding sources within the federal government that should be explored first. Ineligible businesses include those of a speculative nature or those involved in illegal activities.

> **Notes and News**
>
> The SBA website has detailed information on which companies are eligible and which are not. You can find this information at: www.sba.gov/financing/subfiles/type_of_business.html

Use of Proceeds

Money from a 7(a) guaranteed loan can be used for a wide variety of legitimate business purposes. You can use the money for working capital or to purchase real estate, equipment, or an existing business. One of the most important aspects of acceptable usage is that proceeds can be used to start a business. If you remember in Chapter 18, I said that banks don't lend money to start-ups, however if you use the 7(a) guarantee, banks are more willing to fund business start-ups. You still must meet the other qualifications, including a substantial injection of personal equity into the business. The loan guarantee can make a start-up loan happen when it wouldn't happen before.

There are some limits on the use of proceeds. You cannot use the loan for purposes that don't benefit the business. These could include repaying the owner for certain expenses or capital injections. You also can't use the funds to pay off delinquent state or federal taxes.

You can find a more comprehensive list of what does and does not qualify at www.sba.gov/financing/subfiles/use_of_proceeds.html.

Availability of Funds

The availability of funds qualification essentially says if you or your business has the funds or assets to provide all or a substantial part of the financing needed, the SBA does not consider your application. Unlike commercial lenders who jump at the chance to loan money to people and businesses that don't need it, the SBA confines its resources to businesses that have run out of reasonable alternatives.

Financial Aid

The SBA looks at the personal financial status of every owner to see if they have the resources to fund the project before it accepts an application. People who have the means to fund projects are not accepted into the 7(a) program.

Maximum Loan Amounts, Guarantees, Interest Rates

The 7(a) program has a maximum loan amount of $2 million with a maximum guarantee of 75 percent. Other loans have caps on their guarantees of 50 percent. For loans of $150,000 or less, the cap rate is 85 percent, although other programs might have lower rates. Some specific circumstances can call for different loan amounts and interest rates.

Interest rates may be fixed or variable and change according to the amount borrowed and length of the term. The fixed rates are linked to the prime interest rate, which is the rate the bank's best customers pay. Although these rates are subject to change, they fall into these categories according to the SBA:

- Fixed rate loans of $50,000 or more are capped at prime plus 2.25 percent if the maturity is less than 7 years, and prime plus 2.75 percent if the maturity is 7 years or more.

- Loans between $25,000 and $50,000 have maximum rates not to exceed prime plus 3.25 percent if the maturity is less than 7 years, and prime plus 3.75 percent if the maturity is 7 years or more.

- Loans of $25,000 or less, the maximum interest rate must not exceed prime plus 4.25 percent if the maturity is less than 7 years, and prime plus 4.75 percent if the maturity is 7 years or more.

- Variable interest rates are tied to either the lowest prime rate or SBA optional peg rate. Your banker can explain how these rates are chosen and see if your loan has a variable rate.

Fees and Pre-Payment Penalties

The SBA charges you a fee if you use the 7(a) program, which is based on the size and maturity of your loan. The fee can range from 2 percent to 3.75 percent of the amount of the guaranty of the loan. For example, if you had a $500,000 loan with a 75 percent guaranty, the fee would be $11,250, based on a 3 percent fee (500,000 × 75 percent = 375,000 × 3 percent = 11,250). Regardless of the upfront fee, there is a 0.5 percent servicing fee on the balance of the guaranty for the life of the loan. These fees can be charged only for SBA loans.

Financial Aid

The fees for SBA program guarantees typically roll into the note rather than show up as a bill in the mail.

Unlike most commercial loans, some 7(a) loans have a penalty for prepaying the loan. This penalty mainly applies to loans with maturities longer than 15 years. Check with the SBA or your bank for more details on which loans carry a prepayment penalty.

CDC/504 Loan Program

The Certified Development Company (504) Loan Program is a long-term financing tool used by communities to spur economic growth. The SBA works with a Certified Development Company, which is a nonprofit organization that works in the community to generate economic development.

The CDC/504 Program

The CDC/504 program provides businesses with long-term fixed rate financing for major fixed assets such as buildings, infrastructure improvements, and equipment. The funds cannot be used for working capital, inventory, or debt refinancing for example.

The program targets areas of communities where business growth can have a major impact on revitalizing the area. In addition, the 504 program targets businesses that veterans, minorities, and women own.

How Loans Are Structured

According to the SBA, a typical CDC/504 package might include a senior note from a private commercial lender covering 50 percent of the project, a junior note from the CDC (backed by a 100 percent guaranteed SBA debenture) covering 40 percent of the project, and 10 percent equity coming from the owner. Fees run around 3 percent of the SBA debenture.

How large the CDC/504-program loan can be depends on the business involved and the project. Contact your bank and local CDC for specifics on your proposed project.

MicroLoans

The third main type of loan that the SBA provides is the MicroLoan program, which targets small businesses—either start-up or established companies with very small notes.

The Loan

MicroLoans have a maximum amount of $35,000 and are made through nonprofit community-based lenders. These intermediaries make the loans available to local businesses. The average loan size is $10,500, according to the SBA. The local nonprofit lender makes all credit decisions and interest rates are based on costs plus prevailing rates.

Collateral and Training

Each nonprofit sets its own requirements for collateral and requires a personal guarantee of the owner. In addition, the nonprofit provides training and technical assistance to the borrower. Some borrowers may be required to complete training classes before the nonprofit approves the loan.

The Least You Need to Know

- The SBA provides loan guarantees to commercial lenders.
- SBA loan programs cover a wide variety of businesses.
- The SBA 7(a) loan guarantee program is the most flexible program for small businesses.
- Special loan programs like the CDC/504 and MicroLoan programs target economic development opportunities.

Chapter 20

Other Government Programs

In This Chapter

- ◆ Incentive funding
- ◆ City programs
- ◆ State programs
- ◆ Federal programs

There are a variety of local, state, and federal programs designed to help small businesses. It takes some digging, and the programs vary from location to location, although, it can be worth the effort. This chapter is divided into local, state, and federal programs, however as you go through, you notice that many of the programs are combinations of two or more levels of government that work together. There are too many programs to list them all, but this chapter points out major examples of each. You can learn more information if you use the resources listed.

Found Money

The Small Business Administration (SBA), which we looked at in Chapter 19, is not the only governmental agency interested in small businesses. You can find a number of governmental and quasi-governmental organizations at all levels of government with programs and money to help small businesses. Many of these programs target a narrow segment of the business community, although others are open to just about any business. Some of the programs exist not just to help small businesses, but also to create jobs and spur economic development.

Financial Aid

All levels of government agencies understand the value of creating and retaining jobs. Working with government agencies can take some patience, although it can be worth the wait.

It wasn't too many years ago that business and government were natural enemies and some would say they still are on many issues. However, government at all levels has come to understand that job creation and retention is important to the economic health of communities. Businesses have acknowledged that government can play a positive role in helping them grow. When the two work together, it's a win-win situation.

Local Programs

Local programs include those on the city or county level, which work with small businesses to help them start up or expand operations. Local programs frequently use and leverage money from federal or state programs. These programs typically have two main objectives: they provide resources to grow small businesses in the community and they encourage economic development in particular geographic areas of the community.

Growing Their Own

Most of the people employed in a community work for a small business (as defined by the SBA). Communities act in their own self-interest when they provide assistance to businesses. Most communities have a chamber of commerce or some other business organization that can help you identify resources and programs that provide assistance for small businesses.

Nonprofit groups affiliated with governmental bodies target small businesses for state and federal grants and low-interest loans to create jobs in the community. In some cases, the loans and grants are for special groups, such as veterans, minorities, or women. In other cases, their criteria are much broader.

Some of the programs have money for specific purposes, such as training. These programs provide dollars for training workers for specific job skills either on your job site, in a certified training facility, or both. If you hire a person for training, the program subsidizes his salary for a specified period. These programs usually target people on welfare who want to work, although lack job skills. These programs can use federal or state dollars to fund the training.

Cities Want Businesses

The other main objective of communities to work with small businesses is to attract new jobs to the community or to specific areas of the community. All communities want more jobs for their citizens. More jobs mean fewer people on welfare and more tax revenue. Communities can be very competitive to attract new businesses.

If you can or want to relocate your company, you should see what surrounding communities will offer for relocating your business there. If you employ a reasonable number of people, communities, especially smaller communities, often extend incentives to attract your business. These incentives may include free or low-interest loans on land in an industrial park, a

Notes and News
Local communities get excited when a new business comes to town. However, most new jobs in a community come from the expansion of existing businesses.

long-term, cheap lease on space, infrastructure improvements at little or no cost (streets, utilities, and so on), and other financial incentives. Relocating your business is a big decision, and there many other factors to consider in addition to some freebies a community might throw your way. However, all other things being equal, you may be able to cut a good deal if you relocate.

Many communities also work hard to redevelop certain areas that have fallen on hard times. Maybe it's an old industrial area or a downtown that has been abandoned for suburbia—the community wants to improve conditions and is willing to put some money behind its wishes. Communities use incentives to spur activity in these "re-development" areas. One of the tools they use is the CDC/504 program from the SBA we looked at in Chapter 19. That model is typical, and it involves three partners: the SBA, a nonprofit lender, and the business owner.

Notes and News
Another place to find information, especially in rural areas, is through the utility company that provides electricity to the community. The utility company may not have financial assistance available; however, they are usually good sources of information. Many utilities have economic development departments or at least a person on staff with that title—start here with your questions.

Some urban re-development programs use a partnership that consists of the community and a private developer. The community is the funnel for federal or state funds and oversees the project. The goal of these projects is to lure businesses back to the re-development area. Grants and low-interest loans are often available to either renovate existing buildings or build new facilities. Some of the projects have returned once grand sections of communities to their original condition. Service businesses in particular may be attracted to these downtown projects, although light manufacturing or distribution companies may find a good fit in renovated industrial districts.

You can find information on these projects in your community through the chamber of commerce or through the city, which might have an economic development department (or something similarly named).

State Offerings

Incentives and tangible help offered to small businesses on the state level vary from state to state. However, most states have in place a number of programs to encourage the growth of small businesses. Some of these programs operate in partnership with local communities and some work directly with the business. States, similar to communities, understand the benefits of encouraging business growth and acknowledge that most new jobs come from small businesses. What follows are generic descriptions of the types of programs available in most states. States call them by different names, although the majority of states have some form of these programs. You can get a complete listing of the programs offered in your state if you go to the state's website.

Labor Shortage Training Programs

These programs target small businesses in industries where there is a shortage of trained labor. The programs provide tuition reimbursement for all or a substantial part of the cost of training employees in critical skills areas. The training usually must take place at a state certified facility (often a technical school or two-year college), in addition to some other requirements.

Community Development Block Grant

This is one of those programs that involves the federal, state, and local governments. The Community Development Block Grant (CDBG) program provides grants to communities funneled from the federal government through the state to communities. Communities under 50,000 in population use the grants to promote local job creation and retention. The potential number of new jobs drives the funding of business projects.

CDBGs can be an effective tool because they focus on small communities that don't often have the resources to provide other incentives to small businesses.

Industry Specific Programs

Some states have programs that support specific industries important to that state. These include funds to upgrade technology or production standards and resources to help meet changing federal guidelines. Industries such as dairy farming, fishing, and certain manufacturing businesses, can benefit from these incentives in certain states.

Financial Aid

If your industry has a strong trade group, it may have information on industry-specific financing programs at the state and federal levels.

Ownership Loan Programs

These programs help a group of employees purchase an existing business that is about to downsize or close. The program can include money to help with professional assistance to structure the deal and coordinate other resources to make the deal work. The idea is to save jobs if the business is viable and the employees are willing and able to run it.

Enterprise Development Zone

States use enterprise development zones to encourage growth in high unemployment areas and areas of economic disorder, such as declining property values. These zones are frequently used in conjunction with communities in their redevelopment efforts.

The program creates a physical zone that awards tax credits for certain business activities that happen within that area. For example, hiring disadvantaged workers or cleaning up an environmental mess would earn your business tax credits if it were located within the zone. As you might guess, there are rules to follow, although the tax credits can be worthwhile.

Industrial Revenue Bonds

Industrial Revenue Bonds are generally available in most states and provide manufacturers with long-term, fixed-rate financing for plants and equipment. You are responsible for repaying the bonds, but because they issue through a community and the interest is exempt from federal income tax, you get a better interest rate than conventional financing.

The municipality sells the bonds and lends the money to the company. There is a substantial amount of work on the company's part to make the bond sell, and there are limitations imposed by federal and state regulations. This is definitely not a do-it-yourself process; however, the savings on a manufacturing facility can be significant.

Rural Development Programs

Many states have economic programs targeted at helping start or expand small businesses in rural areas where new jobs are often hard to find. If your business is located in a rural area, your state may have resources to help you expand or other resources if you want to relocate to a rural area.

Environmental Clean Up Funds

States offer help to companies that want to locate or expand to sites with environmental problems, especially if the sites are in areas in need of economic stimulation. These funds can be used to rehabilitate buildings or remove pollutants from the ground before building. Some of the programs offer outright grants, although others may offer low-cost loans. In either case, the state works with the community to identify areas in need of economic stimulation that are stymied by environmental problems to attract or assist small businesses to clean up the problems and create jobs.

> **CAUTION**
> **In the Red**
> Before you assume responsibility for an environmental cleanup, make sure you have an expert opinion on the ultimate cost and you have adequate funds to cover the expense.

Low Interest Loans and Grants

The assistance offered at the state level varies from state to state, although all have some programs that are designed to create or retain jobs. There is nothing a politician likes better than to brag about the number of jobs he is responsible for creating or saving. Look at your state's website for information on the types of programs available. Some states have a dedicated department of economic development, although others house this function in the department of commerce or treasury.

In many cases, there are numerous hoops to jump through, however states have money to help small businesses, and if you can put up with some bureaucracy, some of it could be yours.

Federal Government

The role of the federal government to provide financing for small business falls primarily on the Small Business Administration, which I covered in Chapter 19. However, there are other sources within the federal government for help.

Beyond the SBA

As we've gone through the programs for local and state governments, I sure you noticed that several of the programs involved funding from the federal government. The local or state program acted as the funnel to disperse the funds. In most cases, this is the way the federal government works. It typically does not work directly with individual businesses. However, there are numerous programs that go beyond the SBA to provide loans and other financial assistance to small businesses. The difference is that many of these programs come from particular departments within the government and target businesses that fall under their care. For example, the U.S. Department of Agriculture (USDA) has numerous loan programs for farms, ranches, and agricultural related businesses.

Where to Find Help

Knowing the federal government may have help for your business and finding that help are two different things. There are two ways to approach your search. If your business clearly falls under a department, such as the USDA, you can go to that website (www.usda.gov) and begin your search there. In that case, you'll find your answer by clicking on the link "Rural and Community Development" on the left side of the site. From that page, click on the "Business and Community Development" link on the right side on your screen. That will take you to a page titled Business Opportunities that discusses the several programs available, including a guaranteed loan program.

You can also find information on government programs through the government listings in your local telephone book. In most communities, the federal government listing will include the Department of Agriculture and other agencies (if not, directory assistance can provide you with a toll-free number to the department's information desk). You can also find telephone listings through your local public library.

Another way to find help is to go to The Catalog of Federal Domestic Assistance (www.cfda.gov). This site, as the name implies, is a clearinghouse for numerous federal programs, most of which do not concern you. However, if you go to the FAQ link at the top of the page, it takes you to a page of helpful questions and answers. One question is "Where can I find assistance to start a business?" The answer has several links that take you to listings of all the agencies that provide direct loans and guaranteed/insured loans. Armed with that information, it is much easier to track down the ones that apply to you. If the website fails you, use the government listings in the phone book or resources at your public library.

Although there are specific loans available for certain industries, for most businesses the SBA remains the primary source of assistance for financial help.

The Least You Need to Know

- When businesses and government work together, it benefits the businesses, the government, as well as the community.

- Communities often work with businesses and offer them attractive financing packages, because if the business grows, the community grows.

- States work with communities, especially smaller towns, to provide assistance to businesses in the form of financing packages.

- The federal government has numerous specialized financing programs beyond the SBA for small businesses.

Chapter 21

Sources of Alternative Debt Financing

In This Chapter

- ◆ Finding more money
- ◆ Financing cash flow
- ◆ Financing assets
- ◆ Financing inventory

There are several sources to finance debt besides the bank. These alternative means of financing might or might not work for your company. Some industries use them as a matter of course, although others seldom do. This chapter explains the one common factor among the businesses that use alternative debt financing; it requires an operating business.

Expensive Found Money

If the term "expensive found money" seems a contradiction in terms, you are correct. The financing alternatives discussed in this chapter tend to be costly; however, there are times when the alternative (you can't pay your bills) is more costly. Alternative financing means another method besides a traditional bank loan. Banks offer some of these alternative solutions as do specialized lenders. Some industries use these debt-financing plans as a regular business practice with great success. With rare exceptions, these financing plans are for ongoing businesses, not start-ups.

Using Alternatives

In general, alternative financing choices are more expensive than traditional bank options. This is not categorically true, although it usually works out this way. One of the reasons is that businesses tend to fall back on alternative financing because it is

Financial Aid

Don't shun alternative methods of debt financing just because they fall outside your traditional views of banks—they are perfectly legitimate and businesses in your community use them daily.

their last resort in desperate situations. In many cases, a company has run out of cash and traditional ways of accessing more cash (bank loans) are not an option. At the risk of sounding like a broken record, this is why managing your cash is so important. It is not unusual for businesses to find themselves with a lot of business; however, they have no cash. The more business that comes in, the more cash (for materials, labor, and so on) the company needs.

Other Methods

If you cannot or choose not to use traditional lenders, the alternatives for your company to generate cash tend to fall into several categories. The main and probably best-known category is factoring, or accounts receivable financing. Other categories include inventory financing, floor plan financing, revolving credit, purchase order financing, and so on. Banks offer many of these forms of financing along with other lenders that offer only alternative financing. This list isn't complete, as some industries have their own specific financing programs, although it does give you an idea of the main alternatives available.

Although there are many programs to explore, you should do so with caution. Some of these alternatives can be lifesavers in a cash emergency; however, you probably don't want to get hooked on them as a regular way of doing business. If you are forced into a corner, you might not have that many choices. Do your homework before you take on one of these alternatives. Work through the math or have your accountant run the numbers for you so you know exactly how much it will cost you.

Financing Cash Flow

Among the most popular forms of alternative financing is "selling" anticipated cash flow to a third party at a discount. These programs work on the principle that discounted cash now is more important to you than full value cash in the future. Factoring and accounts receivable financing are the two best known of these financing programs.

Accounts Receivable Financing

Here's a common scenario: Business has been good—in fact, it has been too good. You have done a ton of work and more is coming in, unfortunately, collections are not keeping pace. You must pay for materials and labor to fill orders, although cash is running low. You are tapped out at the bank and your personal accounts are no help. What do you do? A quick source of cash is to factor or finance your accounts receivable. This gives you a quick shot of cash to pay for the material and labor to fill the new orders, but at what cost?

Here's how accounts receivable financing works. Accounts receivable financing uses the money that is due to your business as collateral for a short-term loan. A bank or commercial lender determines how much it lends to you for each account and then you pay the money back as you collect the bill from the customer. The lender might give you 75 percent of the face value of a bill that is less than 30 days old. Invoices that are 31 to 60 days old might qualify for 60 percent of their face value. Accounts much over 60 days usually won't be considered unless there are unusual circumstances. These are just examples to illustrate that the lender will "age" the accounts, and lend more to those with fewer outstanding days and less to those outstanding for longer periods. The creditworthiness of the debtor is another consideration in how much the lender will allow on an account.

Financial Aid

Don't wait until it is too late to set up your alternative debt financing. If you let your business slide too much, you might not be able to bring it back.

Interest is calculated by applying a daily interest rate on the outstanding balance of the receivables. As you collect a receivable and repay that portion of the loan, your interest charges will drop. You must pledge the receivables to the lender as collateral and, in some states, notify your customer that you have done so. If you default on the note, the lender can seize all of the pledged receivables for collection.

Factoring

Factoring is similar to accounts receivable financing except instead of pledging your receivables as collateral for a loan, you sell them outright to a company or factor who then collects them from your customer. In this sense, it doesn't belong under the umbrella of this section, which is debt financing because there is no repayment involved. However, it is so close to accounts receivable financing that the two are easily confused and you might want to have both options to consider before you make a decision.

You usually need at least $10,000 in receivables to get a factor's attention and more gets you a better deal. What rates you get depend on how old your receivables are and how credit worthy your customers are. Most factoring deals are "nonrecourse," which means you sell the receivable to the factor and have no more responsibility. It is up to the factor to collect the money. Some states permit "recourse" factoring, which means the factor can hold you liable for repaying invoices it can't collect in a reasonable period. Be sure you know the exact terms of the agreement and any liability you have after the sale.

Financial Aid

Read your factoring agreement carefully and have an attorney review it. Make sure you absolutely understand what you are committing to when you sign the document.

Similar to accounts receivable financing, the factor advances you a percentage of the invoice's face value—usually 70 percent or more for current clients with good credit history. As the invoice is collected by the factor, you receive a final price that might equal between 90 percent and 95 percent of the original invoice. If the invoice proves uncollectible, you may not receive anything beyond the initial 70 percent and may face lower future advances. Factors are not interested in taking your uncollectible accounts; they want all of your receivables.

The downside of factors is that it is more expensive than traditional debt financing in most cases. A 5 or, more likely, 10 percent discount off every invoice can add up to a significant finance charge. Another problem with factoring is that some customers may find the relationship unsettling. Factors are not particularly interested in customer relations, although the more professional organizations are sensitive to your needs. However, the factor doesn't make any money until the invoice is paid and that's where aggressive collection techniques may cause some strain between you and your customer.

The upside of factoring is that it is a quick source of cash. After you have an established relationship with a factor, you can get your initial cash very quickly. Because factoring is a sale, not a loan, there is no repayment and no debt on your books. It also eliminates the task of collecting on late invoices, because the factor now has this job.

Some industries regularly factor their invoices, although it is not as common in other industries. Before you jump into factoring your receivables, consider all of the other options, and consider the impact on your customers.

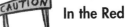 **In the Red** _____

Consider the consequences of the factor upsetting your best clients with harassing collection phone calls.

Purchase Order Financing

Purchase order (P.O.) financing is a form of anticipated cash flow financing that can help you fill a big order if you use a purchase order as collateral for a short-term loan to buy materials to complete the big order. The problem is not uncommon for small businesses: an opportunity to bid on a big job comes along, although you are reluctant because of the payment structure that requires you to front the cost of the materials, which is beyond your cash flow. Vendors want to be paid upfront for materials; however, you won't get paid until 30 to 60 days after the job is finished.

P.O. financing might be a solution to that problem. P.O. financing uses the purchase order itself as collateral for a short-term loan to finance supplies or materials to complete the work. Obviously, the P.O. has to be from a solid organization for this type of financing to work. Some industries use this type of financing as a regular way to do business. If you work with customers, such as government agencies, on large projects, this type of financing can be just the ticket.

The terms are negotiable and depend on the creditworthiness of you and your customer. The loans are typically short term—90 days or less. Often the company who does the financing pays your suppliers directly with a letter of credit or some other method so you can get your needed supplies quickly.

Asset-Based Financing

Several asset-based lending programs are more specific than the general bank loan that is collateralized by company and personal assets. These programs target specific assets and are often tailored to specific industries.

It is common to pledge your assets in debt financing, however, in asset-based financing, some of the pledged assets are the accounts receivable, although others are big-ticket items on the showroom floor.

Inventory Financing

Inventory financing is a way for retailers to maintain full showrooms of expensive merchandise at affordable rates. This type of financing is often extended through the manufacturer, although administered by a third party. The terms of the loans are such to encourage retailers to remain stocked with merchandise. For example, an appliance store with 100 major appliances at an average cost of $750, has $75,000 in merchandise on the floor and maybe that much again in the storeroom. It might be difficult for a small store to carry $150,000 in inventory if the owner had to pay for it upfront (even at wholesale prices).

Inventory financing lets the store stock that much inventory with little or no carrying costs (interest) for an initial period. It is in the manufacturers' interest to have a store full of merchandise, so the terms of inventory financing can be quite generous. Think about car lots and RV dealerships where there may be hundreds of vehicles. Most businesses couldn't afford to pay cash for those inventories.

You will find a wide variety of terms and conditions for inventory financing depending on who the lender is and what its stake is in the success of the product. Many different industries use this type of financing with terms that match the products held in inventory. Items that typically don't move quickly (recreational vehicles, for example) may have different terms than major appliances, which sell more rapidly.

Floor Planning

Floor planning is another form of inventory financing for big-ticket items, especially those that can be uniquely identified by serial numbers, such as automobiles or boats. Under this financing arrangement, a lender lends the money for the merchandise and the retailer holds it in trust for the bank. When the item is sold, the retailer pays off the lender and pockets any profit. Big-ticket items that may take some time to move are the focus of floor planning financing. This is the only way small (and not so small) businesses can afford to carry a reasonable display of merchandise.

Conclusion

This is an overview of the alternative financing sources for debt financing. I have not attempted to cover every alternative—that would take too long and many of the others I haven't listed target specific industries or are located in particular geographic areas. You don't have to settle for "no" from a single bank or any of these areas—with some imagination and hard work it is possible to combine one of more of these resources into a viable financing plan.

The Least You Need to Know

- There are a number of alternative debt financing resources available to you if you're willing to do some legwork.

- Accounts receivable financing and factoring bring in money quickly, although can also cause problems with customers if you're not careful.

- Asset-based financing is a way to raise money using existing assets as collateral.

- Inventory financing and floor planning are ways for your company to stock big-ticket items.

Part 5   Financing Your Business with Equity

For some small businesses, there comes a time when bringing in equity partners is desirable. How you go about preparing for talks with potential investors starts with your financial statements. Although lenders and investors are concerned with many of the same financial details, there are some important differences. What is the end game? How will investors get their money, and interest out of the company? This section is full of tips and guidelines for working with investors.

ANY OF YOU GUYS WANT TO *HELP* ME OUT WITH *THIS?*

Chapter 22

Do You Want Partners?

In This Chapter

- ◆ Equity financing explained
- ◆ What investors expect
- ◆ The investor package
- ◆ Benefits, drawbacks of investors

Some small businesses start with investors or partners from the beginning, although others take on investors later when they need to raise money. What do potential investors want to see in terms of financial projections and other information? Taking on investors or partners has some implications that can change the way you run your business. This chapter examines the good news—bad news of taking on investors.

Equity Financing Explained

In previous chapters, we looked at various ways to borrow money that you need to run your business. Equity financing is another method to raise money for your business. It differs from debt in that you do not have to pay it back. This money buys part ownership in your business, which entitles

Financial Aid

Equity investing in this chapter covers people who make an investment with the expectation of a return. This differs from equity investment from a friend or family member. This commonly occurs when a business starts out; however, that is really a loan in disguise. In this situation, the lender hopes to be paid back some day, but doesn't want to burden the new business with a debt, so they call it 10 percent of the stock.

the part owner to participate in the growth of the company because the initial investment grows as the company's value increases.

Although it is common to think of a single person starting a small business, in some cases two or more people pool their resources to form the company. In this situation, the company has multiple owners from the beginning. The other situation occurs when a small business owner wants either an injection of capital or to bring a working partner into the business. In these cases, an equity investment is made and a percentage of the company's stock is conveyed to the investor. In both cases, no owner controls 100 percent of the company's stock.

What Investors Expect

If you hope to attract investors in your company, you need to understand what their expectations are and how their view of your company differs from your view. Investors want a return on their investment commensurate with the risk involved and in a reasonable period. You need to show how your company's growth can provide that return and how the investor can cash in on his investment.

A Reasonable Return

Investing in a small business is a risky proposition. Even companies that are healthy today can suffer disasters tomorrow that can cripple or slow their growth. People who invest in small businesses on a regular basis understand the risks and factor those into their expectations. As a pure investment, small businesses would be at the top of the risk list, which means investors demand extraordinary returns for this risk. If you invest in a small business, the expected rate of return is much higher than the rate of return expected if you invest in the stock market. How do investors calculate the needed rate of return? There are many ways to figure a needed rate of return given a certain level of risk; however, here is a simple model to help you understand investing in a small business from the investor's point of view.

Investors first determine what is the safest rate of return they can earn on their money. Normally, they use the 10-year U.S. Treasury Bond as a benchmark because that the safest investment you can make. If the 10-year bond pays 4 percent, any other investment that is riskier than the bond must pay more or a risk premium. The greater the risk, the greater the premium and the higher return the investor will insist on before investing. An investor might ask this question, "If I can't make 10 percent on this stock, it is not worth the risk over the 10-year bond."

Financial Aid

Given the high failure rate of small businesses, to expect a high rate of return on an investment is not out of line. Even if the business doesn't fail there is a good chance it won't achieve the growth it needs to meet projections.

Given the high-risk nature of small businesses, it is not unusual to seek investors wanting big returns over a five- to ten-year period in exchange for their investment.

An Exit Strategy

One of the downsides to investing in a small business is the stock has no ready market—no place to easily sell your shares when you want out. Some investors expect the company to eventually "go public," that is, grow big enough to have a public offering of stock. When this happens, early investors have a chance to cash out, often at a huge profit if things go well (more about this later). However, the overwhelming majority of small businesses don't go public. Their stock remains closely held among a few investors and there is no open market. Investors who don't want to own the stock forever (and many don't) want an exit strategy or a way they can cash in their shares for a profit—they hope. Even before then, death and divorce can force the need to sell shares if possible.

An expert in this field must value shares of privately held companies. It's not quite as simple as looking at the financial reports and doing some math, because those numbers don't reflect potential growth in value, which is one of the main determinants of share price. After a fair and impartial share price is established, a buyer must be located. In some cases, purchase agreements include clauses that give existing shareholders the right of first refusal on any shares before they are sold or allow the company to buy back the shares.

Financial Aid

Outselling shares of a privately held company is difficult because the shares have no ready market. You must provide an exit strategy in the future so investors can see how they will get their money out of the company.

When establishing a plan to sell shares to investors, think about an exit strategy for shareholders and also from the company's perspective. Consult with a professional in this area because there are laws concerning how you go about this as well as safeguards for the investors and your company to consider.

An Emphasis on Growth

In Chapter 17, I cautioned against wild projections of growth. Although I still caution against unfounded projections of growth, you need to understand that investors look for numbers that are above the norm. Companies that are growing 5 to 10 percent a year are not likely to attract investors. Most investors want to see an emphasis on growth and the market to sustain substantial growth in the near future. These ingredients need to be in place:

- **A large and sustainable market.** This market can accommodate your company's growth and won't disappear tomorrow (no fads).

- **A unique and defendable position in the market.** Your product or service must be in a strong position to serve this market. Your company must keep the cost of entry high enough to discourage competitors from quickly duplicating your product or service. This could be a national or regional market.

- **A delivery system to service the market.** You must have a way to get your product or service to the market in an efficient manner. This system must be in place and appear transparent to the consumer.

- **A capital structure to finance growth.** Your company must have the money, which includes the investor's, to finance rapid growth without running out of cash.

Some investors might word these criteria in a different way or add some points, however, the essence is the same. Rapid growth, as I have noted in several other places, can be a dangerous time for your company if you are not on top of your finances.

Preparing an Investor Package

Similar to the discussion in Chapter 17 on how to present your idea to the bank officer, you need to sell investors on why they should put money into your business. The package can be a variation of the same material you used for the lender with some obvious differences. The loan package focused on how your business would use the proceeds and how it would repay the loan. The financial projections were for three years.

When you prepare an investor package, you need to focus on the future, because that's what investors are buying. If your company meets the criteria listed above, your financial projections should show substantial growth in the near future. The projections should include the infusion of invested capital you are trying to raise to show investors the affect their money has on the growth potential of the company.

Financial Aid

Your investor's package must demonstrate a clear and convincing path from "here to there." This means you must show how your small company can replicate what it is doing on a much larger scale and still make money.

Financial Projections

Financial projections the should look five years out and show how you predict your growth rate will vary from year to year. These projections should be built on solid assumptions that reflect the market and your company's ability to capture and defend market share. Sophisticated investors question every assumption and every number in your projections, so it makes sense to employ professional help when you prepare these financials. Before you meet with potential investors, have a knowledgeable friend grill you on the numbers and assumptions to make sure you thoroughly understand the projections and have credible answers.

Investors pay particular attention to operating income (income before taxes) and gross margins. They might care little about net income in early years because they are more motivated to build the size and value of the company than to "book profitability." What they want to see is their $200,000 investment become a $1,000,000 investment in five years.

After you have been grilled by professional investors you might feel discouraged. However, it can be an educational experience, even if the investor chooses not to put their money into your company. You will gain an unvarnished, unemotional assessment of your company and its future prospects. That's something that many owners find difficult to do. A common pitfall for small business owners (and managers of big businesses) is to fall in love with an idea. When you're in love, you don't always think clearly and you don't want to let go—two conditions that can spell disaster for any business. If you have an idea that blinds you to a serious flaw, you can be sure a group of professional investors will bring you back to reality.

Market Projections

Part of the package you present to potential investors is a serious discussion of the market(s) for your product or service. If you want to bring investors into your business, it typically means you believe it can grow much bigger, much faster. This means you need to serve a market that is big enough to reasonably accommodate the amount of growth you want. For example, if you want to go from $1 million in sales to $10 million in three years, your market must be large and growing. The companies in this market currently aren't going to sit still and let you take that much market share without a fight.

As I discussed in Chapter 14, you need a credible estimate of your current market share if you compete in established markets. If you are preparing to raise significant equity, it is worth your time and money to seek professional help to determine your current market share—this also adds credibility to your proposal. Your growth plans and market share plans all fit together. Of course, if you have a unique product or service, you'll create a market where one doesn't exist.

If your proposal says you plan to increase market share by 25 percent the first three years, you need to express that in numbers that work with your sales projections. For example, your current sales are $2 million in a market estimated at $40 million, which gives you a 5 percent market share. You project sales to increase 20 percent the first year, which gives you $2.4 million. You also want market share to increase by 10 percent per year. How fast must the market be growing to accommodate your growth in market share?

New market share = 5.5%

New sales = $2.4 million

New market size = 2.4 ÷ .055 = 43.64

New market size = $43.64 million

New market ÷ old market - 1.0 = 43.64 ÷ 40.0 - 1.0

In the Red _____

You don't have to have a completely new idea to raise equity. In fact, that can be a problem because it is untested in the market. What you must have is a product or service that has a unique selling point—service, quality, price, and so on—that you can defend.

New market growth rate = 43.64 ÷ 40.0 = 1.091 - 1.0 = 0.091

New market growth rate = 9.1 percent

The market must be growing at the rate of 9.1 percent per year. This rate of growth accommodates your increase in sales and market share. If the market isn't growing at this rate, it is more difficult for you to hit your projections because every sales dollar has to be won from a competitor.

Selling Your Vision and Yourself

Although you must make the numbers and market projections work for investors or not much is going to happen, it is equally important for you to sell yourself. Investors must feel confident that you are the person who can make all of this happen; that you have the skills, the drive, and the vision to see this through. Although there is a strong emphasis on the numbers, that is not all that goes into investing decisions. A business that has great numbers with an owner with no passion or energy for the business is not likely to attract much money. Though drive and commitment are important, so are flexibility and the willingness to listen to advice. Few business owners single-handedly bring all the skills needed to run a rapidly growing business to the table. Have you made good hires? Have you found people with the skills you lack to fill key management positions and do you listen to their advice?

Different Types of Investors

The next three chapters discuss different types of investors and their particular needs for information. Much of it is similar, however, you will find some differences, mainly in their investing approach and end game.

Financial Aid

It is important that you and your investors share a vision for how far you believe the company can go and what happens when it gets there. For some businesses, success means the company grows large enough to become an acquisition candidate of a larger competitor, although, other businesses hope to keep growing and become a publicly traded company on a major stock exchange.

Investors: Good News—Bad News

Similar to most alternatives, investors can bring many positive aspects to a company; however, they can also cause more problems. Much of this is subjective. What one business owner thinks is a negative, another owner might welcome. How you view investors and their role in your company in large part depends on your personality.

The Good News

If you take on investors, it can have a significant positive impact on your company's financial statements. An injection of cash that you can use for anything you want and never have to pay back is a wonderfully flexible tool. It is also a valuable resource that you don't want to fritter away. Besides making your financial reports look good, cash gives you tremendous options that you don't always have with other investments. For one thing, if conditions aren't immediately right to execute your growth plan, you are under no repayment pressure to do anything. You can put the equity cash into a safe investment until you are ready to move ahead without the bank breathing down your neck.

If your plan calls to borrow money in addition to an equity investment, lenders look with favor on companies that attract equity. It bolsters your financial statement and is a vote of confidence in your business plan from people who are willing to back their assessment with their own money.

There is another nonfinancial benefit to take on investors. Some investors are content to put their money in and monitor the company's progress from a distance. Other investors are willing and eager to lend their expertise to the company in an advisory capacity. They might be retired executives with years of managerial experience willing to listen to your ideas and offer suggestions. They might have experience in particular areas that you lack, such as marketing or finance.

Financial Aid

You might consider setting up an advisory board of investors and noninvestors who meet several times a year and serve as a sounding board for new ideas.

You need to approach these arrangements with some caution. Clear boundaries about roles and responsibilities lessen the possibility of conflict. Be honest with yourself about how you handle criticism and how well you can take advice that contradicts your vision of how a project should flow. However, if you can work in a give and take atmosphere and have an investor who can truly contribute to the company, it makes sense to take advantage of that expertise.

The Bad News

The image of a small business owner as the "Lone Ranger" who builds a business by the sweat of his brow and the strength of his will is idealized in our society. (Numerically, most small business owners are still men, but fortunately, that is changing as more women join the ranks.) The single-mindedness needed to build a small business is a great asset, however it can become a problem if the "Lone Ranger" needs to raise investment capital for expansion. Although investors may value the drive and dedication of the owner, there is a potential conflict in the making. Investors, by definition, are owners too and are entitled to current information on the company's performance. An owner used to answering to no one may find the notion of stockholders uncomfortable at best and infuriating at worst.

Even if the owner retains control of the company, the other investors have a right to information. If the owner is unlucky enough to get an investor who believes their money entitles them to much more than passive information, a real conflict can occur. Ask yourself how well you might handle an investor who calls frequently with "great ideas" for the business or criticisms of how you are running the business. If you have always been a "my way or the highway" kind of manager, how kindly can you take unsolicited advice and criticism?

There is a definite shift in how a business runs when you take on investors. In most cases, the change benefits the business, however owners need to be honest about their personalities and how well they can deal with the give and take of additional owners in the business.

Types of Investors

The following chapters cover three different types of investors. Each type might have somewhat different needs and characteristics than the other two. Their information needs build on what has been presented in this chapter and I will look at their motivation, which is different for each of the three and why your approach should recognize those differences. The three investor types are:

- ◆ Angel investors
- ◆ Investment groups
- ◆ Venture capitalists

These three groups represent the sources for most equity funding for small businesses beyond individuals.

The Least You Need to Know

◆ Equity financing means you bring additional investment capital into the business from outside investors whom become part owners in your business.

◆ Investors expect a reasonable return commensurate with the risk, an exit strategy, and an emphasis on growth.

◆ Financial projections and market share are an important part of your investor package.

◆ Taking on investors has both benefits and disadvantages that you should weigh before you make your decision.

Chapter 23

Angel Investors

In This Chapter

- ◆ Defining the angels
- ◆ Angels with hearts
- ◆ Angels only part-time
- ◆ Full-time angels

As the name implies, it seems as if angel investors often come from heaven. Many times they are friends or family. Other angel investors may be wealthy individuals who enjoy funding start-ups with small (for them) sums, or they may be more sophisticated angels who can bring more than money to your business. This chapter looks at this heavenly group of investors.

Angels Defined

Angel investors are often the first investors a small business attracts. These investors, whose backgrounds and motivations vary, usually don't invest large amounts, however, they invest in companies that are out there on the risk scale. The term "angel investor" comes from the theater community where wealthy individuals stepped in to finance productions. That's often the case with small businesses—angel investors are more likely to put money in when others have said no.

Financial Aid

The three categories of angels—amateur, semi-pro, and pro—are terms that I created, however, I think they serve the purpose to divide angels by motivation.

You can roughly group angel investors into three groups, which I call …

♦ Amateur angels.

♦ Semi-pro angels.

♦ Professional angels.

The investors' background and motivation to become an angel investor distinguishes each group. However, the common denominator for most angel investors is a modest investment. Because of the usually high-risk nature of the investment, most angels don't initially put a lot money into the business.

Amateur Angels

I call the first group amateur angels because, for the most part, they invest with their heart and not their head. These are friends and family, although that doesn't mean you should be casual about the relationship.

Usually Friendly Investors

This group of angels often comes into play just as a business is struggling to get off the ground. The owner may have trouble coming up with enough in the way of personal capital (it always costs more than you think) and banks have said no 15 times. Friends and family can be angels with a rescuing investment in the business. They may tell you that this is an investment and they want to make a lot of money, but this is most often an investment of the heart. They believe in you and want to help you succeed. These investors are tolerant and patient unless you promise them something you can't deliver.

The Strain on Family

Not all family angels will be tolerant forever. If your business doesn't go well, it can cause a strain in your family. What was offered as an investment may now be referred to as a loan and questions raised about repayment. Common wisdom says borrowing money from family is not a good idea for this reason, however, for many people starting a small business, friends and family may be the only resources available.

The Relative Effect

The other side of the coin can also cause some problems. For example, Uncle Fred is your angel investor and the business takes off. Your company is successful, thanks to Uncle Fred's investment to get you going. One day, Uncle Fred pushes you to hire his son, Fred, Jr. Unfortunately, Fred, Jr., doesn't have sense enough to come in out of the rain, although you feel an obligation to Uncle Fred because he believed in you when no one else did. In addition, now that Uncle Fred is retired, he wants to help you in the day-to-day operation of your business. The next section discusses how to handle your own Uncle Fred.

Financial Aid _____

Some families work extremely well together, although others do not. That reality won't change because you want it to. If your family gets along well as long as the subject of money doesn't come up, find an angel somewhere else.

Don't Be Casual

One of the ways to avoid or minimize the Uncle Freds of the world is to be very clear about what the angel investor's role in the business is and what he is getting for his investment. If you don't specify in writing what percentage of the company the angel is getting for their investment, you may face legal trouble in the future. The best course of action is to come to an agreement with the angel about what his investment represents in terms of ownership. Have an attorney set this out in writing for your corporate records so everything is clear and legal. If the angel says he really doesn't want any ownership in the company, have an attorney draw up a loan agreement that calls for repayment out of future profits. That way the angel won't feel as if you are pressured to repay immediately, and you do not need to worry about repayment until the business is profitable. The important point is to get the relationship down in writing so that everyone understands what is expected.

Semi-Pro Angels

Semi-pro angels are wealthy individuals or groups of individuals that invest in risky start-up businesses, mainly in the same community where they live. These angels may be successful professionals or other small business owners who enjoy the thrill of something new.

Involved and Not So Involved

Semi-pro angels run a wide spectrum from people who are still active in business to retirees. Some of the angels want to be involved in the business, although others are more content with a silent role. However, as a rule this group is more interested in the business in a healthy way than the Uncle Freds from the previous section. They may not be involved in micro-managing the business, although want some voice in major decisions. If you hook up with the right angel, you can gain years of experience in addition to some needed capital.

Financial Aid

How much do you want your angel involved in the business? Some people welcome as much assistance as possible, although other folks would just as soon go it alone. Decide which type you are and take that into consideration when you hunt for an angel.

For the most part, these semi-pro angels understand business and what it takes to succeed. They enjoy the creative aspects of building a business and want to contribute to the process.

What They Expect

Semi-pro angels may be less demanding in terms of the documentation and plans than other investors may. What they want to see is the vision and possibilities grounded in a business reality. When they step into a company, it usually has little, if any operating history. They understand that it may take several years before the company can project with any certainty a five-year plan; however, that's part of the attraction. It is most important that the business owner articulate the concept in a manner that suggests this business has potential to be much bigger than it is today. For example, many small businesses start because the owner has a talent at doing or making something. This product or service can be in high demand and profitable, although the future is limited unless the owner can find a way to replicate the product or service many times over with the same quality and market appeal. Baking world-class muffins a couple of dozen at a time is one thing, but can the same quality be achieved in a plant baking 500 dozen at a time?

This is usually not a problem in a manufacturing business, because that's what manufacturing is—making the same product over and over. However, if the product is a custom design or involves some degree of craftsmanship, it is not always easy to translate this to a mass produced operation. Professional service businesses are really at a disadvantage, because they are often built on the reputation of the owner and every client wants to work with the owner. This obviously limits the potential growth of the company.

Semi-pro angels (and the pros, too) look for businesses that can double or triple in size every year, and they look for owners who have a realistic vision of how that can happen. Great ideas are a dime a dozen—the Internet boom and bust of the late 1990s is proof. What is rare, are business owners who can see the big picture that includes how marketing, distribution, and all the other pieces can fit together. When Amazon.com was just getting started, the founders realized that in addition to the book selling business, they were in the materials handling business. Even though they ran the world's biggest bookstore with no walls, they still had to get the books to their customer. That meant an order ticket, packing slips, pulling inventory, packaging, shipping, and all the other pieces that went with handling millions of packages each year. For a virtual company, they had many physical problems.

Financial Aid

Seeing the potential for your business is similar to playing chess—you have to see what the board will look like several moves into the future. If you want to grow from a corner store to a regional chain in a few short years, you must think in much more complex terms than simply adding 20 new stores. It's that type of thinking that angels want in the business owners they back.

How To Find Them

Semi-pro angels don't advertise their services. They are selective about the deals they do and usually avoid any public mention of their activities. The result is they can be hard to find. Many semi-pro angels won't even talk to a business owner unless a trusted associate recommends the person. Similar to many business situations, a referral is often the best way to find a semi-pro angel. You can start with your accountant and attorney. They may know of someone who you can talk to about your business. Even bankers who turned you down might know of a semi-pro angel. You can also ask other business owners if they have any contacts in this area. Not every community has a large body of angels. Smaller communities might not have any, in which case you can try nearby larger towns. If your business plan is compelling enough and you are able to get it in front of enough people, there is a good chance you will get your meeting with a angel.

Professional Angels

The third group I call professional angels because they do this fulltime, even though many are retired business executives. You can think of them as early round venture capitalists because that more closely describes the way they approach their angel duties.

Very Involved

Professional angels, for the most part, want to be heavily involved in the business. They also want a substantial piece of equity for their investment. They also take an active role in the management decisions of the business. Many bring years of business experience to the table and can offer much to improve the operations of the company. If you are weak in an area where they have some strength, the union can be of great benefit to the company. Many pro-angels view their role as that of an advisor to the owner, although others may want a stronger role and controlling interest in your company.

What They Expect

Pro-angels are more demanding than the other two groups. They insist on up-to-date financials and a well-done business plan, or at least a business owner who can think beyond the next two steps. They look for people who work hard and want the rewards of being successful. Pro-angels tend to be people who "have been there and done that." They have had success in business and are used to doing things their way. You want to be cautious about relationships with angels that want to take over your business and do it their way. There is a fine line between following good advice and working for someone else. Many small business owners left corporate situations where someone else called all the shots because they believed they had a better idea. Don't let an overbearing angel put you back in the position of following someone else again.

Your pro-angel will most certainly demand a payout for his investment. Although most angels invest as partners, they can structure the deal as a loan, also. Either way, expect the angel to want a written agreement that covers how and under what circumstances he will be paid back, as either a return of investment plus some interest or as a loan pay off with interest. You may want to continue to plough earnings back into the business to finance growth, but don't expect the angel to be on the same page.

> **Financial Aid**
>
> Professional angels may be hard-nosed about your business, and that can be a good thing. Don't be surprised if they recommend spending cuts. Business owners tend to get comfortable with their surroundings and may not see where costs could be shed.

How to Find Them

Pro-angels are easier to find that you might expect. Because these people make a living or a second income out of their angel activity, they are easier to find and might even be listed in the Yellow Pages.

Go Online

One of the best places to start looking for pro-angels is online at Active Capital, a special website that was created to bring small business owners and angels together. The website (activecapital.org) is the result of over ten years of work and legal steps to allow investors and small businesses to come together in a nonprofit environment. The Small Business Administration started this site to help small businesses find equity investors. Typical equity investors, such as venture capital groups, are not interested in businesses that are in the $5 million and less range. Without a common marketplace, it was difficult for businesses to meet angels interested in funding deals under $5 million.

Active Capital provides a meeting place with none of the hype of commercial sites. It also offers education and training for small businesses to help them prepare for equity investors.

Close to Home

There are certainly pro-angels in larger communities if you want to stick close to home. Your attorney or accountant might be able to help you identify one, although pro-angels are easier to find than you might think. If you have a viable business idea that has the potential for serious growth in a hurry, they can find you.

> **CAUTION**
>
> **In the Red** _____
>
> The Internet is full of all sorts of sites that proclaim they can find money for your business or present your business plan to investors. Virtually every one of these sites is bogus. Somewhere in the pitch is a fee, they want a deposit, they want banking information, or the site wants something of value to secure your funding. Don't bite—it's a rip-off.

Advantages and Disadvantages

Who can complain about angels? With a name like that, they have to be good for you and your business, right? Well, like everything else in business, don't count on it. Angels can provide the money for your business to take off, although sometimes the price may be higher than you want to pay.

Disadvantages

Let's get the negative stuff out of the way first. Angels can be annoying. Maybe you can put up with annoying; however, it can get worse. How many times do you think you can listen to Uncle Fred tell you how you should run your business because "that's the way they did it in the old days and it ought to be good enough for any business my money is bankrolling …."

If you hook up with the wrong angel you may find your every decision challenged and questioned by someone who has been around much longer than you. Even if you are sure you are right, it wears on your self-confidence eventually. What if you are desperate for the money and this overbearing angel says sure, however he gets 51 percent of the business?

Taking on an angel is a risk on your part, too—you do not want to buy a series of headaches and frustrations.

Advantages

For everything negative about angels, there is a positive side. You might find an angel who is a sharp businessperson, who is willing to listen to you, and offers suggestions and guidance in a manner that respects your vision. This angel can bring years of business experience—maybe in an area where you are particularly weak—and be a true blessing in addition to his money.

Rather than challenge your decisions, he listens to your reasoning and, if you reciprocate, share his reasoning that can lead to a different conclusion. This type of collaborative relationship is healthy for you and your business.

Get in with the right angels and you can find a world of different financial structures that provide the investors with the incentive they need, while making sure you have the proper financial motivation. Deals can be struck that blend debt and equity in a variety of creative ways.

The Least You Need to Know

- ◆ Angels are usually wealthy individuals who like to invest in young companies and help them grow.

- ◆ Friends and family are often the angels that get a new business off the ground.

- ◆ Some angels invest as a part-time activity while continuing their job or profession. They usually are not involved in the day-to-day operation of your business.

- ◆ Professional angels look for dynamic young companies in need of money and their expertise to move to a much higher level in a short period.

24

Investment Groups

In This Chapter

- ◆ Defining investment groups
- ◆ Angel networks
- ◆ Other investment groups
- ◆ Specialized groups

The second stage of investor participation for most small businesses occurs with a group of local investors. You get to know these investors through a network, which includes your banker, accountant, and lawyer. Some of these investors might bring years of business experience in addition to their money to the deal. This chapter discusses how to find these investors and how they can help you.

Types of Investment Groups

Investment groups are another source of equity funding for small businesses. The term is generic in the financial world and means different things depending on the type of investment. For our purposes, an investment group is a formal or informal organization of investors who are interested in funding small businesses at start-up or second stage. The group can be private or loosely connected to a governmental agency.

Investment groups usually have more resources at their disposal for companies needing larger equity infusions. They are also easier to find than individual investors. Some investment groups have no particular guidelines about the type of deal they consider, although other groups specialize in certain types of investments. Although it is not categorically true, most investment groups require their members to meet the standards that the Securities & Exchange Commission requires of an *accredited investor*.

Money Talk

Accredited investor is under the Securities Act of 1933, as amended, and includes the following definitions about individual investors: "Any natural person whose individual net worth, or joint net worth with that person's spouse, at the time of his purchase exceeds $1,000,000;" and "Any natural person who had an individual income in excess of $200,000 in each of the two most recent years or joint income with that person's spouse in excess of $300,000 in each of those years and has a reasonable expectation of reaching the same income level in the current year."

Formal or Not

Investment groups can range from a small group of people who meet for coffee and discuss deals to a highly structured organization (some even have paid staff) that handles most of the legwork. Formal or informal, there are certain tasks all investment groups must complete.

Member Screening

This is not an absolute requirement as noted above, although if all members of the group are accredited investors, it takes pressure off the business owner. Why? Because at some point presenting highly risky investment propositions to people who are not "accredited investors," can become problematic. This is not a book on securities law, although there is a line you can cross that puts you as the business owner in a risky position if a nonaccredited investor should sue because he lost all his money. Before you make any presentation to an investment group, consult with your attorney about what legal steps you need to take. If the club certifies that all members are accredited investors, it should take some of the burden off you.

Due Diligence

Due diligence is an investment term that means checking out things before you invest any money. If an investment group is interested in your plan, a member of the group or a staff person spends a great deal of time going over every detail. They also want to know all about you. When they thoroughly understand what it is you are proposing and all the strong and weak points, they make a report to the group with possibly a funding recommendation. Due diligence is important because everyone that puts money into the deal will do so with the same information.

Money Talk

Due diligence is the process of examining the details of an investment proposal and asking questions of the principals involved. If an advisor recommends an investment without proper due diligence, he or she may face a lawsuit if something goes wrong.

Funding and Administration

Some investment groups don't require members to invest in every deal they approve. Members are given a chance to participate and there is usually a minimum participation level. Smaller, more informal groups tend to be all or nothing—that is, everyone is in the deal or the group doesn't do it. Part of this is practical because it keeps administration simpler. The other side is that smaller groups may need every member in each deal to have enough money to make it work.

After a business is funded, the group must administer the investment, which means one or more members are assigned to follow the progress on the company and report back on a periodic basis to the rest of the group. This removes the rest of the members from the personal contact with the business, which some prefer and others regret.

The Biggest Investment Groups

The biggest investment groups of all—not surprisingly—are made up of angels. That's right; the same people we discussed in Chapter 23 make up the largest number of investment groups. There are several reasons for this and they all make logical sense. Not only do angels make up investment groups, they have taken these groups and created networks within states to work even better. Later in this chapter, I discuss this network and how you can access it.

What Type of Angels?

In the previous chapter, I talked about three types of angels: amateur, semi-pro, and pro-angels. The amateur angels were family and friends who invest in or lend to business owners when they are trying to get the company off the ground. These folks are not likely candidates for joining angel investment groups.

The semi-pro angel who could be an executive or another business owner or a professional is a candidate for a passive angel investment group. In fact, this is the primary target for this group. These people want the involvement and hope for financial rewards, although many don't have the time to do their own due diligence (and consequently make bad investment decisions on their own). An investment group that can relieve them of some of the burden is just the ticket for their investment needs.

Financial Aid

Some angels always work alone; however, many angels find that the combined resources and shared risk of a group make it a better deal for the angels and the business owner.

The pro-angel might be the person who organizes the investment group and serves as the paid or unpaid staff. He wants more resources (read that money to invest) to use in doing deals and this is a way to bring more to bear on second stage funding deals. The pro-angel and the semi-pro angel might both want hands-on involvement with the companies that the group decides to fund. Because of this, the investments tend to be regional in nature.

Filling the Gap

A significant problem in small business development has been finding sources of funding for companies that are out of the start-up stage, but are still too small for most venture capital groups to consider. This gap represents a funding level too high for many individual angels, although works nicely for angel groups. Here's where the need is:

Stage	Funding Source	Amount
Pre-seed	Owner/Friends/Family	25,000 – 100,000
Start-up	Angel	100,000 – 500,000
Funding Gap		500,000 – 2 million
Funding Gap		2 million – 5 million
Later	Venture Capital	2 million – 5 million
	Venture Capital	5 million – plus

As you can see from this chart, individual angels can cover most of the initial early funding up to about $500,000. At this point, it becomes difficult for individuals to bear the burden on their own. The two funding gaps represent a shift in the attention of venture capital companies that swings; it depends on where they find the better deals. Venture capital companies tend to choose the more expensive investments.

Angel investment groups fill that void because they provide the funding of multiple angels for a single project. When they combine their money and their forces, angels reach deals that are outside the boundaries that most individuals face.

Networked Angels

Angels have become such an important factor in small business development. In fact, thanks to ActiveCapital.org (a Small Business Administration prototype), most states have put together networks of angels and angel groups. It shouldn't be hard to find or tap into these networks. Between Active Capital, which is national in scope, and your state network, you should be able to find numerous angels and angel investment groups in your area. A search on Google (the Internet search engine—google.com) for "investment groups" turned up numerous hits.

The Trends

Because of their combined resources, angel investment groups account for a large amount of the equity invested in small business start-ups through second stage funding. These groups attract investors to the angel market who would not participate by themselves. What difference does this make to you, the small business owner?

The trend toward groups is generally positive. It has brought more capital into the angel market than was readily available before. Groups make better decisions, which means they are more likely to survive financially to fund another business tomorrow. Groups make it easier for you to reach accredited investors and that solves some problems for you.

However, groups might also make more conservative funding decisions. Typically groups tend to be more conservative than individuals. This can leave some businesses that are on the fringe without a funding source at the stage they need it the most. I hope this trend doesn't develop.

Financial Aid

Are you better off with an individual angel or an angel investment group? That can depend on how much money you need—if the figure is up there, a group might be your only choice.

Other Investment Groups

Angel investment groups aren't the only sources of investment capital for your business. There is a variety of private and quasi-private investment groups that can be potential sources of equity for your company. Some are easy to find, although others operate in quiet modes and can require an introduction.

Small Business Investment Companies

Small Business Investment Companies (SBICs) are investment firms connected to the Small Business Administration. They are privately owned firms that leverage money from the SBA to lend money and invest equity in their community. SBICs often are preexisting investment firms that take on the role of SBIC to gain the advantage of the SBA association. This relationship gains the firm access to capital under favorable conditions, particularly if they are doing business with disadvantage companies (minority and women-owned businesses).

SBICs are classified as venture capital firms, however, their services tend to span a broader spectrum than the typical venture capital group, and their motivations (often community and economic development as well as financial return) are different. Many SBICs fund start-ups with small loans and provide interim financing in small amounts if needed. Venture capitalists aren't interested in these markets.

Regional Investment Companies

Another potential source of equity for your company is through regional investment companies. These are often broker/dealers (stockbrokers) by trade who also put together what are known as private placements. Private placements are investments that are not offered to the public for sale, but are prepared, in the case of small businesses, with a limited number of investors in mind. There are a number of ways the investment company can structure the deal—a stock sale, limited partnership, or other legal organization. This is usually an expensive way to raise money, so it's not practical for small sums. The investment company takes a fee for its services, which is either a percentage of the offering, a straight fee plus expenses, or some combination. Your accountant or lawyer might be able to point you to someone in your community who can tell you what services they provide and at what cost.

Strategic Investors

Strategic investors are those who want something from your company and they usually show up after you have started to make a name for yourself. Technology companies often find these folks sniffing around. Although they may not precisely fall under the heading of investment groups, they are a factor in the market. Strategic investors may know something about your company because they have a relationship with you—as a partner on a project or as a vendor or even as a customer. Be careful because they may have a hidden agenda. For example, they may want to invest a big chunk of cash, but want you to agree not to sell to a certain company, or they may want you to make your technology available to them. Be very cautious about any agreement that limits your options.

> **In the Red**
>
> Be careful of a strategic investor. It is possible that a larger company buys a smaller one just so it can keep an eye on the technology for the parent company.

Specialized Investment Groups

Although many investment groups have few criteria for prospective businesses, others are specific about the types and sizes of businesses they consider.

By Industry

Some investment groups are organized around an industry. Professionals in that industry pool not only their money, but also their talent and experience to find the right type of businesses to fund. These investment groups can focus in on narrow targets because they understand the industry and can see opportunities. Investment groups that fund certain technology, health care, or media companies are examples of specialized investment groups.

By Other Factors

There are investment groups that focus their attention on certain groups of business owners such as women or minority-owned businesses. These groups usually have other motivations than a return on their investment, although that doesn't mean they are charities either. They want to fund viable businesses that have a chance of surviving, however are overlooked in the normal funding process.

By Geography

Cities and states use their muscle to encourage economic development in areas where there is a need, such as inner city neighborhoods and rural communities. They often work with private or semi-private groups to provide incentives for businesses to locate or expand in designated areas. In some cases, these incentives include access to equity investments or low-interest loans coupled with tax breaks. If you are interested to locate or expand in one of these areas, check with local or state officials about any incentives that may be available.

Caution

As noted in the previous chapter, there is no shortage of "loan brokers" and other dubious enterprises promising to put your business plan in front of qualified investors. These folks usually promise some "secret" shortcut or inside connections that makes your funding almost guaranteed. All you need to do is send in a small handling fee or retainer and they'll do the rest. If you want quick action, they recommend you upgrade to the "premium" service, which promises even quicker results for only a few dollars more.

Needless to say, these are rip-offs, so don't waste your money. If you retain a professional (attorney, CPA, and such), expect to pay for their services; however, they won't promise you funding for your business other than their professional services. Some of the angel networks may require a registration fee. However, the first time anyone or any organization promises you funding for a fee, you know it's a rip-off.

The Least You Need to Know

- ◆ Investment groups can be formal or informal, but have a common interest to fund small businesses.

- ◆ Angel investment groups and their networks are great places to look for second stage funding.

- ◆ SBICs act as venture capital companies, but they also fund start-ups.

- ◆ Specialized investment groups may have motivations other than return on investment when they fund certain small businesses.

Chapter **25**

Venture Capitalists

In This Chapter

- Venture capitalists defined
- What they want
- What they expect
- Advantages and disadvantages

Many small businesses are just too small to catch the eye of the venture capitalist community. However, if you have an ongoing concern and the next great idea, but need significant funds to go from local to global, venture capitalists are the place to start. This chapter gives you an overview of what venture capitalists look for in a deal.

Venture Capitalist Defined

A venture capitalist (VC) is seldom an individual anymore. In today's market, most VCs are partnerships or corporations formed to invest significant sums of money in businesses that have the potential to return a significant profit. VCs typically invest in companies that are ready to move from a local or regional presence to a much grander stage. Their funding often takes the company to another level where it is ready to "go public"

Financial Aid _____

Venture capital firms get more media attention when the stock market is hot; however, they continue to invest even when you don't see them in the news-paper every day.

and issue stock on the open market, which is when the VCs typically cash out for a bundle if things go the way they plan.

VCs appear and disappear from the headlines. During the tech boom of the late 1990s, VCs were hot. Their investments fueled much of the growth and it seemed they couldn't find deals fast enough for all the investors who wanted in on the boom. Many of the VCs made obscene amounts of money for their investors during this hyper-inflated market. Of course, when the boom went bust, the venture capitalists faded off the front page and retreated to the background where they continued to invest, however, at a much reduced pace.

How VCs Are Organized

Venture capital firms can be organized many different ways, although one of the more common is to raise money to invest through limited partnerships. The firm sells shares in the partnership to wealthy individuals, however many target institutional investors, such as insurance companies, pension funds, and so on, that want a small percentage of their portfolios in a more aggressive investment. After the limited partnership is fully subscribed, the venture capital firm evaluates companies as potential funding targets for the partnership. Similar to any good investor, the venture capital firm diversifies the partnership's investments over several different types of companies. When the company goes public, the VC cashes out the investment and distributes the proceeds to the limited partners according to its ownership percentages.

What the Venture Capitalist Wants

Similar to angel investors, the venture capitalist firm wants a significant return on its investment—more precisely, the VC wants a home run. If your deal shows a solid 10 percent to 12 percent growth rate, don't bother taking it to a venture capitalist.

Size and Speed

As in any business, there are different types of VCs with different needs and goals. There are some venture capitalist firms that want only big deals—deals where they can put $25 million or a lot more in and expect a lot more out. They won't look at any business that doesn't have the potential to at least double every year for the next five years, for example. (This would turn a $25 million a year company to $800 million in five years.)

There are other venture capitalist firms with more modest requirements in terms of size and growth rate. They tend to look at regional companies that may not appear on a national radar, although have promising futures nonetheless. Many of these firms have more individual investors and smaller limited partnerships than the national VCs. Most small businesses probably have better luck with these regional firms.

Some VCs like to fund start-ups and are often referred to as Series A investors. These firms take the greatest risk, because your company is young and unproven. Consequently, they expect the biggest return—often ten times or more what they invested. Other venture capitalist firms prefer to come in at later stages of a company's development. The later they come in, the less return they expect compared to the Series A VC. It is possible to have several rounds of venture capital funding before the company goes public or is sold.

Financial Aid

When the stock market is down, there are fewer companies going public and venture capital firms must hold on to their investments longer than they might want to under normal circumstances.

Significant Ownership

Capital from VCs does not come cheap. They are notorious for demanding significant pieces of equity, including controlling interest in some cases. They take this position because they have a responsibility to protect their investors' money. Should things go amuck and the business owner becomes incapable or refuses to take corrective action, the VC steps in and takes control of the company. It is not a given that they want controlling interest in your company, however, don't be surprised if that's part of the deal. You may have to ask and answer a hard question: Would you rather own 100 percent of a $5 million company or 49 percent of a $100 million company? If the VCs money could vault your company to those heights, would you give up control for that much potential? There is no right or wrong answer to this question—there's just your honest answer, which is the only one that counts.

Even if the VCs take control of the ownership, it doesn't necessarily mean much has to change. Unless they think you are a problem, you still run the company on a day-to-day basis. However, there are great differences between running a $5 million company and a $100 million company—the VCs might question if you can handle that responsibility. The skills it took to build a company from scratch to $5 million are not the same skills needed to run a $100 million company. If you can adapt, you'll stay on, however, if you try to stick to your $5 million ways, the VCs will likely bring in a professional manager that can run a $100 million company.

An Exit Strategy

When we discussed angels, the exit strategy was some type of payout from future earnings. That doesn't apply for venture capitalists. Although there is some variation, most VCs have one of two possible strategies in mind when they invest in a company. The plan is to build the company up to a point where it either can go public with a stock issue or be sold to a competitor. In each case, the VC sells its stock or most of it and distributes the profits to its investors.

When a company first issues stock for public sale, it is called an Initial Public Offering or IPO. IPOs were all the rage during the Internet stock boom and still draw much investor interest for certain companies. If a company is really "hot," investors bid up its stock in the open market over the initial offering price. After the stock is in the public market, its price is subject to the same market influences as other stocks and it rises and falls accordingly.

However, now that the stock is in the public market, the venture capitalist can sell all or some of its shares at the appropriate time. This solves the problem angel investors have with a privately held stock and no market for it. The VCs stand to make a tremendous profit if they have backed the right company. Of course, not all the companies they back do well.

Financial Aid

Although the venture capital firm may think that the company should be sold to a competitor, occasionally the opposite happens and the funded company buys out a competitor. The much bigger company is then in a better position to go public or be bought by another larger company.

The other strategy is to build the company up so that a larger competitor will buy it out. This strategy works for companies involved in businesses that are not easily explained to the investing public and unlikely to attract much investor interest.

As a strategy, this is not without some risk, because you won't know for sure if there will be a competitor with the means available to buy you out at the appropriate time. Nevertheless, this is an attractive strategy, because there is considerable expense and hassle to take a company public, although selling your company outright to a competitor is relatively easy.

What They Expect

VCs are demanding, and you better do your homework before you present to them. It might not be difficult to find venture capital firms, although getting your deal in front of them is something else.

Getting to Know Them

Most VCs find prospective deals through referrals from a trusted source, either other VCs, people they have funded in the past, or bankers, attorneys, or CPAs, and so on. The odds are slim that your deal gets in front of anyone unless someone known to the VCs refers it.

So you must first get to know someone who knows someone. However, especially in the case of regional VCs, you probably already know someone who can make an introduction for you or at least can introduce you to someone who knows someone. You get the picture.

Know Your Target

Don't waste your time and the VC's time knocking on doors where there is no fit. If a VC is interested only in technology companies and you have a new retailing concept, don't bother it. You make a better impression if you come to a venture capitalist firm with a proposal that falls within the type of deals that it has funded in the past. This is where your "friend of the VC" and some research can pay off handsomely.

Know Your Stuff

Venture capitalist firms expect drop-dead presentations, so this is the time to spend some money on a professional job. Remember, these folks are not going to be wowed by a dazzling PowerPoint presentation, but rather by the content. Still, the slides should be professionally designed for a consistent look and color hard copies should be available for handouts. In most cases, if you get this far, you will present to a group of VC professionals who want your whole deal in less than an hour and closer to 30 minutes. You can leave hard copies with more data in the appendix, although they look for concepts that can be articulated clearly and concisely and for owners who can do the articulating.

Make sure you do not gloss over the barriers to entry or what obstacles can prevent your plan from succeeding. Be honest, because if you're not, your credibility is gone and so is any chance for a deal.

> **Financial Aid** _____
>
> Make sure your financial projections are professionally done, because the VC professionals will challenge your assumptions and projections, especially for young companies. The financial projections that VCs want differ markedly from what a loan officer needs. Valuation estimates, which project what the stock of the company will be worth at some future date, are a key part of the financial presentation and unless you are an expert in this complicated field, don't do this yourself. Hire a professional valuation firm to prepare these estimates and make sure you understand and can explain the assumptions and conclusions.

A Team Player

The VCs expect business owners they fund to be team players who are willing to work with an active board of directors (where they will have seats) and bring strong managers on board who will share in the running of the company. Business owners who must remain in sole control are probably not good candidates for venture capital funding.

An A Team

There are many factors a venture capital firm evaluates when it decides to fund a company. One of the most important factors is the quality of team that the business owner has put together to run the company. An owner who has surrounded himself with smart, experienced people is ready to take the business to the next level. If the owner has to be the smartest person on staff and everyone else waits for his instructions, that person has probably limited the future of the company and is not a good venture capital candidate.

Advantages and Disadvantages

For some owners, it comes down to the question: do I want to be a big frog in a small pond or a small frog in a big pond? Maybe that question isn't exactly right, although it makes the point. When you ask yourself what's your vision for the company, if you want to move to a bigger pond, maybe it's time to work with a VC.

Disadvantages

The biggest disadvantage of venture capital funding is that few small businesses qualify for it. Due to size minimums and growth expectations, many small businesses simply don't fit the VC profile.

For those small businesses that do fit the profile, there are other drawbacks, including the loss of a significant amount of equity if your company. This loss can be so great that you no longer control the company you founded. For some owners, that is a price too high to pay for the additional equity investment.

Venture capital firms have high expectations for growth, which might not sit well with your vision of how you thought your life would be. Growing a company that is doubling its revenue each year takes a toll on the owner.

At some point in the not too distant future, the venture capital company wants to take the company public or sell it to another company so they can cash out of their investment. Where does this leave you? You can be out of a job if the company is sold, and you might dread the thought of managing a publicly traded company with all the regulatory oversight and stockholder hassles.

Financial Aid _____

If the thought of giving up control makes you sick, a VC investment is probably not for you. There is nothing wrong with this feeling—many people share it. Just don't waste your time chasing something that is going to make your miserable.

Advantages

Did I mention that you don't have to pay the money back? Gaining an investment from a venture capital company can push your company to a new level in many ways. Not only do you get a shot of cash, but also you get the expertise of the VC professionals, many of whom are industry veterans. They become your champions in the industry and make introductions that can lead to sales and contracts.

Your board of directors now has more expertise than you could amass in several lifetimes. These business and industry veterans have seen and solved many of the problems you'll face as you manage a rapidly growing company. They can offer shortcuts and solutions months before you'll think of them because of their experience.

If you lack the skills or experience in critical management areas, they know people who have those talents who can be recruited to work on the team.

An investment by a venture capital firm is no guarantee of success, however if you work with them you have a much greater chance. If you choose to go with a VC, you have decided that partial ownership of a $100 million company is better than total ownership of a $5 million company.

The Least You Need to Know

- ◆ Venture capital firms manage pools of investor money and fund young, rapidly growing companies.

- ◆ Venture capital firms look for companies in large, rapidly growing markets that have the potential to grow at a fast rate.

- ◆ Venture capital firms expect owners that will work with them and are open to suggestions from an active board of directors about the operations of the business.

- ◆ Funding from venture capital companies can push your firm to the next level; however, that assistance comes with a price, which includes giving up a significant portion of ownership.

Afterword

In This Afterword

- ◆ Where we've been
- ◆ What to do now
- ◆ Next steps
- ◆ Looking ahead

Numbers are your friends. They tell you much about your company that you can't get anywhere else. I hope that if you haven't made friends with your numbers yet, you'll at least give them a chance to prove how good a friend they can be. When you let your numbers work for you, you can build planning budgets that make real sense and use them to help you arrange financing for your company.

Math Stinks

Americans have a love/hate relationship with math—they love when they are out of school and don't have to deal with it and they hate it while in school. Many business owners let this strained relationship get in the way of a powerful tool that can put real money in their pockets.

Cash Rules

The first nine chapters of this book can be summed up this way: protect your cash at all times. Although it sounds crazy, cash is more important than "book" profits, because you can show a net profit and still be out of cash thanks to accounting conventions such as depreciation and other noncash expenses you can deduct. The financial reports you receive from your accountant every month or generate from your accounting software tell you what happened in the recent past. This is helpful information, but if you really want to know what's going on beneath the surface, you have to dig, and the tool you use is simple math.

There is no reason for you to find your company in the position of being very busy, but suddenly out of cash and not knowing why. This happens to small businesses every day—don't let it happen to yours.

Knowledge Is Power

Which products are profitable? How much does that store contribute to the bottom line? Who are our best customers?

You may think you know the answers to these questions or you may lay awake at night wondering how to answer questions like these. In either case, until you have applied some analysis to the problem, you may never know the correct answer. Business owners must make important decisions every day. How do you make those decisions when you don't have the facts? If you understand your company's finances, you have the tools to gather the information you need to make decisions and not guesses.

Budgeting for Success

When you have a firm grip on your company's current financials, you can plan with confidence. Without an understanding of where you are it makes little sense to plan to go some place else. Strategic planning and budgeting is about making every dollar you spend count—remember, cash is everything. When you plan against a set of goals, you focus your spending and limit expenses within those goals. This keeps your company on track to accomplish important goals and prevents using resources for nontarget expenses.

Making It Grow

If your dreams are bigger than your current reality, you're going to need more money to finance your growth. Whether it's securing a loan or raising equity, your job is to put together a convincing package that presents your vision for the company in a compelling and thoughtful manner. Integral to this package are financials and financial projections. You must be able to talk intelligently about your company's numbers and defend your projections to a potential lender or investor.

It's All in the Financials

Everything you need to run your company better and more profitably is in your monthly financial reports. When you have the tools to pull out the information you need, you'll make better decisions and there won't be any financial surprises.

Financial Aid

How embarrassing is this? You sit down in front of a banker for a loan interview and he or she can spend a few minutes looking at the financial statements you included and know more about your company than you do.

Practice, Practice

Becoming comfortable with your company's financials isn't going to happen immediately. It will take a little time to get used to looking at the numbers, in addition to deciding which tools are the most helpful for your business. Get your most recent financial reports (income statement, balance sheet, statement of cash flows) and go through the first chapters of this book. Look at my examples and your statements. Don't be surprised if they don't look exactly the same. The main elements will be the same. Use some of the ratios found in later chapters and see how your company does. If you have trouble making sense of what the ratios are telling you about your company, visit with your accountant for some specific training relative to your company. Manufacturing, service, and retail businesses will have very different ratios in some areas.

In the Red

Don't practice reading financial statements using the ones you find in annual reports from publicly held companies. Although there are similarities, these reports lack the detail your company's reports have and are designed to meet regulatory reporting requirements.

What's Next?

I hope I've impressed upon you the importance of staying on top of your company's finances. A small business is particularly vulnerable to cash flow problems and often doesn't have the resources to weather lengthy cash shortages. Even if you have an accountant or financial person on staff, it is still your job and one of your top priorities to protect the company's cash and head off problems before they happen. The only way you can do that is by understanding your company's finances. Don't rely on someone else to be the sole monitor of this vital function—it's too important.

You will need to decide how often you look at reports, but it should never be any less frequent than monthly. Larger businesses will want certain information weekly and cash intensive businesses, such as retail, will want some daily reports. It will take some time, but you will get to a point where there is a standard set of reports that you look at on a regular basis. The time for studying these reports should be built into your schedule as often as the reports come out—don't let them sit on your desk or in your briefcase for days, because you lose the point of seeing them on a regular basis.

Looking Ahead

Running a small business is a dynamic and challenging effort. As your business grows, so do the challenges, and keeping up with the finances doesn't get any easier. However, the rewards for understanding your businesses financials are significant. Not only can that knowledge put real money in your pocket, it can also stop small problems from becoming big problems.

When you talk to potential lenders or investors, an understanding of your company's finances sets you apart as an owner who is serious about succeeding. You can approach the future with confidence because you know where your business is financially. You can speak with confidence about how your company is going to grow, because you can demonstrate, in terms lenders and investors understand, the financial dynamics that can make it happen.

Many small business owners have dreams of growing their business. Dreams are wonderful things—they give us the courage to leave comfortable salaries and start our own businesses. However, your dreams will only become your reality when you fully understand the finances of your business.

The Least You Need to Know

- Protect your cash at all times.
- Plan and budget to protect your cash and to stay on task to accomplish your major goals.
- Practice reading your financial reports and doing the appropriate ratios.
- The rewards of understanding your company's financials are realizing your dreams.

Glossary

This glossary contains definitions for the terms in this book, plus a few more for good luck.

accounts payable   Accounts payable is found on the balance sheet and includes the bills the company owes, but has not paid.

accounts receivable   Accounts receivable is found on the balance sheet and includes the outstanding bills owed to the company for products or services rendered.

accounts receivable financing   Lenders let a company borrow against the value of its accounts receivable for short-term loans.

accredited investor   The Securities Act of 1933, as amended, includes the following definitions about individual investors: "Any natural person whose individual net worth, or joint net worth with that person's spouse, at the time of his purchase exceeds $1,000,000"; and "Any natural person who had an individual income in excess of $200,000 in each of the two most recent years or joint income with that person's spouse in excess of $300,000 in each of those years and has a reasonable expectation of reaching the same income level in the current year."

accrual accounting   Accrual accounting is a method of accounting that ties the expense and revenue of a transaction, regardless of whether cash has changed hands or not.

aging schedule   This management tool tells how long the company has waited for payment from customers. It shows the effectiveness of the company's collection efforts.

angel investor(s)   An individual or group of individuals who invest in start-up businesses and often provide counseling to the business owner as well.

assets   Resources of value that the company owns.

balance sheet   One of the three important financial reports along with statement of cash flows and income statement, the balance sheet shows all of the company's assets, liabilities, and equities at a single point in time.

Bottom line   The bottom line is the same as net income.

capital   A broad financial term, but used in this book to refer to money needed to start or run a business.

capital structure   The capital structure of a company looks at the mix of debt and equity to determine if a company has too much debt.

cash accounting   Cash accounting is a method of accounting that records an expense when it is paid and revenue when it is received.

cash flow   The amount of cash the business generates that it can use to run the business is called cash flow. To calculate, add net income and depreciation together.

closely held corporation   A closely held corporation is a company with a limited number of stockholders. There is no ready market for the stock. In most cases, the majority stockholders are active in the management of the company.

collateral   Assets used to secure a loan are called collateral. If the loan is not repaid, the lender may seize the collateral.

cost of goods sold (COGS)   The cost of producing the products or services that are sold to produce revenue. These are the direct costs tied to the actual product or service and do not include general administration or overhead costs.

current assets and liabilities   Found on the balance sheet, assets that might be expected to convert into cash within one year. Current liabilities are those that the company expects to pay off within one year.

current ratio   Calculated as current assets divided by current liabilities. It gives a measure of the firm's ability to meet its short-term financial obligations.

depreciation An accounting convention to charge off an asset over a period of years using a variety of schedules, depreciation is an expense that reduces current earnings, but does not involve cash.

due diligence Before making an investment, due diligence is the process of examining the details and asking questions of the principals involved. If an advisor recommends an investment without proper due diligence, he may face a lawsuit if something goes wrong.

earnings Earnings are the same as net income.

EBITDA This stands for earnings before interest, taxes, depreciation, and amortization and is the equivalent of operating income.

equity For financial reporting purposes, equity is the business owner's stake in the business and usually consists of what the owner originally contributed plus the growth of the business. It also refers to any additional owners' or shareholders' money invested in the company.

factoring A form of financing where accounts receivable are sold to a factor at a discount from face value. Some factors assume the collection risk (nonrecourse), although others hold the company liable for collection (with recourse). It's an expensive form of financing.

financial statement Often called the financial report, these three documents summarize the company's financial position at the end of an accounting period. The reports include the income statement, the balance sheet, and the statement of cash flows.

fiscal year The 12-month cycle of the business used for accounting purposes is called its fiscal year. It may or may not coincide with the calendar year.

fixed assets Assets that are expected to be in service for many years are fixed assets. They do not necessarily have to be "fixed" to a particular location—a truck is a fixed asset, for example.

fixed costs Some costs do not change with the level of business activity. The rent for example stays the same regardless of whether sales are up or down.

gross margin Also known as gross profit, gross margin is calculated by subtracting the direct costs of producing a product or service from the sales. The gross margin is found on the income statement.

income   Also known as earnings, income is what remains after expenses are paid—in other words, profits or earnings.

income statement   Sometimes called the profit and loss statement, the income statement shows revenues less expenses and indicates a profit (earnings) or loss for the period.

initial public offering (IPO)   A company's first offering of its stock to the public is its initial public offering or IPO.

inventory turnover   Calculated as the cost of goods sold divided by an average inventory level. It measures the efficiency of inventory management.

leverage   Leverage is the amount of debt the company uses to finance its assets and operations.

liability   Any obligation of the company is considered a liability, which may be short or long term.

liquidity   The term liquidity refers to how easily an asset can be converted into cash. Common stocks are highly liquid because they are quickly sold on the open market, although land is highly illiquid because it can take a long time to find a buyer. It also can refer to how easily a company can generate cash to pay bills or meet other obligations.

liquidity ratios   Financial ratios that indicate a company's ability to pay current bills. These include the quick ratio and the current ratio.

net income   Calculated as revenues minus all expenses including taxes, interest, and depreciation. Net income is also known as earnings, or the bottom line.

North American Industry Classification System Codes   The North American Industry Classification System Codes are six-digit numbers that uniquely identify different types of businesses. These numbers help distinguish similar, but different types of businesses from one another.

operating income   The company's profit before one-time events such as income taxes and any unusual nonreoccurring events.

pro forma   A financial statement that reflects an anticipated change of some sort in the business' condition. The results may or may not work out as projected.

profitability ratios   Ratios that show how well or poorly a company earns money.

quick ratio   Calculated as current assets minus inventories divided by current liabilities, the quick ratio is a liquidity measurement.

ratio analysis   A way to measure the financial health of a company using ratios from groups of numbers from its financial statements.

return on assets (ROA)   Calculated as net income divided by total assets. It is a way to measure profitability and asset use.

return on equity (ROE)   Calculated as net income divided by equity. It is a way to measure profitability combined with asset use.

return on sales (ROS)   Calculated as net income divided by sales revenue. It is a measure of profitability.

revenue   Money received from selling a company's products or services. It is also called sales, but more properly referred to as revenue.

risk premium   When evaluating an investment, the risk premium is the return over a "safe" investment an investor expects for the risk he takes when investing. The riskier the investment, the higher the premium.

Small Business Administration (SBA)   An agency of the federal government, the SBA is primarily charged with assisting small businesses through education, advocacy, and financial assistance.

statement of cash flows   Also known as a cash flow statement, the statement of cash flows traces where cash has come from and where it flows through a business during an accounting period (month or year, typically).

variable costs   Costs related to production and sales that change with the level. For example, the cost of materials will rise and fall with the level of production.

venture capitalist   A person or firm that takes an equity position in new, high-risk businesses in search of high returns.

working capital   The money a business needs to operate on a day-to-day basis is known as working capital. Many small businesses struggle to keep enough on hand.

Appendix B

Resources

You can generally find help online for many of the major topics mentioned in this book. Here are some websites that can help you:

Websites

These websites offer resources and information on a variety of topics for small businesses.

- **The Small Business Administration—www.sba.gov**

  The Small Business Administration's website is full of useful information about its programs and services. It also contains a tremendous amount of educational material for small businesses. Click on your state's map and go to a state-specific SBA page to find offices in your area as well as much more information.

- **Active Capital—www.activecapital.org**

  Active Capital is a national, online network of angel investors that you can access when looking for equity investors. The organization grew out of the SBA's interest to make it easier for small business owners to identify interested and qualified angel investors.

◆ State Economic Development Departments

Almost every state has an economic development department somewhere in its structure. Go to your state government's website to find it. If there is no link on the home page, enter "economic development" in the search box.

◆ City Economic Development Departments

Many communities have economic development departments that can assist your business. In fact, there might be more than one. You can often find it on the chamber of commerce website as well as on the city's website.

Books

Here are some books that will help you with your small business:

◆ Marks, Gene. *Small Business Desk Reference*. Alpha Books, December, 2004.

A handy and ready source of information no small business should be without.

◆ Moran, Gwen, and Sue Johnson. *The Complete Idiot's Guide to Business Plans*. Alpha Books, October, 2005.

This comprehensive guide walks you through the planning process in detail.

◆ *The Ultimate Small Business Guide*. Ultimate Business Library, November, 2004.

A collection of reference articles on a wide range of issues important to small businesses.

◆ Paulson, Edward. *The Complete Idiot's Guide to Starting Your Own Business*. Alpha Books, December, 2003.

How to get your business idea off the ground.

Different Legal Structures

Ownership Alternatives

Your business needs a legal structure to operate within the rules and regulations of local, state, and federal guidelines. No surprise there. Fortunately, you have several legal alternatives to consider when organizing a new business. Each has its own merits and limitations and what works well for one business may not fit as nicely for another.

Although the legal structure you pick for your business is important, it isn't final. Many businesses start out as one legal entity and later switch to another as business conditions warrant. Therefore, this discussion is not just for new businesses, but also for existing businesses that may find a different legal structure better suits its evolving needs.

Why It Matters

It may seem to you that picking a legal form for your business is more a matter of what's cheapest and fastest, than anything else when you are starting up. In many cases, you would be right. Trying to get a new business off the ground and profitable is difficult enough without adding extra burdens and, if you've gotten nothing else out of this book so far, it's that you should guard your cash and question every expense.

Will some legal papers get you closer to profitability or are you going to just waste time and money jumping through regulatory hoops when you need to build your business? The answer to that question won't be the same for each business. For some, the legal filings can be done in a few hours or less, whereas other businesses need and want a more complicated legal structure.

> **CAUTION In the Red**
>
> Here is some legalese of my own. This discussion is of a general nature and should not be considered as favoring one form of business organization over another. The laws in each state differ on the terms and conditions of business organizations, so you should absolutely consult an attorney about what form of legal structure is best for your company. Money for sound legal advice about important matters is a good investment and could save you many times over the expense in future headaches.

The Five Types

There are five legal forms a business can adopt to present itself to the public. Each form has its own advantages and drawbacks; however, to do business you must choose one of these legal forms to give your business an identity at the local, state, and federal level. The forms are:

- Sole Proprietorship
- Partnership
- Limited Liability Company (LLC)
- Subchapter S Corporation
- C Corporation

> **Financial Aid**
>
> Over 72 percent of all businesses are organized as sole proprietorships or partnerships, mainly because that's all the legal structure they need.

These five legal structures run the gamut from very simple to complex. One will be appropriate for your business. Just because your business is in the start-up phase doesn't mean the simplest form is automatically right for you, just as mature businesses may not need the more complex structures.

Sole Proprietorship

Most small businesses are organized as sole proprietorships. It is the most common form of legal organization and it is the simplest of all. You can form a sole proprietorship in most states simply by saying you're in business. However, there are a few other steps most states require and this form of ownership has its own set of benefits and drawbacks.

How to Do It

Unlike other forms of ownership, you are the business and the business is you in a sole proprietorship. There are usually no direct documents to file declaring the existence of a sole proprietorship; however, there are certain tax filings and possibly local requirements.

The most common requirement is filing an assumed name, which is also known as a D.B.A (Doing Business As) certificate, usually with the county clerk or some other office. This simply states in a publicly filed document that you are doing business as your business name. For example, John Smith D.B.A. as Smith Plumbing. You shouldn't need an attorney to file this document.

In some localities, this information must be published in the local paper. In any event, for a small fee you will receive a certified copy of the D.B.A., which many banks require before you can open a business account under your company name. It is a good idea to get your D.B.A. early in the process of setting up your business so that your bank account isn't held up.

You'll want to make sure the name you pick for your business is not in use by another company and doesn't infringe on trademarks.

Financial Aid

Your local Chamber of Commerce is usually a good source of information on what you need to do to start your business. Some offer special information kits for entrepreneurs that list all the local governmental agencies you might need to know.

Other Requirements

After you have your assumed named registered, you can proceed with securing the various permits and licenses required by state and local governments for your business. Even though you and your business are legally the same, you'll want to register everything in the business name.

The reason for keeping everything in the business name is two-fold. First, it presents a more professional image to your customers and vendors if your bank accounts, permits, and so on are in your business name. Second, in the future you may want to convert to a more formal legal structure. It will be easier if all the agreements and permits are already in the company's name.

If you don't plan to have any employees, your Social Security number will serve as your federal tax number. However, if you plan to hire people, you'll need a federal employer tax number. If you need a federal employer tax number, you can apply online at www.irs.gov/businesses/index.html. Click "Employer ID Numbers" in the left column and it will take you to the section of the site you need. You can apply online and get an immediate response. You can also call 1-800-829-4933 and an IRS employee will take your information over the phone and issue an immediate number.

Advantages and Disadvantages

The sole proprietary form of ownership has some real advantages for many small businesses, especially in the start-up phase. However, it doesn't work for all businesses and, for larger companies, it can be a roadblock to growth.

Advantages of Sole Proprietorships

One of the main advantages of organizing your business as a sole proprietorship is there is almost no organization involved. If you follow the few steps I outlined previously, and any that are unique to your area, that's it. No lawyers need be involved in filing papers or drawing up agreements.

If you clear the necessary permits (which you'll need regardless of the legal organization of your business), you're ready to go.

Beyond the little paperwork involved, there are other advantages of being the sole owner. One of the major benefits is you don't have to answer to anyone else, as in no partners, stockholders, or others with an ownership interest in your business. This is why many people go into business for themselves in the first place—to be their own boss.

You also get to keep all the profits. Again, there are no partners or shareholders with any claims on your earnings. You also can make decisions quickly because you don't have to consult other principals of the company on major decisions. This makes it easy to act quickly when needed.

Financial Aid _____

Sole proprietorships are usually the best choice for start-ups (unless your attorney tells you otherwise). It costs almost nothing in fees and expenses, so you can focus on growing your business.

Sole proprietorships are as easy to close as they are to open. After your accounts are settled, you simply close the doors and that's it. With other forms of ownership, closing can be much more complicated.

Disadvantages of Sole Proprietorships

Of course, there is a downside to being the Lone Ranger. You are out there by yourself. Because there is little legal distinction between you and your business, the risk factor is high and you must bear it all. You can buy insurance policies to protect against certain liabilities, but nothing will protect you from bad business decisions or plain bad luck.

When you are on your own, there is no one to share the risks just as there is no one with any claim on the rewards. If things go badly, often your personal assets back the business and are at risk in the event of failure.

The business may be limited by your skills and abilities. You can hire employees, but there is only one "you." Often it is difficult to hire key employees unless you can offer them some ownership in the business. This is particularly true in professional service businesses, such as law, accounting, engineering, architectural practices, and so on.

In the Red _____

If you need a lot of structure and feel more comfortable when your work is orderly and laid out for you, then perhaps you're not cut out to run your own business, which can be chaotic at times.

Tax Considerations

Because you are the business, the profits and losses of your business flow through your personal income tax return. There is no separate filing for the business.

This eliminates the potential "double" taxation of corporations, but also does not offer all the potential tax breaks available to corporations. However, it is extremely important to keep your business and personal expenses separate because there is a schedule for filing profits and losses from a business and you want to account for all the company's expenses.

Partnerships

You might think that the next step above a sole proprietorship is a partnership, however, that's not quite correct. There is not much difference as far as the outside world is concerned between a sole proprietorship and a partnership. A partnership can be two or more individuals. This is a far less common form of ownership than sole proprietors are. This is a more formal structure that requires an attorney to draw up the agreement and is complicated by defining ownership, roles, and relationships.

Most businesses operate as general partnerships with all the partners participating in the active management and decision making of the company (and sharing unlimited liability). Limited partnerships are usually investment vehicles, whereby a general partner assumes management responsibility and limited partners supply investment funds. The limited partners do not participate in the management of the company and are usually liable only up to their invested capital.

Getting Started

Starting a partnership is surprisingly easy. In fact if you and one or more people start operating a business, you've formed a partnership in the eyes of the law. This may not be what you intend because without a written agreement, it is assumed all partners are equal.

Financial Aid _____

A partnership is like a marriage: the best ones are built of honesty, trust, and a lot of effective communication.

Therefore, the very first step is to draw up a detailed partnership agreement. An attorney familiar with these agreements will be a big help in pointing out areas that the partnership agreement needs to cover. Expect that the document is going to be detailed and cover all sorts of possibilities, such as what happens if a partner dies or wants to leave.

Advantages of Partnerships

Partnerships are often associated with professional services, such as when people pool there talents to form larger organizations with the partners sharing in the profits and losses. The partners also share in funding the start-up of the organization, which is a major advantage. The partnership agreement should define all the roles and relationships of the partners.

Partnerships are a good vehicle to bring not only capital, but also highly talented people together. Compensation structures can be complicated in partnerships, but also highly rewarding to the partners if the group is successful.

Disadvantages of Partnerships

Partnerships spread out the decision-making and, unless all the partners get along well, can by acrimonious. Partnerships don't have to be structured where all partners are equal, as long as the relationships are fully disclosed before partners buy in. This can solve some of the decision-making blockage by giving one or more partners superior status.

If you don't like working and making decisions in committees, a partnership is probably not for you. Partners, even if they own a minority position, have legal rights that you can't ignore.

Before you form a partnership, consult an attorney to make sure this is the best legal structure for your business and to learn all the legal rights and obligations.

A greater concern is the liability issue for partners. Partnerships share the personal liability problem with sole proprietorships. The partnership itself offers no protection against business liabilities. Each partner is responsible for all of the partnerships' liabilities. If one partner is sued, all partners can be made to pay.

Partnerships present particular management and people skills. Depending on how many partners are involved, decision making may become cumbersome. Some management experts suggest that one or more partners be "more equal" than others to facilitate decisions.

CAUTION

In the Red

Be aware, that in a general partnership, all partners are responsible for the actions of each other. If your partner causes an accident, you can be sued.

Special Cases

Some states offer professional service providers a different class of legal structure that gives the participants some more options in how the business is organized. Some states call them Professional Service Corporations and they have many of the characteristics of partnerships, but change some of the rules for unlimited liability.

Each state, if it offers this option, writes its own rules so it is important to consult an attorney when considering this option.

Closing the Doors

Unlike sole proprietorships, partnerships may be difficult to shut down. Some states have laws that dictate what happens to partnerships when a partner dies or leaves, unless you have these contingencies spelled out in the partnership agreement.

Part of the problem comes in placing a value on a departing or deceased partner's share. In some cases, this will require a specialized valuation by a skilled professional. How this is handled should be spelled out in the partnership agreement, along with appropriate insurance policies to help fund the ownership transition.

Taxes

Partnerships pass through income tax liability to the partners. Earnings show up on partners' personal income tax, even if some or all are retained with in the partnership. The partnership does not pay income taxes itself.

Limited Liability Company

After sole proprietorships and partnerships come various forms of corporations. One of the newer and more popular forms is the Limited Liability Company or LLC. The significant difference to the owner is the limited liability a corporation offers that is not available to proprietorships or partnerships. The corporation and the owner are separated.

Unfortunately, in the real world there is little protection behind the corporate shield for small business owners. It is almost a certainty that if you want a loan from the bank or any substantial credit, such as a lease, you will have to give your personal guarantee. So much for protecting your personal assets.

Getting Started

The LLC is a hybrid form of corporation that offers small businesses some of the advantages of incorporating, while avoiding one of the major drawbacks—double taxation on earnings.

There is not much difference between the LLC and S corporations, which I discuss next. Some of the wording is different, but they both accomplish the same major goals.

Financial Aid

Limited Liability Companies are the newest legal organization type and can be found in all 50 states. However, the rules in each state may be different, so be sure you check with an attorney familiar with local statutes.

Advantages of LLCs

The LLC form of organization is a flexible way for small businesses to operate that need more legal structure than a sole proprietorship. A single individual can own an LLC or it can have multiple owners. The LLC can raise capital by selling ownership interests (a different word for stock), something a sole proprietorship cannot do, and a partnership has to take in new partners or existing partners must get out their checkbooks to raise more money.

Even though there is not much protection for the small business owner, the limited liability feature is attractive and can prove its worth in certain cases.

Financial Aid

LLCs were formed to help small businesses find legal ground that was between a sole proprietorship and C Corporations, but without some of the restrictions of S-type corporations.

Disadvantages of LLCs

If you do not intend to sell stock and don't want to be bothered with shareholders, an LLC may not be necessary. Given the reality that you will probably have to personally guarantee most significant debt, incorporating may not be worth the expense and paperwork.

Like partnerships, LLCs with multiple members may become awkward to manage. Ownership interests of closely held corporations are often difficult to value to everyone's satisfaction. Because the interests are not traded on any open market, the holdings may need an outside appraisal for valuing. If someone dies or wants out, how do you determine the value? A procedure needs to be in place, but even that may not satisfy everyone.

Taxation

LLCs are taxed just as partnerships; that is, the profits and losses flow through the company's books and directly to the owners' personal tax statements.

The earnings are taxed only at the owners' personal level, so there are no corporate income taxes to pay. In most cases, this works out find, however, this is not always the case. Always consult a competent tax advisor before making any tax assumptions.

Closing the Doors

Like any corporation, closing an LLC is not a simple matter. Consult an attorney to determine what the exact requirements are in your state.

S Corporations

Sub-chapter S corporations, also known as S corporations, are another simple form of incorporation for small businesses. This form has been around for many years and, until the recent arrival of the LLC, was the most popular corporate organization.

Advantages of S Corporations

S corporations share the same limited liability protection for owners as LLCs. They also offer one advantage over LLCs that may be significant for some companies: stock options. This factor can be critical in attracting key employees to certain types of businesses.

Financial Aid

Sub-chapter S Corporations are the oldest small business-friendly corporate organizational type. They are in widespread use, but may be losing their popularity to LLCs.

One strategy often used with start-ups is to begin as a Sub-chapter S corporation when the company was likely to lose money so those losses passed through to the owners. As the company turned profitable, the company could switch to a C Corporation and take advantage of possibly better tax rates on earnings for corporations.

Disadvantages of S Corporations

In many people's eyes, the disadvantages of S Corporations far out weigh the advantages. One of the reasons LLCs were created was to get around some of the limitations of S Corporations.

Although you can issue stock in S Corporations, you can have only 75 stockholders. This limits the size of your investment pool considerably. These investors must be people, which means you can't partner with another company in an equity arrangement.

Profits and losses must be distributed to stockholders according to their holdings, which may seem fair only on the surface, but may not be the way you want to share profits in the early stages of your company based on contributions over and above capital.

Taxation

Taxation of S Corporation earnings is the same as an LLC—the profits and losses are passed through to the owners based on their percentage of equity. The company files an information return, alerting the IRS about profits or losses and what the owners received.

Closing the Doors

Like the LLC, consult your attorney for the proper procedure for closing an S corporation. Your state and the IRS have certain procedures that must be followed to protect all investors.

The C Corporation

The C Corporation or regular corporation is usually reserved for larger companies, although a fair number of small businesses opt for this form of organization. It is the most complicated and costly to organize and maintain; however, there are businesses and circumstances that make it the wise choice.

C Corporations are distinct legal entities from their owners. Their profits are taxed directly

CAUTION

In the Red

There is no reason to organize as a C Corporation unless your attorney or accountant tells you it is to your advantage to do so. Don't jump into this expensive form of organization without professional advice.

and, if the company pays dividends to investors, those are taxed again at the individ-ual level. It is important to understand that the law views a C corporation as a legal entity, which means it has rights that are separate from the owner(s). If one person owns all the stock in a C Corporation and that person dies, the company lives on with new owners who are heirs to the stock.

Getting Started

Incorporating a C Corporation requires the services of an attorney in most cases, although there are many services that will file all the papers for you. However, you should consult with a business attorney about the need for this type of structure before you spend the money and time to make it happen.

Corporations require a board of directors, annual meetings, minutes, corporate tax returns, and so on. Even if you are the sole stockholder, you still must fulfill all the legal requirements. Depending on the complexity of your corporation and the state requirements, you could easily spend several thousand dollars setting up the corporation.

> **CAUTION**
>
> **In the Red**
>
> If you take on stockhold-ers, even just a few, you take on a fiduciary responsibility and that means accurate bookkeeping, recordkeeping, and report filing. Mess up and you could find yourself facing a shareholder fraud suit or worse.

After the corporation is set up, the fun continues. When you want to borrow money or establish credit, you may be asked by the lender for a resolution from the board of directors authorizing you to obligate the corporation, even though you are the only stock-holder.

Advantages of a C Corporation

There are three major areas in which C Corporations differ from proprietorships and can offer limited advantages to the business owner.

The primary one is the protection of limited liability for the owner provided by the corporate shield. In theory, the corporation is a separate entity from the owner and that provides protection to the stockholders. However, as I have already pointed out, in the real world, small business owners are almost always going to be required to personally guarantee major debts to the company. This eliminates any protection the corporation can offer. Stockholders who are not active in the business may be shielded by the corporate veil from liability.

Another advantage, of sorts, is in the way earnings are taxed. Because the corporation is a legal entity, it pays its own taxes. In most cases, owners pay themselves a salary out of the corporation, which is taxed like any other salary. However, if the company distributes dividends to the shareholder(s), those are also taxed, which means they have been taxed twice—once at the corporate level and again at the personal level. Careful planning can avoid most of these problems. In addition, the owner's salary is usually deductible to the corporation as a business expense.

C Corporations offer the best vehicle for raising money if that is your goal. Companies that plan to grow rapidly and want to attract equity partners prefer the C Corporation structure because of the flexibility in issuing common stock. If you picture your company on a fast growth track, borrowing to get there is probably not realistic. Taking on stockholders is a common way for young companies to generate the capital they need to fund growth. With the right idea and initial funding, your company could eventually "go public" and have your stock listed on a major stock exchange.

Disadvantages of C Corporations

It is relatively expensive to set up and maintain a C Corporation. Beyond the initial start-up fees to an attorney, there are filing fees and other expenses associated with individual state requirements. This is why it is so important to be clear in your mind about why you need to have a C Corporation rather than one of the other forms discussed earlier.

If you plan to have no or only a few employees and are in a business that is seldom sued, there may not be any reason to choose a C Corporation.

If you are going to be the owner-operator, there is almost no chance the corporate shield is going to protect you from being sued along with the company—so what good is paying for the "protection" of a corporate shield?

Financial Aid

You may be able to file a simple return for a C Corporation, however, if you have many employees, a benefits package, inventory, depreciation and other charges, you will probably need an accountant to prepare or review your tax return.

You must follow the administrative rules in your state, which probably mean keeping corporate minutes of board meetings, even if it is you and your spouse. You will definitely have to file corporate income taxes, which are no piece of cake to complete.

You have to be extremely careful not to mix any business and personal assets or pay for any personal services out of corporate funds and so on. If you do, it could be used in court against you to argue that you aren't running a true corporation and have no protection from lawsuits.

Taxation

As mentioned previously, corporations file their own income tax returns, separate from stockholders' returns. The forms are not easy to complete and may you may require an accountant to help you. Because of the legal status of corporations, you must keep very careful and complete books. These books will help at tax time, but are also expected, especially if you have stockholders.

Closing the Doors

Because a C Corporation has a legal "life" of its own, you can't just shut the doors and call it done. There are forms to file and procedures to go through to shut down a corporation, including paying all outstanding permits, fees, fines, and charges, if any. Of course, you'll need a resolution from the board of directors.

How to Choose

How do you decide which is the best legal organization for your business? For most businesses, it probably doesn't matter much which form you pick. However, your best bet is to spend some time and a little money with a business attorney just to make sure it really doesn't matter all that much from a legal perspective.

If there is no compelling legal reason to choose one form of ownership over another, then you should weigh what benefits a particular form may offer.

Single vs. Multiple Owners

One of the considerations is the number of current or eventual owners you foresee for the company. If all you want is a one-person operation, then you will probably want to stick with a sole proprietorship.

On the other hand, if you have partners or investors or can see a time in the future when you would like to bring those into the company, consider one of the other forms that allow multiple owners.

Self-Funded vs. Outside Capital

Do you see your company growing on internally generated cash and your investment or do you envision selling shares of stock? The answer to these questions will push you towards a particular organization.

Earnings vs. Salary and Dividends

In a sole proprietorship, partnership, S Corp and LLC, all the earnings pass through to your personal account (unless you decide to keep them in the company to fund growth). This means you pay income tax on all the earnings.

In a C Corporation, you pay yourself a salary and the board of directors (which could be you and your spouse) decide if the company is going to pay out dividends or retain the earnings in the company. Because dividends are usually taxed at a lower rate than ordinary income, you must be careful how you structure your pay. The IRS will not let you play games with your salary and dividends (for example, take a $1 salary and $60,000 in dividends).

Financial Aid

Before you go out and begin selling shares in your company, consult with your attorney. There are specific rules to follow, even for closely held corporations and it is easy to violate security laws if you don't know what you are doing.

Not the Final Word

As I noted at the beginning of this appendix, it is not uncommon for companies to start in one legal form and switch as the business changesd. In most cases, the switch is not a big deal, but it will probably involve an attorney and your accountant. The hassle factor is not a reason to avoid the change if it makes good business sense.

When to Switch

The most common switch is from a sole proprietorship or partnership to one of the forms of incorporation. This often occurs after a company moves out of the start-up phase and experiences rapid, but planned growth.

A corporate form (C) of organization may make more sense when the number of employees begins to grow. There are some tax benefits that corporations can use in terms of deduction benefit programs and such that are harder for unincorporated businesses to use.

Because a C Corporation files its own tax return, some businesses find that as they grow, it makes more sense for the owner to take a salary and retain earnings in the company to fund growth. An accountant can help you make the decision about when it makes sense to switch to a C Corporation.

Other Choices

You have two other choices (LLC and S Corporation) to consider if you are looking for some of the advantages listed for these types of organizations. Although taxes may not be the reason, there are other considerations.

You may want to offer ownership interests (stock) to a limited number of investors to raise capital as with the S-type Corporation or an LLC. You can use stock options to attract key employees.

Buy-Sell Agreements

Regardless of the type of organization you choose, if there is more than one key principal in the business, you should have a well written and funded buy-sell agreement in place.

What It Is

A buy-sell agreement details what happens if one of the principals wants to leave or dies. All the principals (owners) of the company sign this agreement and they should all agree to its terms. The agreement can head off major disputes that could disrupt the company to the point of failure.

What It Says

The buy-sell agreement details how the principals will determine the value of the business in the event one wants to leave or dies. This method will set the value and state how the departing owner or the owner's estate will be paid for their share.

Many companies maintain life insurance policies on the principals payable to the company to help buy back a deceased principal's share. Of course, life insurance doesn't help if the principal just wants to leave. Under these circumstances, the agreement may spell out the terms of payment to the departing principal.

Financial Aid

Buy-sell agreements are another example of why you should know a good business attorney. This is not a do-it-yourself exercise.

Establishing Value

There are several ways a closely held company can be valued, depending on the nature of the business and other factors. There are specialists in this field who can help you establish the value of your company.

The buy-sell agreement should spell out the method for valuing the business. If the principals don't agree on the value, arbitration should force a conclusion so the business can keep moving forward.

Know the Owners

Another important part of the buy-sell agreement that most small businesses insist on states that principals must sell their shares back to the company rather than strangers.

This protects the remaining principals, who are likely a close-knit group and may not want a stranger in their midst.

Conclusion

Organizing your business is an important decision and should be made with thought and help from professionals, such as your attorney and accountant. However, your decision is seldom cast in stone. If you change your mind as your business grows, you will be able to reorganize your company into a new legal form that better suits your growing needs.

Index

D

K-L

Q-R

S

Check Out These
Best-Sellers

Read by millions!

Grammar and Style

1-59257-115-8 • $16.95

Buying and Selling a Home

1-59257-120-4 • $18.95

Being a Groom

0-02-864456-5 • $9.95

Learning Spanish

0-02-864451-4 • $18.95

Personal Finance in Your 20s & 30s

0-02-864374-7 • $19.95

Organizing Your Life

1-59257-413-0 • $16.95

Total Nutrition

1-59257-439-4 • $18.95

Positive Dog Training

0-02-864463-8 • $14.95

The Bible

1-59257-389-4 • $18.95

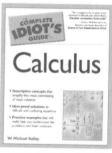

Calculus

0-02-864365-8 • $18.95

Music Theory

1-59257-437-8 • $19.95

The Perfect Resume

0-02-864440-9 • $14.95

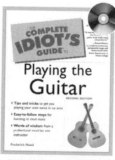

Playing the Guitar

0-02-864244-9 • $21.95

1-59257-335-5 • $19.95

Knitting and Crocheting

1-59257-089-5 • $16.95

More than *450 titles* available at
booksellers and online retailers everywhere

www.idiotsguides.com

ALPHA